BUD

ian mulgrew

INSIDE CANADA'S MARIJUANA INDUSTRY

INC.

VINTAGE CANADA

VINTAGE CANADA EDITION, 2006

Copyright © 2005 Ian Mulgrew

Published in Canada by Vintage Canada, a division of Random House of
Canada Limited, Toronto, in 2006. Originally published in hardcover in
Canada by Random House Canada, a division of Random House of
Canada Limited, Toronto, in 2005. Distributed by Random House of
Canada Limited, Toronto.

Vintage Canada and colophon are registered trademarks of Random
House of Canada Limited.

www.randomhouse.ca

Library and Archives Canada Cataloguing in Publication

Mulgrew, Ian, 1957–
Bud Inc. : inside Canada's marijuana industry / Ian Mulgrew.

Includes bibliographical references and index.

ISBN-13: 978-0-679-31330-4
ISBN-10: 0-679-31330-3

1. Marijuana industry—Canada. I. Title.

HD9019.M382C3 2006   338.1'7379'0971   C2006-902098-1

Text design by Kelly Hill

Printed and bound in Canada

2 4 6 8 9 7 5 3 1

For Alexander, Paul, Deanna and Christopher,
who always make me high

CONTENTS

INTRODUCTION

STEPHEN EASTON SAT in a small Spartan office behind a desktop cluttered with computer printouts detailing his latest calculations. A senior scholar at Canada's conservative think-tank, the Fraser Institute, and an economics professor at Simon Fraser University, Easton was astonished by the numbers his formula spat out. If they were correct, marijuana was Canada's most valuable agricultural product. Forget iconic wheat—golden shimmering symbol of the country's farming heartland. Stinky, lime-green pot contributed more to the economy. Much, much more.

"Over the last three or four years, I think most people now would say my estimates are low," he laughed. "Especially the police."

By 2000, Easton figured, Canadian cannabis consumers annually spent at least $1.8 billion on bud. That's almost as much as Canadians spent on tobacco—$2.3 billion. And it meant consumption in the previous decade had doubled. Easton also believed exports to the United States dwarfed those figures.

He projected the size of the B.C. export market alone at 1,433 metric tons worth $2 billion dollars in 2000—almost 3 per cent of the provincial GDP. By way of comparison, that was nearly the size of the B.C. mining and oil-and-gas sectors combined. Easton added that the total intentionally understated the value of the industry because he used only wholesale prices. It didn't reflect the final sale price, which included markups and the cut that goes to every middleman no matter what the commodity. If you looked at the true value of the crop in 2000, Easton thought, you could plausibly produce a figure between $5.6 billion and $7.1 billion.[*]

The latest figures are as staggering. Pot production in B.C., which grows the lion's share of the country's crop, has more than tripled during the past seven years—from an estimated 19,727 kilograms in 1997 to 79,817 kilograms in 2003. In Ontario and Quebec, the growth in hydroponic production has been exponential. Growing pot indoors has become uncomplicated and highly profitable—in just three months, a closet, a basement, a bedroom, a barn or a bathroom anywhere can produce a down payment on a house. In most cities, towns, villages and rural areas across the continent, someone is doing it. The same is true in Europe. Hydroponic sales in sunny Spain are skyrocketing—and the growers are not producing heirloom tomatoes.

Easton estimated that based on the most recently available 2003 figures, wholesale marijuana was worth about $2.2 billion to the B.C. economy—$7.7 billion retail if consumers paid top dollar. That's larger than the province's legitimate agricultural sector. Across the country, he estimated that the industry was worth $5.7 billion wholesale and $19.5 billion if high-end retail pricing is assumed. That's about the size of the Canadian cattle industry ($5.2 billion).

---

[*] All dollar amounts are Canadian, unless otherwise noted.

"The dollar figures would be much higher had there not been economic factors during this period such as a low U.S. dollar and the fall of the wholesale marijuana price in the face of a glut market," Easton said. "But here's the kicker—looking at the most recent numbers, the police are clearly changing their behaviour in that they are not responding to as many calls as they did before. The police have obviously reached an accommodation in their own mind. And they have prioritized in a way that is very unfair."

Last year, more than 25,000 growing operations across British Columbia came to the attention of police, but they investigated fewer than 17,000 and only about half of those were prosecuted. More than half of the grow operations police raided over the past seven years resulted in seizures but no charges. Police are charging people in fewer and fewer cases and seem to be increasingly reluctant to act at all. The same is true elsewhere in Canada.

Prosecutors and the judiciary also look like they are throwing up their hands. Large numbers of marijuana cases are dealt with via stays of proceedings and conditional sentence- or probation-based plea bargains. Nearly half end in conditional sentences, up from roughly one in ten people receiving such a penalty in 1997. Only one in ten of the 3,364 convicted in 2003 were imprisoned and on average they were jailed for less than five months. That's about half the ratio of those jailed in 1997. British Columbia is Canada's most lenient jurisdiction, but across the country the judiciary is vexed about the question of sentencing in marijuana cases.

Nationally, 225 offenders were imprisoned for cultivation at the end of 2000—and on average such inmates spent less than a year in custody, or eighteen months if they were convicted for importing. Traffickers on average spend only two years inside.

"One can see how you could easily slouch into legalization," Easton said. "You just slump into it in some sense. That may ultimately be the most graceful way it could happen."

Consider that half of those convicted in British Columbia alone would have been jailed for five years or more under U.S. sentencing guidelines. Fully 77 per cent of those convicted would have served at least three months if caught in the United States.

But even in jurisdictions where tough sentences are meted out, marijuana cultivation is a fact of life. The law is no longer a risk to growers, it is an operating cost. Jail penalties be damned: consumers want to have good dope, and in most places the only way to do that is to grow your own— which has the benefit of allowing you to sell the excess to your friends and pocket the profit.

It's time to admit the cannabis prohibition is a failure. More and more, it is revealed as a public policy disaster, a crisis for our communities and local politicians, and a legal quagmire for police and judges. The damage prohibition causes is exacerbated by the violence endemic to the pernicious black market it spawns, eroding confidence in law enforcement and respect for the courts. Taxpayers must deal with the problems of the illicit pot industry but receive no benefit, and as long as it's underground, we have no ability to regulate it or control the commerce.

Decriminalization, which is Ottawa's strategy, is a halfway house that makes users feel more relaxed but does nothing to eliminate the underground market and its attendant horrors. Stiffer sentences and more jail time are not a realistic answer, though justice and public safety ministers from Ottawa, Washington and European capitals continue to insist on them. There are far too many people involved. We cannot build enough prisons and we cannot deal with the social fallout.

In 2003, police in B.C. investigated more than 15,000 individuals—mainly men in their thirties. If we assume they got everyone involved in the one in ten grow operations the police claim to be busting—a generous assumption—that means there could be as many as 150,000 people involved across the sprawling, sparsely populated province. Consider how many people that would be across the country, and at what scale. Consider a sampling of recent newspaper reports:

- In Barrie, Ontario, a former Molson brewery was converted into the largest grow-op in Canadian history—more than 25,000 plants producing an estimated $100 million a year in revenue.
- In Edmonton, police raided a warehouse, seizing 5,600 plants.
- On Vancouver Island, police arrested two men and seized 6,700 plants.
- In Halifax, police found 4,000 plants in coordinated raids on nineteen sites.
- In Winnipeg, police busted the second-largest grow-op in the country—10,000 plants worth some $11 million—only a block from their HQ.
- In Calgary, police seized $4 million worth from three locations.
- In St-Rémi-d'Amherst, Quebec, police seized 12,000 plants.

Every day brings a new list of seizures. Every day. With the kind of profit pot promises, people are lining up to get into this game.

The phenomenal rise of the domestic marijuana industry at the end of the 20th century—call it Bud Inc.—is a study in market dynamics and real-life supply and demand economics.

The kaleidoscope of shifting social and political forces at play, some visible, some subterranean, fascinates me.

I have participated in the cannabis industry since I realized as a fourteen-year-old you could buy a bag of reefer, make $20 profit middling joints and still have plenty to smoke; thirty-four years later I, too, am astonished at how it has blossomed. But something else heightened my interest in the public policy debate.

In recent years, I have lost three friends to various cancers. Each found marijuana the only effective medication for defeating the nausea of chemotherapy. When my mother was diagnosed with bowel cancer, I flew back to Ontario with a bag of B.C. Bud to help her through the treatment regime. Those experiences left me seriously questioning our public policy.

As someone who has often written about marijuana and as a long-time consumer, I have watched the industry develop. Initially, it was a microscopic subculture. Up until the mid-sixties, marijuana was invisible and pot prosecutions were rare. There were users, but they were well insulated within fringe communities. Until, as we all know, a revolution occurred.

Jazz, rock 'n' roll, reggae, the popularity of romantic literature, pick your catalyst. Charles Baudelaire, Louis Armstrong, the Beats, Hugh Hefner, Allen Ginsberg, Lenny Bruce, Bob Dylan, Jimi Hendrix, the Beatles, the Stones, John Prine, Margaret Trudeau, Bob Marley, Willie Nelson, Cheech and Chong, TV, Hollywood, Toronto's Rochdale College, the media in general—they all helped spread marijuana like a virus. It became an avatar of that particular sixties and early seventies cultural and political rebellion.

Initially, it wasn't much more than rich kids returning from exotic destinations with a couple of keys. Some ran Mexican dope up the coast to Vancouver, others carried it to Toronto. I know people who by 1970 were driving truckloads of hashish from Morocco to Amsterdam, where it was stuffed into the gas tanks of expensive cars and shipped to Montreal. Within a few years they graduated to transoceanic operations, bringing in tons of cannabis through Montreal, Vancouver and Halifax. In the late 1970s and until the early 1990s, there were mother-ships offshore unloading Thai-stick onto fishing boats, and shipping containers arrived stuffed with Afghani and Nepalese hash. There were a thousand ways to get it into the country. The word on the street was that at any one time as much as $20 million worth was floating in Vancouver Harbour. Then the lights went on and no one had to import it any more—you could grow it here. And the outlaw biker gangs were always involved.

People have cultivated marijuana outdoors in Canada since the 1960s, and some immigrant communities nurtured it for medicinal and cultural reasons long, long before that. There were even legendary commercial harvests throughout the 1980s—and there continue to be. But the arrival and spread of hydroponic expertise in the 1980s and 1990s and the profitability of indoor growing put the industry on a steroid program, pumping up yields per plant, stoking THC levels to new stony heights and priming profits skyward. Today Bud Inc. is a hardly invisible going concern worth billions of dollars and complete with its own emerging barons. Anyone can see that. No wonder it scares the hell out of the establishment, especially the Bush administration in Washington.

With Ottawa's permission, the U.S. federal government has deployed Drug Enforcement Administration operatives on the ground in Canada, ostensibly to work with local police forces on eradicating pot. Both nations have beefed up border patrols and inspections, established a tighter air-defence system and heightened surveillance of the sea routes. The world's longest undefended border is no more. Internationally, the DEA is exerting pressure on the United

Kingdom, the Netherlands and other countries to be tougher on cannabis. Washington and its allies also have ramped up the public rhetoric—marijuana hasn't been quite this demonized since the days of *Reefer Madness*.

Nothing could better illustrate the visceral nature of the discussion than the response from American and Canadian anti-cannabis crusaders upon learning four officers from the Royal Canadian Mounted Police were gunned down in March 2005 in northern Alberta. Without waiting for a full briefing, RCMP Commissioner Giuliano Zaccardelli blamed grow-ops and said they were a "plague" on society. Public Safety Minister Anne McLellan fumed about evil pot growers and Liberal MP Dan McTeague fulminated, "I think it's time for Parliament to target marijuana grow operations."

The Americans were still fingering pot growers a week later. *The New York Times* even blamed a rising murder rate on the drug battles this potent pot caused—only to correct itself later, saying the Canadian murder rate was stable. Trouble was, none of that was true, and the RCMP commissioner certainly should have known that. A pedophile and psychopath well known to police committed the murders. The killer had no connection to organized crime and had been a local menace for decades. The police officers were guarding an auto chop-shop discovered on the farm—the grow-op was serendipitously found and was not why the police were on site. But, as often happens in the cannabis prohibition debate, facts were the first casualty.

A loner described by his own family as evil, the perpetrator was armed with several guns even though he was prohibited by law from possessing firearms. No one pointed out that Alberta was the staunchest provincial opponent to federal gun-control laws. Little attention was paid to the failure of the courts to imprison a long-term violent offender. It was as if the pot plants themselves crept out of the shed and shot the police.

The international debate, in my view, is similarly coloured by ideology rather than insight. Canada's ascendancy as one of the world's primo producers, for instance, earns it the kind of verbal slagging the United States usually reserves for Colombia or Pakistan. Forget terrorists using the country as a staging area, the Bush administration would have you believe pot growers are creating a budding Sodom that endangers Homeland Security and the American Dream. And it's having little effect. So far they've nabbed: teenagers on a cross-border school bus smuggling kilos at a time; crooked Canadian and U.S. customs officers using the cloak of their uniforms to move hundreds of pounds; commercial boats carrying salmon stuffed with pot exempted from customs inspection by fisheries laws; kayakers paddling across Boundary Bay with loads of marijuana; helicopter pilots risking high-alpine passes, white-out weather and treacherous terrain to deliver thousands of pounds a week. In the summer of 2005, U.S. authorities discovered a sophisticated tunnel running under the border from Abbotsford, B.C., into Washington State. It was the first discovered in Canada, although nearly a score have been located under the Mexican–U.S. border. Truth is, Mexico sends much, much more marijuana north, and California produces as much pot as Canada.

A friendly, gregarious academic with white hair and glasses, Easton came to the pot industry by accident. His first interest as an economist was in the alcohol prohibition. He loved tales of gangsters, black markets and how they operated. He now is convinced history is repeating itself. And it isn't pretty.

I liked talking with Easton because he is one of the few disinterested observers of Bud Inc. with a big-picture view and no particular stake in skewing the facts. He was trying to determine how much booze was produced during Prohibition and the nature of the alcohol market in those years. We were both taken by the similarities between what happened with alcohol and what is happening with cannabis. The parallels are stunning. Back then, as now, police and judges did little to rein in bootleggers, and the rule of law began to collapse, given broad community support and collusion.

Prohibition in North America, Easton explained, was a strange beast, and most people don't fully understand it was a weird public policy griffin. It lasted from 1920 to 1933 in the United States. But, outside of PEI, Newfoundland, which was a separate entity, and Quebec, which appears to have simply ignored it, the Canadian ban was much briefer.* That led to the rise of a lucrative and widespread domestic alcohol industry that is the root of many family fortunes. The Bronfmans, the Seagrams, the Kennedys and the Rockefellers all profited mightily from the alcohol prohibition. Easton and I were amazed at the relevance to current debate.

In the twenties, with high unemployment, distilling illicit liquor and smuggling it became a way of life across Canada. Rum-running was lucrative, and the underground economy was no more subterranean than is today's pot industry. Al Capone bought almost all his lager from the Windsor magnates, Harry Low, Charles Burns and Marco Leon, who ran the Carling brewery in London.† On the West Coast, for

---

* Dry times lasted in Yukon three years, in B.C. four, in Manitoba seven, in Alberta, Saskatchewan and Newfoundland eight, in New Brunswick 10, in Ontario 11, and in Nova Scotia 13, and on Prince Edward Island for nearly half a century.

† Craig Heron, a York University professor, is the expert in this area and has written a brilliant and scintillating history of liquor and alcohol regulation in Canada called *Booze*. I am indebted to him and his work.

instance, one company had an export permit to send liquor to Tahiti but the boats left B.C. ports and were back in a week—hence their nudge-nudge reputation as "extremely fast" vessels. They sailed into U.S. waters and unloaded. Today, pot smugglers use the same routes, running a more sophisticated (but basically the same style) gauntlet of Coast Guard and U.S. Navy vessels.

Hypocrisy back then, as now, was rampant. Future prime minister and father of the country's first anti-drug law Mackenzie King voted to tighten Prohibition in 1921, reportedly on the same day he took delivery of a shipment of whisky. One nefarious bootlegger is said to have told police: "Yes, I voted for prohibition, and I'd vote for it again. I went broke farming."

The alcohol ban was clearly good for the economy but it was difficult to quantify, Easton pointed out, because data were hard to obtain. When a Royal Commission on Customs and Excise held cross-country hearings to investigate the sales and profits of the industry, it found the brewers and distillers had cooked their books. Records were destroyed so there would be no incriminating evidence.

Conservative economists have long worried about the corrosive influence of any kind of prohibition. Every introductory economics course inculcates the rule that prohibitions necessarily breed black markets. The profitability of such markets ensures that even if you caught more people, they would not disappear because there's always a lineup of eager new entrants. Still, economists have long had difficulty describing these shady dealings in terms that quantify the consequences for society—they are rarely able to accurately measure or gauge such activity because of its murky nature. Some factors are easy to discern. The alcohol prohibition in North America was particularly profitable for those willing to take risks, because Canada and the United

States adopted different kinds of public policy. The 18th U.S. amendment shut down all production and retailing of alcohol. In Canada, only retail sales were interrupted and production continued. "No one in Canada went thirsty," Easton quipped.

Under the alcohol prohibition in Canada, doctors prescribed it for all kinds of ailments, church wine consumption skyrocketed and mail-order services sprang up. Sam Bronfman stole Sears's catalogue idea in 1916 and opened an import and distribution business. If you lived in Calgary, you ordered booze from Fernie, B.C., or Maple Creek, Saskatchewan, and it was delivered to your door. In Manitoba, two-thirds of the liquor stores changed their names to "Warehouse" and began "wholesaling" instead of "retailing"—legal legerdemain that put them under federal protection.

With all this activity, Easton wanted to know: How much alcohol was actually produced—especially during the era when Canada was wet, America dry and smuggling rampant? He devised a computer program to figure it out.

"I tried to develop a methodology to determine how many stills were in operation," he explained. "I developed a technique and said: 'Well, there is no way to test the technique to see if it is correct or not. It's just a mechanism.' So I said: 'Why don't I try it on something like marijuana and see if it comes up with a reasonable answer?' I decided to build the prototype on the contemporaneous marijuana business because we could find out more about that than about the alcohol business eighty years ago."

The difference between tough, punitive U.S. federal anti-drug laws and Canada's more liberal treatment of pot has produced a similarly artificial situation as the alcohol prohibition. The law and the courts encourage marijuana growers to operate on this side of the border and ship their products south. Within Canada, Easton pointed out, growers migrate to British Columbia because its judiciary is among the most lenient when it comes to pot offences. The particularly profitable situation that the alcohol prohibition produced has arisen again because of the cannabis prohibition policy differences between the two countries. And no one who truly wants a reefer goes without.

Easton said his technique is of no use with cocaine or other imports because there must be local production. His model uses profit maximization, the economist's favourite idea, which says an illicit industry will continue to grow as long as its rate of return is at least equal to that generated by a small business.

For his calculations, Easton began with the estimated total number of users, which was available from a variety of health and census reports. He plugged in consumption numbers based on estimates of usage (available again through various studies and surveys), and he came up with a ballpark size for the internal market: about two million consumers.

Next he turned his attention to grow-ops. He chose British Columbia because that's where police intelligence said most were located. It is the centre of the industry because it is the California of Canada, with a social culture that is cannabis friendly. Police believed the number and spread of grow-ops in Ontario and Quebec was of a similar order, but the pot culture was simply less prominent.

Between 1997 and 2000, the number of grow-ops across British Columbia dismantled by police more than doubled, from 1,251 to 2,808. Nearly 80 per cent were indoors. Working with the police numbers, Easton factored in other parameters—four harvests a year, $2,613 a pound, 33 grams of dried bud per plant, $18,000 rent a year, $10,000 investment in equipment for a hundred-plant show, $2,500 in electricity, $70,000 in labour and security costs . . .

He figured per-harvest revenue from a modest hundred-plant show was slightly more than $19,000, or $76,000 in gross revenue a year. That was fabulous return on investment—55 per cent even with the most conservative assumptions. But that didn't include risk factors. If 10 per cent of grow-ops were busted by police, competitors or thieves, then the rate of return was actually closer to 40 per cent, Easton said. Still not bad if you can get it.

But how many grow-ops were out there?

If you crunched the numbers and fiddled with your estimate of the percentage busted by police, Easton credibly suggested there were between 10,500 and 17,500 across B.C. alone. Remember, these were commercial grows, not homes with fewer than fifty plants. There were some limitations on the calculation, but it provided a starting point in terms of making economic sense about the market activities.

Moving from the number of grow-ops, and refining his formula, Easton was able to estimate the total quantity of marijuana grown. According to the numbers, Easton said, marijuana cultivation and production are so pervasive that the prohibition is doomed. As with alcohol a century ago, Easton concluded pot is too easily produced and too easily exported to be controlled by law enforcement. The return on investment is simply too high. For every grow-op police shut down, another will spring up. It's an economic inevitability.

I had recently returned from a tour of grow operations—one was massive, housing 6,000 plants or more. We saw over a dozen in a day, all within a few kilometres of each other. I visited barns that once sheltered animals—barns where chickens once roosted, where cattle once were milked—now rigged for growing pot. The biggest was underground, with generators powering lights that ate up so much gas the owners bought a gas station to hide their conspicuous consumption.

"That scares me," Easton said. "Because if something is unenforceable and widespread then what you get is capricious enforcement, which is exactly what the rule of law is supposed to deny. Secondly, you have a situation in which the police could devote an infinite number of resources to this, so the decision about how many resources to devote becomes much more complex and really is a decision I don't think the police feel very comfortable making. They could devote all their resources to this and there would still be grow-ops out there. Why would you want to shut down the kidnapping squad or the murder squad or the robbery detail in order to investigate this one activity? They don't. As a result, they're being called upon to manage their resources with something that is increasingly growing."

Two things bothered Easton and me about the current approach. First, that the police and anti-marijuana political propaganda is obvious baloney.

"I used it," Easton said. "I'm still doing things. I didn't turn into a frog. I mean, I'm a real person, I did this stuff, I smoked marijuana in high school and, yeah, it made me nervous." So he quit; it didn't make me nervous so I kept smoking for years.

Second, both of us believe that the current policy is nurturing not combatting organized crime.

"Marijuana is the low-hanging fruit," Easton explained. "It is the real source of enormous amounts of revenue for criminal organizations. People talk about heroin and these other hard drugs, but the amount of those drugs and the number of people who use them are very, very small. It may be a higher return in terms of the volume and so forth, but it's still nothing like the return generated by the marijuana trade."

The alcohol prohibition ended, he suggested, because it was impossible to enforce. Booze was available everywhere; as a consequence, Prohibition had an acidic influence on people's attitude toward police and the courts because the law was often ignored or treated as a misdemeanour. The dirty money generated by the activity was equally caustic.

"It's unimaginable that those kind of funds flowing through the system won't have a terribly corrosive influence on public servants," Easton said. "There is what I would characterize as the potential for widespread corruption. It was certainly true of Chicago in the 1920s. It was certainly true across the U.S. in the major cities, and I don't see why we should be immune today. We might have the attitude that it can't happen here, but I think that is naive."

It already has. Not only have law enforcement and border agencies seen their own members tempted, but even high-level bureaucrats have been linked to cross-border marijuana smuggling. And money from organized crime has bought influence and tainted political party leadership races.

Still, what is the best replacement for the current prohibition and what would be the economic implications of this alternative policy regime? With legalization, the production, distribution, sale and possession of marijuana would all be legitimate and pot would be treated as any other commodity. With decriminalization, possession is not subject to criminal sanctions but it remains illegal to grow, produce, distribute and sell. Is one better than the other?

The case against decriminalization is identical to the central complaint about the Dutch approach. Since the mid-1970s, it has been legal in the Netherlands to buy, possess and smoke small amounts of cannabis, but the underlying wholesale transaction required to support the market is not. That doesn't really make sense. Decriminalization keeps the industry underground and perpetuates the unwanted side of the business—crime, corruption, violence and the collateral damage. The only benefit is, users can relax.

The same criticism can be levelled at those pushing for a medical regime wherein marijuana is controlled by doctors and distributed through pharmacies, as occurs with prescription medication and the pilot medical-marijuana programs run by Canada and the Netherlands. This provides patients with a legal supply and reduces the black market—and might even considerably shrink it if doctors were to take the same approach as they used to with booze. But there are limits to such a parlour game, and a lax prescription process would continue the corrosion of respect for the law and perpetuate the myth that somehow marijuana is dangerous and only allowable for medical reasons.

I think full legalization makes better sense than any other proposal. It is also the policy urged by most non-partisan inquiries into the use of marijuana. Conservative senator Pierre Claude Nolin, as chair of the Senate Special Committee on Illegal Drugs, was the latest politician to urge legalization. He oversaw the most exhaustive study of Canadian cannabis policy since the LeDain Commission of the 1970s. The government put his report on the same shelf as LeDain's.

Although President Jimmy Carter along with Prime Minister Pierre Trudeau and his successor Joe Clark all nominally favoured changing the marijuana laws, none ever spent the political capital to do it. By the 1980s, the conservative tide flowing across both nations militated against the issue coming forward. Most of the users from the sixties and seventies also had jobs, had moved to the suburbs and were in no danger of being busted—so who cared?

The National Organization for the Reform of Marijuana Laws (NORML) even became dormant in Canada. The AIDS crisis and the political activism of gays in California, with their drive for cannabis to be reclassified as a legal medication, resuscitated the issue. The medical marijuana movement is the most potent force pushing for legalization on both sides of the border. And it is growing fast.

The current Liberal government's approach—which is to lessen penalties for possession while stiffening production and manufacturing sentences—is probably one of the worst policies the country could consider. The law will have a net-widening effect and exacerbate current social ills. It will encourage the growth of organized crime and put more money in criminals' pockets.

The problem: the Canadian government is afraid of Washington and hamstrung by international legal conventions, to which it is a signatory, that classify cannabis with cocaine and heroin. The United Nations agreed at a special assembly in 1998 to eliminate—or significantly reduce—by 2008 the cultivation of cannabis, coca and opium. That commitment was reaffirmed at the March 2003 session of the UN Commission on Drugs, yet these three substances are by no means equivalent. Employing the same approach is fraught with pitfalls.

The best estimates that have been generated suggest that marijuana legalization in the United States might save roughly US$7.7 billion a year in enforcement costs (US$5.3 billion of which would accrue to local governments, US$2.4 billion to Washington). In Canada, the savings might be in the order of $300 million.

It's hard to figure out the size of the tax boon that marijuana legalization might produce, but at the very least the government could pocket the current premium on illegality. In other words, the tax man could absorb the risk-reward portion of the profit reaped by illegal growers. In a legal environment, Easton pointed out, prices should normally fall due to mass production. But the government could substitute a tax to maintain the price consumers are used to paying.

"There are questions about how we would collect taxes on exports, and what would happen should the U.S. retaliate against our legalization, but the basic argument would be the

same: we effect no change in price, we only transfer the revenue from current producers."

Now, there are questions in a legal world, such as whether
you allow advertising, whether you impose age restrictions,
whether changes in competition will affect the market,
whether individual growers can be licensed, and so on. But
those can be answered, and the future is not difficult to pre-
dict: in a legal environment, large, sophisticated pot producers will quickly supplant local suppliers offering cannabis
products at lower cost. It happened with alcohol, it happened
with tobacco, it will happen with cannabis.

"The broader social question becomes less whether or not
we approve or disapprove of local production, but rather who
shall enjoy the spoils," Easton said. "As it stands now, growers
and distributors pay some of the costs and reap all of the benefits of the multi-billion-dollar marijuana industry, while the
non-marijuana-smoking taxpayer sees only the costs."

Arguably, removing the alcohol prohibition caused or
exacerbated many social problems, such as addiction, family
dysfunction and homelessness. But such societal ills existed
regardless of the legal status of liquor, and they paled in comparison to the problems that afflicted society as a result of
the power and influence wielded by Al Capone and his ilk.
The profits that flowed to organized crime from illegal
whisky—like the profits that are now flowing into its pockets
from illicit pot—produced as natural by-products political
corruption and violence. Bullying, intimidation, extortion
and murder—these are the tools of organized crime.
Legalization would end some of that. Removing the prohibition on cannabis would permit society to replace today's gift
of revenue to organized crime with (at the very least) an additional source of revenue for government coffers.

"Unless we wish to continue to transfer these billions
from this lucrative endeavour to organized crime," Easton

said, "legalization should be considered. Not only would we deprive some very unsavoury groups of a profound source of easy money, but also resources currently spent on marijuana enforcement would be available for other activities."

Is there an economic value to legalization in and of itself? Not particularly. If you take $1,000 from the black economy and move it to the white economy you get a modest increase in activity because it's more efficient and you have the tools of society to help make that operation work. Beyond that, there may be some other consequences, but no great jump in the GDP or anything like that.

Easton looked up from his computer. "Still, if we don't stop it, this could be a return to the Roaring Twenties."

I think he's right. The numbers alone are a persuasive argument for change. The insidious side effects of today's prohibition provide even more compelling reasons for legalization—from the unsavoury characters who profit from it, the overcrowded prisons and the hundreds of thousands who have been saddled with a criminal record to the crime, corruption and lack of respect it breeds.

If you'd like to see for yourself, let me give you a glimpse inside Bud Inc. It has been my experience that smugglers the world over are of a type. As are farmers. Ditto pot growers. Sure, there are indigenous idiosyncrasies and wrinkles, but the market forces are very similar whether you are in California, the Netherlands or British Columbia—the world of marijuana's three centres. A head shop in Amsterdam carries the same paraphernalia as one in Toronto or San Francisco. A dealer is moving the same strains and products and doing the same thing no matter where he lives. Although more than two hundred groups in North America are fighting for legalization and an end to pot prohibition, only a handful of people are on the bridge—some of whom have been involved in the struggle for forty years.

I have chosen to look at the business of cannabis primarily through the prism of and from the perspective of its British Columbia branch office. The province is a marijuana mecca, and B.C. Bud now stands in a pantheon of pot beside such legends as Acapulco Gold and California Sinsemilla. The globally recognized brand name is sought by cannabis cognoscenti and commands the highest prices—what sells wholesale in Vancouver for US$1,500 will sell for US$4,000 and up in Los Angeles, New York or London. B.C. is a good place to use for a case study on the industry's dynamics. I have watched the business blossom here for a quarter-century, and I'm convinced that what is true here is true across Canada and America and Europe.

THE ROYAL COURT

April 26, 2004

A CHILL WIND SWEPT DOWN Hastings Street, swirling around the cenotaph and filling drab Victory Square with the acrid smoke of a three-alarm fire. The dealers were on the corners already. Their scouts lounged nearby, against the columns of the landmark Dominion Building, once the tallest skyscraper in the British Empire. Those with a job or a destination scurried past, ignoring the open trade.

Bud. Hey, man, looking for bud?

In the historic, if decaying, squat walk-ups around the foot of the tarnished, late-Victorian skyscraping marvel, the neighbourhood has gone to pot. Literally. Nearly a hundred years ago, the good burghers consecrated the small park around the war memorial, and today it remains hallowed ground, the annual focus of Remembrance Day ceremonies, scant moments of respectability. For at least a decade, this swath has formed the dividing line between Vancouver's tourist-friendly business core and the wasteland of its skid road, dubbed the Downtown Eastside, home turf for some five thousand indigent, mentally ill, addicted and poor.

Bud. Hey, man, looking for bud?

A few steps west of the Dominion Building's colonnade and just before the baroque window displays of Dressew, where once stood a two-storey brick heritage building, a ragged vacancy smouldered. From across the street, it looked as if someone had knocked a tooth from the slatternly block's smile. Arson. The inferno consumed Blunt Bros. Café ("a respectable joint"), vintage clothing store Cabbages & Kinx and Spartacus Books, the beloved local purveyor of left-wing literature and propaganda. The Sunday-morning blaze, had it spread to adjoining buildings, would have destroyed the command centre of Marc Emery, de facto leader of the global movement for marijuana legalization and head of the BC Marijuana Party, a legitimate provincial political organization.

Emery was the lightning rod of marijuana culture. Many believed he was the real target of the culprits who set alight Dumpsters in the alley to ignite the fire. Regardless, smoke and water damage to his building and the bookend one on the other side was extensive. Emery's offices, store and television production centre were flooded and soiled with soot.

Looking for bud?

Erected in the flush days of the Klondike Gold Rush of the 1890s, the buildings reflected the contemporary-classical architecture style of the day with its sheet-metal facades and oversized pediments (these days considered more potentially hazardous than decorative). Locally, this is known as the Pot Block, or the Pot Precinct, a thriving if shabby commercial oasis of hemp stores, head shops, bong emporiums, music stores, cannabis-friendly restaurants and grotty street life.

A century ago, this was the thumping heart of a nascent metropolis. Today it's funky at best, rank at worst. People refer to it as Vansterdam, a legal-marijuana limbo nestled between the open misery of the Downtown Eastside and the gaudy affluence of the downtown core. The city's vaunted pedestrian mall, tony cruise-ship docks, five-star hotels, designer boutiques and high-end merchants such as Birks and Cartier lie a few steps west. Travel in the other direction and one finds crackheads in doorways, heroin addicts in the alleys and panhandlers stalking the sidewalk in front of the usual tenderloin pawn shops, cheap beer parlours and 24/7 convenience stores happy to trade in stolen goods.

Bud. Hey, man, looking for Bud?

Around here, seed companies offer a wealth of genetics developed by the province's not-so-underground gardeners—hundreds of unique strains of *Cannabis indica* and *sativa* with names like Blueberry Daydreams, Chronic and Black Death. Some are tremendous mood-enhancers, others are said to be potent medicinals. You'll find products that in the past were enjoyed only by the most well-connected and well-travelled connoisseurs.

If you ignore the street dealers, you can find cannabis-laced cookies, kif, domestic hashish that I think trumps the imported Lebanese or Nepalese that is also available, bubble hash and a spectrum of luscious, crystal-encrusted pot in colours from Day-Glo emerald green to deep purple, not to mention brownie-like K-Nanaimo squares that will fly you to the moon and spacey granola bars that make eating roughage an entirely uplifting experience. All the accessories, ancillary equipment and accoutrements for enjoying, growing, processing or producing your own marijuana are available too. Pollinators ranging in price from $550 to $795 for tumbling your shake—the leaves and trim—to quickly and easily separate the tiny, prized resin glands from the rest of the plant to manufacture hashish. Stainless steel hash presses for $275. Ice-o-lator bags for producing bubble hash — 5-gallon size: two bags for $150, three bags for $225; 20-gallon size: two bags for $200, three bags for $300. For less than $20 you could even select from an unbelievable variety of Herby's Twists, magnetic, plastic grinders painted to look like eight balls, eyeballs, rainbows . . . (The cute, useful novelty won first prize at the 2003 CannaBusiness Trade Show in Germany.) And if you're worried about taking a urine test at work, a plethora of products can ease those anxieties: catheters, synthetic urine to substitute for your own (guaranteed from babies) and contraptions like the Whizzinator, which — well, it's better not to ask unless you need to know.

The Vancouver Yellow Pages features three pages of listings for hydroponic equipment companies — dozens, and a tenfold increase in a decade. More outlets than Burger King in the metropolitan area.

It is easy to understand why Canada's fastest growing and hippest city became an iconic ground zero for the U.S. war on drugs. Vancouver is a crucible for a dramatic shift in treating the "drug problem" that threatens to repudiate Washington's long-standing crusade against dope. Dubbed the Four Pillars approach, it was a product of the left-of-centre, George Soros–funded civil society initiative and its point man, Ethan Nadelmann. Plucked from academia, he used the billionaire's money to create the Drug Policy Alliance. Nadelmann was changing minds and laws around the globe by advocating a simple message: drug use was a health issue, not a criminal problem.

Some elements had been pioneered in Amsterdam, in Frankfurt and in other European cities, but Nadelmann advocated a broad, integrated set of initiatives and Vancouver was a North American test site.

Under the plan funded by all three levels of Canadian

government, the city distributed free syringes, operated a safe injection site and backed a free heroin experiment, and the mayor wanted to legalize and tax marijuana. Vancouver was a crucial battleground for those out to change the way Western democracies regulated drug use and dealt with the fallout of addiction. Millions of Americans who visited regularly were in danger of seeing first-hand what was happening and whether it worked better than the existing prohibition.

Emery's operation stocked just about everything the Bush administration deigns evil: subversive books, hemp clothes, bags, shoes, hats, papers, pipes, magazines, grow chemicals, pot posters, wild psychedelics, grinders, hemp food and anything else you might fancy for sowing, cultivating, consuming or celebrating marijuana. At the back of the store, along with a display of museum-quality opium pipes and drug culture artifacts, the Urban Shaman dispensed "entheobotanicals"—a cornucopia of magical, mystical and sacred plants guaranteed to give you a glimpse of psychedelic godhead: ayahuasca, Iboga root bark, peyote, *Salvia divinorum*, yerba mate and exotic sage, along with other dreaming herbs and fungi.

No one was a more eloquent, enthusiastic or loquacious salesman for marijuana than Emery, one of the original financiers of Canada's Libertarian Party. The self-proclaimed "Prince of Pot," Emery was a darling of the media. He had graced *The National Enquirer, 60 Minutes,* CNN, *The Times of London* and *The Wall Street Journal.* The first time he was busted in Vancouver, in January 1996, was after his appearance in the latter, august financial publication. He contested nine local elections, his most recent a futile challenge to become mayor in November 2002.

From his headquarters in the Rogers Building, Emery controlled the BC Marijuana Party, subsidized most major marijuana events around the globe, financed the U.S. Marijuana

Party, published *Cannabis Culture* magazine, underwrote the Pot TV network, ran the world's largest marijuana-seed brokerage and kept his finger in a dozen other pot-related projects. He had not left the country in a decade for fear of ending up in a U.S. dungeon.

A close friend of Emery's, Howard Marks, the legendary British smuggler nicknamed "Mr. Nice" who two decades ago moved shipments of pot and hash in and out of Vancouver with abandon, was nabbed in Spain in 1989 on a U.S. warrant. He served most of a decade. Marks was in U.S. custody when Canadian authorities stayed charges in a $38-million Vancouver seizure tied to him. Nevil Schoenmakers, another pal who was behind the Dutch Seed Bank, was grabbed on a U.S. warrant in 1990 in Australia when he went to visit family. I too had a friend busted, in a 1991 sting, after U.S. destroyers steamed into international waters, three days north of Hawaii, to seize his Canada-bound, 80-ton shipload of hash. He got twenty-six years in a U.S. prison and served fifteen. Emery did not plan to make the same kind of mistakes.

A loud, insect-like drone reverberated throughout the three-storey brick building when I visited, but other than that, Emery's staff had done a remarkable job of getting things back in shape. The store looked normal in spite of the fire and the demolition work next door. But it was a Monday morning and the normally ebullient Emery was in the back dealing with more than the usual headaches for a marijuana mogul.

He had lost between $20,000 and $40,000 in merchandise, and counting. The building's power supply was cut and muck was everywhere. The "suspicious" blaze had disrupted his operations and piled on expenses, such as the $3,000-a-day buzzing generator needed to keep the Internet television studio and computer servers functioning. Emery had no insurance — no one insures a company operating in a legal shadowland with marijuana in its name. Rent was due: $5,500.

Emery handed a Mason jar of dope to Kaara (Maori for "Star in the Night Sky"), his violet-haired personal assistant. She rolled a large joint.

A sign on the wall read: "Overgrow the Government."

"Marijuana is the best industry any province can have," Emery muttered, fulminating on the motive behind the unsuccessful attempt to burn down the block. "People are damn lucky to have it."

Straights were hauling themselves into offices across the land and keying into their e-mail. The bleary-eyed happy-face of Canadian politics was staring down personnel crises, a seemingly interminable cash-crunch and raging paranoia. Greg Williams, his long-time right-hand man, ignored Emery's pique and packaged seeds while monitoring Internet orders and updating the electronic inventory. A burly visiting grower, slumped on one of the couches, eyes at half-mast, seemed to have heard it all before too. Or was too stoned to care.

"Some Blueberry," Kaara said, sparking the spliff.

"I'm not allowed to touch it," Emery quipped.

He was awaiting trial, as he often is, after he was arrested for passing a joint to another man at a rally in Saskatchewan. Police charged him with trafficking.

Kaara planted her lips on his and blew smoke into his mouth shotgun style. Emery exhaled a long stream, giggled and took a sip of blueberry tea. *A-h-h.* His mood visibly improved. Wake and bake.

"Be back." Kaara waved and disappeared into the front of the store.

As if the bad news of the blaze wasn't enough, Emery had learned his accountant was stealing to support a sordid pornography habit—only one of many ironies in the world of marijuana. In a previous incarnation as a provincial book-seller and publicity hound, Emery helped open access to explicit sexual material in Canada through legal challenges to the obscenity laws. He was also known among staff for boasting of his horny escapades. That didn't make paying thousands in tax penalties because of his accountant's malfeasance any easier to swallow.

The problem added to Emery's cash-flow worries and already high overhead. He provided $2,500 for the Rome rally, $2,500 for London, England, $1,000 for Toronto, $7,000 for Vancouver and $20,000 for the Fill the Hill bash in Ottawa. There was the $15,000 for a public policy conference, $5,000 to $6,000 for Cannabis Day festivities, and $120,000 a year for the Iboga Therapy House, a free facility Emery founded in 2002 that treats addicts with Ibogaine, a powerful psychoactive extract from the bark of an African tree. That's not to mention what he provides in child support—and did he mention taxes?

"I just filed," he said blithely, the gathering clouds parting, "and for the fifth year I will continue paying about $10,000 a month, alas, in personal income tax. I'm the only one who says he gets his money from marijuana. I asked them. They said, no one else. I claim $300,000 or thereabouts, which is pretty well what it takes to live in an apartment and support three of my four kids. Three exes now—it used to be four—and they take a lot of money."

He rolled his eyes theatrically.

Emery had forty-five or so people on the payroll. He supported a full-time lobbyist in Ottawa, advertising offices in Toronto, a circulation department in Port Franks, Ontario, and correspondence offices in the United States and in Nelson, B.C. He funded the U.S. Marijuana Party and he was sending its leader to Moscow to support jailed Russian activists. He had no hobbies other than marijuana and civil liberties. His life was a constant stream-of-consciousness performance fuelled by marijuana, and this was his main court. He fired up a bong as Kaara returned with a short, squat middle-aged man.

"He'd like to buy some seeds," she said.

Emery brightened at the sight of the first customer of the day.

"Come in, sit down." He gestured to the couch, letting out a stream of smoke and offering the bong to the man with spiky yellow hair, who turned out be from Chicago. The visitor took a big toke.

Emery developed his business essentially to finance a revolution. He sold marijuana seeds around the world and took the proceeds to subvert the system. He considered himself judgment-proof. The biggest fine he had paid was $2,000. If they forced him out of business again, he vowed to declare bankruptcy. He said he gave away all his money immediately to provide people with bail, pay legal bills or fund pot-related enterprises. He claimed to own nothing. For instance, he had been unable to sell Pot TV in an elaborate deal with Canadian media celebrity Moses Znaimer because of the hurdles in moving the off-book enterprise into the above-ground world. He also feared police would declare any money that he earned in the transaction to be the proceeds of crime. Emery tries to ensure all his cash is in by noon and out by four p.m. That way there is nothing for police to seize if they raid him.

"Any idea what you're looking for?" he asked.

The American, his cheeks puffy with pot, nodded.

"Remember the name?"

The head bobbed again. The man exhaled smoke. "I'm going to go with the Vancouver . . ." He stopped, his head weaving slightly.

"Vancouver Island?" Emery offered. "Those are all strong *indicas*. Do you remember the name?"

The man released the rest of the toke and grinned. "Burmese Incredible," he said.

"Yeah, those are Vancouver Island," Emery replied. "Not Burmese Fucking Incredible?"

"Yeah. That's it."

"Yeah, Burmese Fucking Incredible," Emery repeated. "That'll be great."

While the man fished a wad of bills from his pocket, Emery reached into a drawer and withdrew a covered plastic tray like one from a small tackle or sewing box. The compartments were filled not with lures or bobbins, but with individually labelled, inch-square glassine bags of seeds.

"Do you guys do Canadian or U.S. money?"

"Either," Emery said. "How many?"

"I'll take a hundred," said the man, who owned a couple of duplexes and a pizza-and-pot delivery service.

"We'll put them in one of these," Emery said, holding up a tiny, stiff mailing sleeve that looked like a thick credit card. "I always recommend mailing them to yourself. There's no ability for them to detect seeds in it and the package contains small sticks to keep them from being squashed in the automatic rollers. You can carry them over the border, and I don't know of any customers who have had trouble, but it's always a possibility. You're going into America. Crazy place, full of paranoia and what-have-you."

He handed the package to the American.

"So okay, a hundred Burmese Fucking Incredible, which are fabulous by the way, just wonderful. You want to mail this?"

"No, I think I'll just hang on to it."

"Just strip away all this paperwork before crossing the border. It's incriminating. You don't have to tell them what these seeds are; they could be any kind of seed. Don't at any point admit they are marijuana seeds. Even if they find them, don't say they are marijuana seeds."

The American put the package in his pocket.

"That's $400 Canadian or about $320 American."

"What's the shelf life?"

"Two years. They're relatively fresh, so that's another two

years away." Emery counted out the bills. "Twenty, forty, sixty . . . Be sure and come back."

The *Hockey Night in Canada* theme song pierced the air. Emery reached for his cellphone.

"Marc speaking . . ."

Reared as a libertarian by two British parents, Emery honed his early life into a veritable homily that would have made his inspiration, Ayn Rand, proud. He turned money from his paper route into Marc's Comics Room, a mail-order business built around Moon Mullins and Beetle Bailey comic books that he resold at hugely inflated prices. He quit school at sixteen, opened a bookstore and started getting under the skin of the local establishment. He was a gadfly protesting everything from the Sunday shopping law to the civic garbage strike.

"I provided a free service because the government union shut down this service," he recalls with glee. "I hate unions, so I took the garbage to a private landfill site. I was charged, but they dropped them eventually. I was also charged for home-schooling my four adopted children in Ontario."

He then discovered marijuana.

Back in the 1980s, the Criminal Code of Canada made it illegal to sell or publish pro-drug literature or periodicals such as *High Times*, the New York–based monthly devoted to promoting cannabis and delivering the scripture to true believers. Emery thought that was ridiculous and sold copies of *High Times* in front of the police station, begging to be arrested. The publicity, as it does today, produced profit. But after a while, Emery threw in the towel and left Canada. He lived in Asia for two years before ending up broke in Singapore, wallowing in self-pity.

"I was trying to decide what to do when I read a Reuters article in the newspaper saying, 'Marijuana blooms in Lower Mainland of B.C.,'" is how he recalls it. "This was 1993 and the article went on to say there were more smokers and growers of marijuana in southwestern B.C. than in all of North America, according to the RCMP. So it was the RCMP who brought me here—they should feel responsible for what has happened." If he tells this anecdote during a speech, audiences laugh heartily.

Before setting up in Vancouver, however, he stopped in Amsterdam to attend the Cannabis Cup, the global marijuana culture's annual harvest festival sponsored by *High Times*. There, Emery met Ben Dronkers, pioneer pot grower, seed seller and progenitor of the Sensi Seeds conglomerate.

Dronkers, a key player in the Netherlands' thirty-year experiment with liberal marijuana laws, is among the most successful of cannabis capitalists. He opened the first seed-and-grow shop in 1985. For Emery, this was the true Saul-on-the-road-to-Damascus moment. Over the following days, he soaked up all he could about the business blueprint Dronkers had created and decided to implement the model when he arrived in Vancouver. He literally said: "I want to be that man. I love that man."

After establishing a business relationship with Dronkers, Emery transported his strategy and tactics to British Columbia in the hope of sparking political change and claiming a beachhead in the emerging cannabis economy. I met him the following year, shortly after he arrived in 1994.

Emery began by selling grow books and *High Times* door-to-door until he could open a storefront operation. His first was in the recently firebombed communist bookstore a few blocks east of his current location.

In a very real way, it was a second front in the War to Liberate the Weed, a new theatre for the ongoing social experiment started in the Mellow Yellow, the Bulldog, the Milky Way and a handful of other Dutch coffee shops twenty years earlier. And one of Emery's main assets was his access and distribution deal with Dronkers and Sensi.

Today, Emery's main revenue stream—between $1 million and $3 million a year, depending on whom you believe—comes from seeds, a grey area of the law. They are a legitimate food product bearing beneficial edible oil and only trace amounts of THC, the key psychotropic chemical sought in the mature plant. They have been used forever in products such as bird chow. Identifying viable cannabis seeds is nearly impossible without sprouting them. So enforcement is damn tough. Emery exploits this situation.

There are others in the same business—Smokinseeds, Kind Seeds Co., AAA Seed Company, Vancouver Seeds ("The finest connoisseur strains from Holland, Humboldt, and B.C.") or Sacred Seed in Toronto, and similar brokers in Quebec, Atlantic Canada and the United States, all marketed on the Internet and in various pot-friendly publications.

Emblematic of the largest seed vendors, Emery's firm offers five-hundred-plus varieties from growers and wholesale seed sellers around the globe, such as Solar Warrior, Soma Seeds, Wild Rose Seeds, Easter Island Seeds, Cash Crop Ken, DJ Short Seeds, Australian Outback Seeds . . . Genetics for all the big, smooth-smoking bud are available by mail: Black Domina, Romulan, Durban Poison, Mississippi Sweet Bud, Afghan Dream, Northern Lights, Maui Mist . . . the list goes on.

Prices range from $40 a ten-seed packet for some Jamaican swag to $345 per pack for something tastier, like Marley's Collie. Each plant, properly nurtured, will yield at least a pound of smokable dope, worth up to $2,500, give or take a few hundred bucks, depending on the market.

Emery is a rock star among the marijuana set and rarely without an entourage of assistants and assorted hangers-on.

Not only does he know everyone, he freely dispenses his information and loves to gossip and name-drop. Journalists, broad-
casters, documentary filmmakers, writers and photographers
arrive regularly looking for a quote, a story or an introduction
to someone in the industry.

As a result, Michelle Rainey, a brash, buxom blonde who
has managed his affairs since 2000, does much of the hard
work. She is rarely to be found lounging around the office: "I
don't have time to sit there with the boys going, 'Don't you
like my tits?' There's a business to run."

Rainey's father died when she was twelve and her Ukrain-
ian mother reared an independent, hard-working woman like
herself. At sixteen, Rainey developed Crohn's disease and at
nineteen decided that curse would make graduating from university impossible. She went to work in the local bank. Nearly
ten years later, Emery strolled up to her wicket.

"I had seen him all over the news as a young woman," the
thirty-three-year-old recalls. "I said, 'Mr. Emery I think you are
a hero and I hope you can keep doing what you do because it's
people like me who need you. I have Crohn's disease and I
have been a closet marijuana smoker for the past few years.
Nobody knows because I want to keep my job at this bank and
I have a mortgage now.' He gave me an autographed magazine with the message 'Overgrow the government!'"

She went home and told her now ex, Bruce, that Emery
was going to change her life someday and she was going to
change his. Two years later, Emery advertised for a personal
assistant. Rainey phoned, and he remembered her.

"He went, 'You're the nice-looking woman with the red
lips and big boobs,'" she giggled. "I said, 'Yes, I'd like to apply
for your job.' Took my ten-page resumé, went to his house,
and we've been together for almost five years."

Back then, Emery had only a few projects on the go.
Vancouver mayor Philip Owen, who still hadn't embraced

the Four Pillars plan, shut down Emery and pretty well chased him to the Sunshine Coast. In those days, Pot TV was little more than a computer in the basement of Emery's house.

"He had a lot of incompetent and failing people that weren't doing what they set out to do," Rainey said. "It was chaos. Absolute chaos. I took a look around. Not only did the house need to be cleaned, not only did Marc's clothes need to be cleaned and he himself need to be pressed, his mistress needed to be taken care of or thrown out. The ex-wives had to be paid, and I think I had a couple of seed breeders coming to the house who wanted to be paid and no one was there to pay them."

She went out, bought a datebook and took over Emery's life, from the bookkeeping right down to the cooking and cleaning. They started the BC Marijuana Party together from the ground up and in the 2001 provincial campaign ran seventy-nine candidates in the seventy-nine ridings. A true accomplishment. Like good parents, they reared Pot TV—bringing Chris Bennett on board and beefing up content. "Almost a billion served right now, I think," she crowed.

But there were a lot of obstacles.

"It's a great big challenge to orchestrate a marijuana world and filter the money to the right places and make the right decisions as to where the money should go," Rainey said. "When you are dealing in an illegal business, you always have the fear you are going to get caught. I have had 30 pounds of pot. I have had seeds. I do everything. That puts me in the position of always being fearful, and in this day and age I don't think any of us should have to worry about pot or seeds."

Every single day there was a threat against the seed business, she confided. If the United States decided to halt the mail, if it developed some way to identify Emery's product and intercept it . . . "Every day there is a threat," she repeated, "and that's what maintains all of this. The only thing that keeps our ship running is the seed business."

She thought Emery and his small knot of companies could make a go of it after legalization. But it would depend on what the government allowed and who got to play. Other companies were already registering copyright names, even muscling in on Emery's long-time use of monikers such as *Cannabis Culture*.

"I see the government hand in the pie, everyone will be taxed," Rainey said. "I guarantee it. We will all have to pay a tax. Just like alcohol. But I also feel we should have the ability to open up our own facilities to sell like the coffee shops in Amsterdam. The compassion clubs should be allowed to service patients like me and recreational users should be able to go to a coffee shop. I'd like Marc and I to have stores across Canada—BC Marijuana Party or Alberta Marijuana Party or just Marijuana Party bookstores all across Canada that feature Pot TV going all day."

She thought the challenges of moving Emery's assets into the light of a legalized economy could be overcome. "I think we will be able to succeed because we already pay a lot of tax," Rainey said. "The government wants that income. We're also the experts and everybody knows that. Marc is known worldwide—in Japan, in Europe, in South America, in the former USSR, in the U.S. Consumers already trust us. They will not trust the CHUM media group to produce Pot TV, or Imperial Tobacco if it offered marijuana."

She considered Emery's asset basket—a magazine, Pot TV, seed sales. Put those together, add a bookstore and a great big festival, the Toker's Bowl. That's not a bad package if it could be vended into a public company and taken to market. "It's a multi-million-dollar industry now and it would be enormously larger if we could be legal and get into the U.S.," she said. "There are roughly 30 million people in Canada, there are more than 300 million just a few miles south. And 80 per cent of our base customers are already American."

***

A stocky, bearded man, Chris Bennett, who runs Pot TV for Emery, emerged from the downstairs studio with a frown on his face. "Have you heard a rare opium pipe is missing?"

Emery nodded.

"I heard [the neighbours] were down there," Bennett continued, indicating the heavies who dealt dope from a nearby office.

The marijuana mafia, who controlled the street traffic, were muscle connected to the Hells Angels, with a bevy of sellers stationed on most corners in the area and manning posts in the neighbourhood bars. Even Emery didn't dare challenge their control of the pot trade on the block.

"I rather doubt any of them care about a rare opium pipe," Emery opined. He shrugged, not relishing confrontation. "Everything is replaceable."

Bennett was among Emery's inner circle, the core group that has kept Emery at the vanguard of the global movement. Emery's greatest strength was his ability to attract passionate, committed people such as Rainey and Bennett. Some considered it a veritable cult.

Like Emery, Bennett was gobsmacked one day about marijuana. Only for Bennett it was about the herb and its connection to the Bible. The vision, and he talks of it in those terms, transformed him from a spaced-out hippie sadhu living on the edge of the rain forest to an incredibly focused television producer and amateur scholar who has authored acclaimed books on ancient religious references to cannabis.

Bennett's transformation occurred years before Emery arrived on the scene. The pot legalization movement of the

1970s was withered and moribund if not stone-cold dead. Bennett resuscitated it and had been breathing new life into it for five or six years when Emery appeared and assumed the leadership. One of Bennett's latest projects was a museum full of artifacts tracing humanity's use of psychotropic substances. That's why the missing pipe bugged him.

"Cheap lesson," Emery continued, nonplussed. "Let's not worry about it. I'm more concerned that the mayor's clip is on the website."

Bennett grimaced.

Vancouver mayor Larry Campbell had appeared as part of a public policy conference sponsored by Emery. He had called on the federal government to legalize cannabis so that it could be regulated and taxed. The speech was all on videotape. But Bennett had a list of shows backed up to be digitized and uploaded. The fire had sabotaged his operation.

"It's all under control," Bennett said. "I'll be back." He disappeared downstairs.

Emery turned to Williams. "Did we get mail today?"

"A little," replied the 50-year-old.

"So not a lot of money in the offing? What about Web sales?"

"It's not looking so good."

Internet sales were a priority for Emery because once the system was set up, customers could serve themselves with delivery from UPS.

"I'm going to go to the Money Mart and see if there is any money there for me," Emery said, standing.

Amy, another employee, arrived from the front of the store. "You heard [the neighbours] stole a pipe yesterday?"

Emery shook his head. "That's bizarre," he said. "They're mafia. We're nice to them because we're nice to everybody. But I'm going to have to go and ask."

Everyone watched as Emery headed off. They waited

in silence. Emery returned moments later to say that the
dealers knew nothing about the pipe.

"So, Amy, you go get those bubblebags. I've got $700 to
$800—you can borrow the rest from the envelope."

"Can't," she said. "We took $230 for the books."

"What books?"

"Books for distribution."

"Oh, great. Well, here's money. I'm going to go next door
and get wire money."

As he counted out the bills, a tradesman arrived—the
electrician who had jerry-rigged the power.

"Funny you should have some money in your hand," he
said.

Emery grinned. "By the end of the day, in a perfect
world, how much should I have?" he asked.

"$2,500," the new arrival said.

"I assure you I'll have at least $1,250 for you."

"Fabulous."

"In fact," Emery said, "Kyle and everyone are back by two
or three, so you might drop by then and see how everyone is
coping with the computers and how it's all working."

"Perfect."

"To the Money Mart, then," Emery said, heading for the
door.

He bounced into the branch smiling at the brace of
tellers behind inch-thick bulletproof glass.

"Hi, Marc," they chimed.

"I'm hoping your till overfloweth," he said in a singsong
voice.

One of the clerks flipped through a manila folder. "Here
you go. It's for $33," she said, pushing the order under the
armoured glass.

The two laughed. The look on Emery's face—his mother
could have died.

"Remember the day you got $9!" one shrieked.

Emery nodded and laughed along.

As we strolled back to the office, I asked him what legalization would mean for him.

"Who knows?" Emery said. "If the government ever legalizes marijuana, I'll be out of business. The big plant shops will have a wall of seeds and most people will want cuttings. Just like today. You go to the plant shop and buy a cutting, you generally don't go and buy seeds for most things."

He thought a lot of people would grow marijuana in their backyards if personal cultivation was allowed. But they would buy cuttings ready to plant and already sexed. Growers only want male plants for breeding; it is the female plant that produces the most prized chemical cocktail. In an illegal environment, cuttings are for the well-organized because they must be nurtured and cared for immediately. So seeds are in demand. They can be planted at a grower's convenience.

"What we've got that's unusual is more than 100,000 Canadians who are really good at growing pot. But today it's 99 per cent risk pay. If prohibition ends, you're going to find not only is the market flooded with pot, but it will cease to have the monetary value it has now. There will be no money in it. Within a season, everybody will grow a shitload of pot, put it in Mason jars like they used to in the old days, and they won't be able to smoke it all. They won't be buying pot. I know 100,000 people who are used to making a living and maybe 1,000 will continue to grow profitably in the legal period. Maybe 1,000."

Growers who were currently earning $50,000 to $80,000 tax-free were going to have to get a job, as far as Emery was concerned.

"For a lot of people who don't co-exist in the regular world, that's a good job when you can grow plants at home and stay by yourself and watch TV. It's a nice life even though there are certain risks of going to jail. These are not people who work well in a factory or office environment anyway. They're not so happy it's going to become legal and nearly worthless."

The lifestyle of growing pot as an underground guerrilla gardener and the economic niche it provides will disappear. He foresaw other repercussions too. Take away the marijuana economy, Emery suggested, and resource-based towns, in British Columbia for instance, will suffer. Growers provide needed cash flow in many rural parts of the province hit by hard times as a result, for example, of the prolonged lumber dispute with the United States or sluggishness in other resource-extraction industries. Pot growers have a penchant for new cars, pickups, adult toys, better lights, carbon-monoxide generators, fertilizers, you name it. With legalization, that flow of under-the-table currency would come to a halt.

"Canadians within twelve months of legalization would be getting it everywhere," Emery said. "It's totally impractical, really, to grow in homes—that's the most expensive agricultural real estate you'll find. Everyone will be growing outdoors or in greenhouses. Let's face it, Saskatchewan is one large sun-lamp. You'd grow there. In fact, I was at a neat greenhouse in Yorkton recently and I thought, this is where you could really take advantage of the sun with massive greenhouses. Cheap, cheap land. That's where you would grow pot—where land is cheap and it makes sense."

Or in the hectares and hectares under glass controlled by the giant agricultural firm B.C. Hothouse, only a few kilometres outside of Vancouver.

Emery said he expected to see coffee shops everywhere in Canada eventually offering small quantities for sale with restrictions regulating export and resale, just as there are in the Netherlands. Just like Starbucks. Maybe even Starbucks.

"People will become blasé about it," Emery mused. "The emerging industries will be the alternative ones. Vaporizers. Techniques where you don't have to smoke. That's why tinctures are back in the marketplace again. Absinthe is a good way to take it but you usually can't move after you take cannabis extract through absinthe. You're usually rooted to one spot, but that's great for people who would like not to be in pain. I think you'll have yogurt drinks—'cause THC is fat-soluble—granola bars, cookies, brownies, cakes, ice cream. There will be so much pot around, people will be cooking with it and adding it to salads."

David Malmo-Levine, who challenged the pot prohibition all the way to the Supreme Court of Canada in 2003, was waiting when we returned to Emery's office. Once dubbed Canada's most flamboyant pot activist, he looked remarkably sedate in oversized glasses with black plastic frames and black hair (perhaps for once dyed its true colour, but who knew, since it's been orange, scarlet, green, blue). An Edmonton-reared thirty-one-year-old with a Woody Allen personality full of ironic wit and humour, Malmo-Levine came to the coast to join Emery's burgeoning pot movement in the mid-1990s. Now, he continued to work with Emery, although he was no longer on the payroll. He was a pot entrepreneur.

He produced his own show on Pot TV, dabbled in multi-media projects and operated a self-styled Herb School that offered a range of seminars. From a storefront base next to a safe-injection site (a medically staffed hangout provided by the city for needle users), Malmo-Levine proselytized like a dozen other inner-city evangelists. Only he wasn't pushing Jesus, he was pushing herb. He offered a mini-museum, a photo display and an archive. He provided grow workshops, colloquia around the dangers of radioactive chemical fertilizers and organic nutrients for sale. Malmo-Levine lectured and also led walking tours for which he charged between $3 and $30 depending on your income.

Vancouver is a young city and almost nothing was here until after the end of the U.S. Civil War. Just a sawmill and a few homes. Legend has it, the first saloon was built when a barkeep named Gassy Jack arrived in a canoe with a keg of whisky. Gastown, the town that grew up to be Vancouver, was named after a drug dealer.

During his ninety-minute walkabout through the gritty side of the city, Malmo-Levine offered his commentary on the significant local events that punctuated what he said was a war against drugs that white, northern Europeans were late to appreciate. Down toward Main Street, for instance, was the site of the infamous Gastown Riot. The melee occurred Saturday, August 7, 1971 as about 1,200 mostly young people with longish hair protested for pot legalization. The Vancouver Police charged the crowd on horseback, chasing demonstrators into stores and clubbing them down. It was quite a scene. Back then everyone thought legalization was imminent—even the prime minister's wife was a stoner flower child. How wrong we were.

I followed Malmo-Levine downstairs to the Pot TV studio and production space, leaving Emery to deal with his seed customers.

"My main argument is, you can teach people to properly use this substance," he said, holding up his knapsack, "so they don't hurt themselves." Ergo, he founded the Herb School. He continued to speak as he undid his bag. "It's all about the harm principle. The criminal law should be used only when there is real harm that can measured."

The B.C. Court of Appeal liked that concept—that the criminal law should be guided by a tenet enunciated by the 19th-century English philosopher John Stuart Mill: "The only purpose for which power can be rightfully exercised over any member of a civilized community, against his will, is to prevent harm to others. His own good, either physical or moral, is not a sufficient warrant . . ."

The B.C. high bench saw marijuana as no more dangerous than alcohol. Unfortunately, in May 2003 the Supreme Court of Canada scoffed.

"They said they didn't think there was any such thing as a harm principle," Malmo-Levine said. "[They said] cannabis consumers are in a debatable legal category—not quite harmful, not quite harmless. I think they are wrong."

Aye, there's the rub. It was their game.

Malmo-Levine was the Peter Pan of the Canadian pot world. The activist who didn't grow up, he grow-opped.

"Would you like to see the selection today?" he asked, pulling a Tupperware container from the knapsack. It held nearly a dozen small glass vials containing bubble hash, a selection of pre-rolled reefers and four kinds of loose marijuana.

"Everything you see is organic," he said, moving his long thin hands over the box like a magician. "This is Blueberry, this is Train Wreck, *ha-ha-ha*, speaking of impairment. This one comes with a warning. Mostly *indica*. These ones have smaller buds so if any of them were *sativa*, it would be these. This one I'm fairly certain is an *indica*. Identification of strain isn't my forte. I'm working on quality control with fertilizers. Later on I'm going to take a course on water-extraction process, the bubble-hash making. That's going to be the latest thing—different flavours of domestic bubble hash in Vancouver."

He chuckled as he removed a state-of-the-art digital scale from a hollowed-out copy of Lee Iacocca's autobiography, *Talking Straight*.

"Let's try the *indica*." He pinched enough for a spliff.

Malmo-Levine spent the first twenty-five years of his life in Edmonton, visiting his dad, who lived in Hamilton and the Gulf Islands, during school breaks. It was a nice, safe, good upbringing for a nerd. Edmonton had a certain charm, for a flat, uninteresting northern prairie city. It had a repertory theatre, a couple of good bookshops, a university and the shabby semblance of a Canadian counterculture.

A mouthy kid, Malmo-Levine argued with everybody, and because some kids didn't like that, he got beaten up a lot. He started smoking at fourteen because he "needed it as a silver lining to my domesticated, sterile, authoritarian-ridden life. I had all these thumbs on my neck, my parents, my teachers, my employers; each one exerted arbitrary authority. I had one boss who used to dangle my cheque in front of me every month and say: 'Here it is, beg for it, come on!'"

The way he figured it, pot dealers didn't have bosses. They worked with agricultural products bought off other people who didn't have bosses. He thought that was a cool economy. He went to Holland and saw it for himself.

Malmo-Levine was a prankster-intellectual who eventually made his way to the University of Victoria, where he studied history and anthropology. He moved back to Edmonton in 1993 and enrolled at the University of Alberta. A fellow student at the time who became a Conservative Party political player, Ezra Levant, remembered him this way for a CBC profile: "He stood out. He was such a radical on the left. But I enjoyed his idealism and I saw it, I saw him as the exact opposite of me on ideas but I saw in him what I like to think I am a little bit of and that is an idealist. We are on opposite sides of the coin but I like his style."

Malmo-Levine's first smoke-in was on July 1, 1993 in Edmonton.

"Me and a whole bunch of really young people organized it, put up the posters, broke the law, blew pot in everyone's face. There was some nudity, some other victimless crimes committed—trespassing, all the things you could do without hurting anyone. It was great fun."

But he was accused of being the skimpiest pot activist in the country and still recalls the jibe: "You could only come up with twenty-five measly joints, probably all seeds and stems!"

He worked hard to live it down.

"The cops figured we would all just go away, and then we started doing smoke-in after smoke-in. We handed out twenty-five joints at one rally, got busted on the way to another rally, got ten hours of community service for that at the Sally Ann."

In 1995, he was spending all his time at the campus newspaper, at the radio station or in the library promoting cannabis. But he had no money. The cash to fund his first big rally came from the *Edmonton Journal*, which paid him $100 for a letter to the editor.

His pizzazz—Jello-inspired hair colours, naked chicks and 3-foot joints—caught Emery's attention. Within months, Malmo-Levine was ensconced in Vancouver, working as a professional pot activist on Emery's nickel.

"It was like, wow!" he recalled. "Here's a bunch of hippies working with a bunch of capitalists and a bunch of, you know, dreamers, thespians, all the youth cultures, one of everybody here, you know, and we're all working together. It was like, wow! I want to join this team. It's like the superheroes team, a Superhero Pot Activist Team. It was a dream come true. Before, in Edmonton, I was spending the money from my minimum-wage job that wasn't spent on rent or food, I was spending that on my pot activism. It was maybe $25 or $100 every two or three months. Here, I got paid to do what I was doing in my spare time with my own money. I had a huge budget. Marijuana flowed like hot and cold running water."

In Edmonton, his biggest rally probably cost $300 for photocopying, brushes, buckets and glue. Now that was lunch.

"We had thousands of dollars. We had enough money to be part of the community, part of the Vancouver community with our own voice. We could take out ads in the *Terminal City* newspaper, or the *Georgia Straight*, even the *Province*. We could afford to take out radio ads; we could do a decent postering with sometimes colour posters. We started to look like everyone else, you know, like another subculture, another subsection of Vancouver."

They started to believe it.

In 1996, California was seized with a full-bore debate about medical marijuana as a result of gay political pressure over the AIDS crisis. Even if no one had defined what "medical marijuana" was, Malmo-Levine wanted to get it rolling in Canada.

"I was thinking if California had medical marijuana, we should have social and recreational, oh-what-the-hell-I-feel-like-getting-high-today marijuana," he said. "Canadians are supposedly a little more progressive than Americans. So not to be outdone by California, we decided to open up the Harm Reduction Club—just go for broke."

He picked a sunny day in the park, set up a table and, as two uniformed police officers watched, signed up members.

"For that day in the park there," he said, beaming, "pot was essentially legal. For all 250 people who signed up for the Harm Reduction Club, on that day, in that park there, it seemed as legal as a lemonade stand. Everyone walked home with a nice fat joint or two or twelve in their pocket and a club membership card printed on hemp paper with a little quote on the back about the Dutch experience. The dream spread from there."

The next day, he started dealing from his house. At first, a neighbour's dog barked a lot because hundreds of people were coming over. He gave the neighbour an eighth of an ounce and bought the dog a humongous bag of doggie treats.

"I said, 'Anytime you need another eighth, come on by, yours are free, you are taken care of,'" Malmo-Levine explained. "Then the landlord came over and we gave him an eighth and said, 'You're the landlord, you're taken care of, anytime you need an eighth, come on over.'"

The neighbourhood was onside, he believed. They needed a good supply of cheap, potent, organic cannabis. Well, Malmo-Levine was a connoisseur and it would take time for police to catch up with him even if he was a publicity hound. His open distribution of bud got more and more media attention until he made every major newspaper in the country and CBC dispatched a crew from the program *Big Life with Daniel Richler*.

Police raided Emery's HQ, then called Hemp B.C., in September 1998. You can still see the footage on the Internet—police carting away Malmo-Levine, who was yelling, "This is not freedom, this is pretend freedom . . . You're breaking the circulation in my wrists, my hands are turning blue."

He was five foot six and 140 pounds dripping wet, and the camera exaggerated his sand-in-the-face-weakling physique. He looked comical as burly cops bundled him into the paddy wagon. As he waited to be transported he teased the officers from behind a mesh window. "You don't have to answer if you don't want to, your facial expression will do enough. The question is: If there was a drug-war truth and reconciliation committee, could you say in your heart that you did all you could to resist this obvious witch hunt?"

"I have no idea what you're taking about," the cop replied.

Malmo-Levine told the camera, "I don't feel free right now. I feel like I'm getting beaten up 'cause I'm opposing torture. If I'm in jail, I won't have to do that any more— I can just write, or write songs, do something like that. I mean maybe if I'm in jail maybe I can call more attention to the issue than if I'm out of jail. I just want the drug war to be over."

Publicity from the raid was better than advertising.

"They threw us in jail overnight, they didn't make us promise to stop selling pot. I figured by the end of that first month of sales, we were doing a pound a day easy, maybe a pound and a half [nearly $5,000 a day, seven days a week] and it was rising at an exponential rate."

The incredible spike in sales occurred after a television news item inadvertently broadcast his phone number. The phone started ringing off the hook. Every time he hung up it rang again. *Do you promise not to disturb the neighbours?* Yes. *Are you over thirteen? Do you promise to read the safer, smarter, smoking guide? Promise not to drive while you're impaired? Okay, the address is . . .*

"We asked those four questions again and again, and if they answered correctly, over they came. The door opened and closed, opened and closed. It was quite a mess. The people upstairs were going crazy. They were about to have a baby. It was just so much traffic." The police raided Malmo-Levine's home a week after they arrested him at Hemp B.C. "Luckily enough, a little place came up for rent at 420 Grove Avenue in North Burnaby."

It was a closed hemp store with time left on the lease. Ba-da-boom-ba-da-bing, Malmo-Levine was in business again. It was RCMP territory this time, so a whole new file had to be opened. The Mounties had to conduct their own investigation and decide whether other crimes were being committed or other drugs sold. Two and a half months more of that, and, of course, the local tabloid newspaper, *The Province*, gave him more coverage, more media followed and more people learned about his business.

"We had 1,600 regular members by the time they shut us down the second time," Malmo-Levine laughed.

He finished rolling a huge spliff. "What do you think of the zine?" he asked, firing the reefer.

His tour came with a hundred-page booklet, a thick version of *Potshot*, his own illustrated black-and-white photocopied magazine. Sold for $4.95, it was an omnibus grab bag of his writing along with illustrations, photographs and clips from his encyclopedic reading habits. Malmo-Levine lived in an impressive warren full of books, some historic, some contemporary, almost all on drugs and the philosophies associated with expanded consciousness.

His magazine had a good selection of material culled from a variety of sources including Neil Boyd (one of the country's leading academics on illegal drugs), Bruce MacFarlane (special council to the Department of Justice and a drug law historian) and a host of others. MacFarlane's survey of changes to the law over the years was essential reading and Boyd's work on the social and legal context for drug policy was fabulous.

Malmo-Levine provided pretty fair review of the legislative record, although it was laced with some wild hypothesis, such as a cabal linking John D. Rockefeller and the Rockefeller Foundation, J.P. Morgan, the Mellons, the DuPonts, William Randolph Hearst, Bayer, the Nazis, modern-day pharmaceutical companies . . .

For the past decade, Malmo-Levine believed, there had been a growing momentum for change again, as attitudes softened.

"Right now, we're the good guys in the mass media. Like we have everyone from the *Saturday Night Live* crew—every successive *Saturday Night Live* crew since Chevy Chase and John Belushi and Steve Martin—to Doonesbury, all the kind, saner voices out there. We have more public opinion on our side."

Compared with alcohol or tobacco, cannabis is benign, he insisted. Caffeine is more dangerous, more lethal and responsible for far greater health costs. Chocolate bars even contain fairly strong psychoactive substances—the xanthine derivatives, theophylline and theobromine. The median lethal dose of cannabis means you would have to smoke 1,500 pounds within fifteen minutes to die. There has not been a single reported death due to its use or a single incident of lung cancer (because of the particular mix of chemicals in cannabis compared with tobacco) associated solely with cannabis inhalation.

Malmo-Levine believes marijuana is a mild, medicinal intoxicant that, used properly, is a performance enhancer. "It doesn't impair, it helps you focus," he maintained. "It helps you dance through the crowds as they busily walk down the streets. I think that is the truth. I know it sounds absurd, but that's because the world has been turned upside down. You can teach people to use this herb properly. The Supreme Court of Canada agreed in Paragraph 100, you can teach people to use it."

He liked the idea of a café-based distribution system offering a variety of strains, supported by a grow industry regulated in the same manner as the wine industry.

"I think corporations will actually find it hard to compete with the hippies in the pot market that evolves. I think they feel threatened by our twenty to thirty years of experience growing this stuff while they are just starting out. I'm not out to put pharmacists out of business. What I'm out to do is give them a job, help the flower people and the botanists and the biologists, helping those people understand the medicine better. If we all work together, figure out what the cannabinols and the terpenes and the flavonols and the volatile oils do, and we figure out what the medicine does and which strains do what grown under what conditions, if we all help figure this out, we'll all do well. The pharmacists will get money through testing, through isolating extracts, through developing their unique products, but they won't enjoy a monopoly. They shouldn't."

He thought some of the nearly $200 billion North Americans spent on pills would shift into the cannabis economy, which was why he thought there was pharmaceutical resistance to legalization. Instead of a few guys in lab coats making billions, it would be ordinary people, Malmo-Levine believed—ordinary people organized and paying taxes and not fighting one another.

"We want dealers with addresses and phone numbers. Dealers you can point to and say, that's who sold me the bad stuff. Dealers who are accountable. If you get accountable dealers, you can regulate any way you want. I think Vancouver is smart enough to draw up some reasonable regulations. I said thirteen with parental permission, but if they started at nineteen and instituted a parental-permission policy later, maybe that's how legalization develops. Maybe I was too quick, too fast, too much, too soon."

Malmo-Levine was continuing to mine away at the next legal challenge with the B.C. Civil Liberties Association. His latest thoughts were to knit together an argument using global conventions on drug control, human rights and anti-genocide into some über-assault on the Criminal Code as an instrument of cultural genocide and persecution. Lots of luck.

In the meantime, he had to make a living. He laughed and tapped on the plastic lid of his pot container. "Yes, I've come out of the closet. I'm a shameless pot dealer again. But it's a good job. It's a noble profession. We need more good pot dealers out there. People who won't mark it up too bad or rip other people off, sell stuff that won't get you high."

He said he didn't have to find customers. The customers were out there clamouring for it; they always found him. But there was turf.

"You have to be a diplomat to realize what is open turf and what is not open turf. I don't want to ruffle anyone's feathers, I don't want to offend anyone. I want to work with all the other dealers in town. Work together to avoid a monopoly mentality and get more of a cooperative community mentality in the dealer community. I want to encourage our best behaviours and discourage our worst behaviours."

He wanted to see civic authorities experiment as much with marijuana regulation as they did with heroin and cocaine.

"I think the international treaties allow for that, I think our consciences allow for that. I think the world is ready for it. I really think if the war drags on, the opportunities become fewer to do this sort of thing. They don't increase; they decrease. Now is the time, now is the time something positive happens. I think we are going to get a Holland kind of world, not a Singapore kind of world. That's my guess."

I went back upstairs to see Emery. Not surprisingly, he was still talking.

"The old paradigm for marijuana will cease to exist when it's legal because it's all about the money," he was saying. "It's very corrupting, the money. The money makes everything happen. It determines whether people chop it down early so they can pay their rent. Pot gets stolen because of money, cops are after it and always boasting about the financial value it has. In a legal environment, pot will look so different. They talk about a tax windfall, there will be nothing to tax except tourists."

On top of that whammy, Emery predicted 100,000 or so units of the provincial housing market would be vacated because they're currently used as grow-ops. No one would need them in a legal environment.

"You'll have a real recession," he said. "Hey, Jordan, what will you do when pot is legal?"

The thirty-something in a baseball cap and anorak looked up from rolling a multi-skin carrot.

"Prices have already gone downhill," Jordan said. "There's tons of pot around. If somebody were interested in 50 pounds of triple-A bud, I can get it for $1,500 a pound!"

Sure it's 50 pounds, but it's only $75,000. If you had that kind of money, sat on it a few months, resold it in 1-pound packages—even at a giveaway price of $2,000—you'd earn $25,000 profit. Tidy. As everyone did the mind math, the momentary silence amplified the giggling from the front of the store.

"What's going on?" Emery called out.

"Midgets on the street," someone replied.

"Midgets!" he shrieked. "Midgets cost me $3,500! We paid $3,500 to produce an episode of *Captain Jackson* for Pot TV."

Emery got up from behind the desk.

"Captain Jackson used to take a bong hit and get super-powers for as long as he was high. Say fifteen minutes. It always wore off just at the moment of crisis. 'Oh my God! I'm losing my sixth strength, getting weaker.' Like the opposite of kryptonite, 'The effects are w-e-a-ring off. Must have T-H-C. Must have T-H-C . . .'

"I paid for eight midgets but they never materialized. God damn midgets!" he laughed. "Maybe it's them. Let me go look."

THE SEED(Y) BUSINESS

reeferman

TWO LANES OF BLACKTOP wound among small truck farms, fields of alfalfa and hay, grazing livestock and second-growth forest. You could be anywhere in rural, temperate North America. I turned off the highway onto a dirt road, the car kicking up a dust devil as I passed the sign, DEAD END. A quarter-mile on, the line of poplars running alongside broke to reveal a rutted driveway leading to a big, two-storey white clapboard home. A toffee-coloured mastiff, lounging beside a late-model sedan, roused himself, baying news of my arrival.

The door opened and an imposing heavyweight of a man with dark hair and a full beard emerged squinting into the sunlight. He wore a pair of ratty black sweatpants and a black T-shirt. He raised a hand to shade his eyes. I gave a wave as the car pulled to a stop.

"Hi, Charles."

"Hey, good you could make it," Charles Scott said, flashing a grin.

I opened the car door and offered my arm to the canine herald loping toward me.

"It's okay, Tacky," Scott cooed, then said to me, "Good to see you, man. Come on in."

Scott, at thirty-eight, was a guru among cannabis lovers and he represented the first level of the business—the producer, the manufacturer, the grower. Without people such as Scott, there is no domestic marijuana business. They are the source not only of cannabis but also of seeds and clones for the consumer who wants to grow.

Scores of seed companies are based in Europe, the United States and Canada. The main breeding work is most visible in Holland and California—and B.C., home alone to dozens of seed firms marketing hundreds of strains. Almost anyone can grow marijuana, but to produce it on a commercial scale takes a modicum of talent, meticulous technique, the best genetic stock and (in an illegal environment) a great deal of luck.

Others, such as Ed Rosenthal, the American grow king, Dave Watson, the legendary Dutch-based cultivator, or Jorge Cervantes, *High Times* grow editor, were more famous than Scott. Ben Dronkers of Sensi Seeds was far richer. But Scott was an up-and-comer. He had spent nearly seventeen years in the business, had amassed a broad selection of original strains and had garnered as much experience as anyone producing the plant, especially on a commercial scale.

Scott straddled generations and worlds. He was a unique, and odd, link between the past and the present, between outdoor and indoor cultivators, small-time and big-time operators, politics and pot. He had grown fields of marijuana and managed the biggest of indoor shows. He had worked independently and for large organizations, including the Angels and the mob. Now he produced primarily breeding stock and plants for medical patients.

He led me through his large eight-bedroom home strewn with children's toys. The former triplex once was home to three welfare families. He had moved in about fourteen months ago.

"Every second neighbour around here grows dope," he said. "I ran the local hydroponics store, so I'm not exaggerating. Every second property is growing."

He threw himself into a leather recliner in front of a computer. The household was in tumult because his father-in-law was dying and his wife of thirteen years, Leanne, and their son were by his side. Leanne was a hard-core pot activist who smoked every day to control the pain and symptoms of spinal disease.

Scott's dark hair was flecked with grey and his blue eyes were bleary-looking from pot. He is big—six foot two, pushing 300 pounds—and has savage-looking scars on his leg from operations on a knee damaged in professional martial-arts combat. He boasts a fifth-degree black belt in jujitsu. Tacky is never far from his side, padding away only to patrol the property. Sensors are planted in the surrounding land, especially near the greenhouse, Scott told me.

"They trigger an alarm. I'll show you."

He touched the computer keyboard. The machine screamed. *Beep . . . beep . . . beep . . . beep . . . bee-ee-ee-ee-eep.* The dog sprang out the back door emitting terrifying howls, barks and growls.

"The paranoia is electric at night when something sets them off," Scott chuckled. "September becomes manic because of thieves and the seismic sensor going off really gets your heart pumping. You're up and racing through the bush in the middle of the night with a mean dog. It's crazy around here. I sit on edge when the crop's ready. Sometimes it's rabbits and stuff that's just stupid. But you never know—people can be violent."

Marijuana is no different from any crop susceptible to blight, bugs and blackouts. Its illicit status adds cops and robbers to those dangers. Scott is representative of the type of person who becomes a seditious grower—independent, libertarian, eager to make a buck and able to juggle the usual farmer's worries and a whole lot of fear. His operation was typical.

"I have a big crew-cab truck and I'll use it to stop thieves," Scott said. "That's my thing. I know it sounds bad but that's the limit I am willing to go to. I don't have guns. I have dogs, and Tacky is incredible. He's a rare find. A mastiff crossed with a so-called pit bull, a Staffordshire terrier. He's like one of my kids. He's totally defensive and hates strangers so he's a great guard dog."

He bent to pet the hulking beast that trotted back into the room.

"I'm buying another," Scott said. "A really exceptional dog from California, a purebred German shepherd, trained in crowd control, building entry, disarming. He's a psycho dog: $8,000 U.S. But he's worth the investment. When I'm out of town, my wife wants it. I don't like firearms."

He got up and returned with a couple of Coronas. "I hate firearms even though I was raised in a culture surrounded by guns. I can strip and assemble an AR-15 like an American soldier can. No problem. Colt .45, same."

He was a true army brat.

"It's a weird thing—whenever you have something that is worth a lot of money, guns become a factor in protecting it," Scott said. "Everybody I know, who I meet through the grow shop or that I come in contact with, I just beg them to not taint our industry with guns and violence. But that's the problem. We can't call the police. An old-timer, a close friend of the family was beat nearly to death last year."

He shook his head. "The availability and cost of cannabis

would drop and it wouldn't be such a valuable commodity to protect if it were legal."

Scott has dual Canadian and American citizenship because his father is American. "I grew up on military bases," he said. "My dad was all over the place, although his command HQ was Fort Bragg. He was stationed in New York State, where he met my mom who is from Ontario."

After twenty-one years in the military, including traumatic combat in the Congo, his dad moved to Alberta to work for the Correctional Service of Canada—at a maximum-security penitentiary in Edmonton. "He taught jujitsu," Scott said. "So did I. That's how I met my wife—after I moved to B.C. She was one of my students."

Scott studied agriculture, finishing his BSc at the University of British Columbia and doing his practicum at the Pacific Agriculture Research Centre at Agassiz, where he bred some of his first herb. From there, he went to the hog centre in Chilliwack to breed swine.

"I've been growing indoors since 1988. My first grow was in North Burnaby. It wasn't because I needed the money. We had just inherited $250,000 from a relative. But this old hippie guy named Wayne was selling me this killer grass and I said I wanted to meet the grower. Her name was Gabriella, a fifty-eight-year-old woman from the British Properties [one of the more exclusive Greater Vancouver neighbourhoods]. He hooked us up."

Scott smiled. "I said I had the money and she said, okay, she was going to take half. I paid for everything and she provided the plants. It was expensive. I paid about $6,000 to set up the room. We got 7½ pounds and I had to give her half, so it was an expensive first crop. These days, when I introduce her to people in the scene like Emery, and Ed Rosenthal, she says, 'I'm the one who taught him to be bad.'" He treasured the friendship. "She's over seventy now," Scott said. "That's how we got a start."

"It has been just a constant love affair—me and the herb. No matter what I was doing I was growing. But the fellow who was my mentor was Wayne, a draft dodger who sold pot in East Vancouver basically since he got here. Wayne Curry was the name he used, but he was a fugitive from the U.S. because of his anti-war actions."

Wayne, in fact, was the real deal—a true sixties radical, one of thousands of young Americans (many of them draft dodgers) who fled across the border in the late 1960s and early 1970s and survived by growing and dealing a little weed. The pot prohibition creates a commodity that desperate people can easily grow or acquire and sell to finance their nefarious activities, or to supplement their income so they can survive off the grid.

The arrival of counterculture Americans in British Columbia caused outdoor cultivation in the province to ramp up in the 1970s, especially in the Interior, which is so large, so undeveloped and so wild, you could drop Germany in and lose it. Before these hipsters came north, there was little domestic cannabis cultivation in Canada—a few insignificant plots of homegrown, especially on Lasqueti Island, but nothing of commercial note. The arrival of these Americans was a fascinating, colourful moment in the history of marijuana in Canada, and Curry was certainly one of the more incandescent among them.

Wayne Curry died on October 19, 1997, ravaged by cancer. In the days following, his close friends in Vancouver learned that his real identity was John Jacobs. He was a co-founder of the Weathermen (a.k.a. Weather Underground), one of the weirder political gangs spawned by the sixties.

Born in New York State in 1947, the son of leftists who

reared him with a hefty social conscience, Jacobs was infatuated with Karl Marx and Russian ideologues, Che Guevara and Castro. By the time he arrived at Columbia University in 1965, he was ripe for revolution. A raving Maoist, he helped orchestrate the infamous Columbia Student Rebellion and Chicago's Days of Rage. Jacobs liked the adrenaline rush of confrontation. A brilliant and chic figure, he was seized with an apocalyptic vision of Imperial Amerika rampant. More than seven hundred were arrested in the rebellion he inspired at Columbia, though his later stunts were not so popular.

In 1969, he penned the notorious manifesto "You Don't Need a Weatherman to Know Which Way the Wind Blows," a line cribbed from Bob Dylan's "Subterranean Homesick Blues." But Uncle Bob, who turned the Beatles on to marijuana, offered a surreal comic perspective of U.S. political Armageddon. Jacobs sounded an earnest clarion call to armed struggle: Rise up, let's bring the war into the streets of America and kick their fascist ass! In Chicago, that talk got your head broken by Mayor Daley's leather-clad stormtroopers.

Jacobs took moral succour from being arrested. Getting his share of abuse proved his mettle and Marxist–Leninist bona fides. Unfortunately, he was not just posturing. He took his own published credo to heart. "We're against everything that's 'good and decent' in honky America. We will burn and loot and destroy."

And they did. They were on the lam for years. Most ultimately would be acquitted or never face charges when they were arrested or resurfaced. Prosecution was too difficult after so much time and given the investigative misconduct that came to light. Jacobs fled to Vancouver and for nearly two decades he eked out a living growing and selling pot.

That he fell in with Charles Scott and was seen as a mentor to him is a true irony. Especially given who Scott was in those days—a budding right-wing racist.

Scott had grown marijuana initially to support his extremist politics. He had met Timothy McVeigh, the bomber, and rubbed shoulders with the inner circle of the continent's most dangerous fascists, including Richard Butler, the septuagenarian head of the Aryan Nations based in Hayden Lake, Idaho, whose Hitlerian ideas motivated the Order, probably the most violent white supremacist group spawned in North America. Former Alberta-based Aryan leader Terry Long was a supporter as well.

Back in the mid-1990s, Scott announced plans to create a private, armed militia, dubbed the Patriot Training Network, and boasted fifty soldiers ready to fight the "Communist, Zionist, anti-Christ government" in Ottawa over its gun registry and gun-control laws. "When they come after our families and our guns," Scott was quoted as saying, "we won't give in without bullets flying."

The Canadian Security Intelligence Service (CSIS) recruited Scott, who was then twenty-nine, and for several months he became their window on that dangerous right-wing world. But on June 12, 1995, Scott received a pipe-bomb in the mail at his home in Yarrow. Stuffed with a kilo of nails, the shoe-box-sized parcel had a mousetrap trigger rigged to detonate upon opening. The crude lettering on the address label gave Scott pause. That pause saved his life.

A month after the pipe-bomb arrived, Scott was named Aryan Man of the Year in recognition of his recruitment efforts. He denounced the movement soon afterward and moved to the Prairies in 1997, where he was busted running a massive grow-op on a pig farm in 1999.

Today Scott maintains those days of racist politics are long behind him, but they continue to haunt him. "I don't like to think of myself as a rat," he told me when I asked about those years. "But I guess that's what it was. I never gave them [the security service] information that led to an arrest, just the seizure of arms caches."

CSIS paid him for about six months, Scott said, and provided $53,000 for a racist-leaflet campaign that brought him national attention.

"I had to get out, man," he said. "I suddenly found myself living like James Bond. Really weird shit. You wouldn't believe it . . . So that's touchy because in this business I don't want people to think I'm a rat. So it's like, what do you do? I don't know how to put it." He paused, picked his words carefully. "I have associated with the Canadian Security Intelligence Service, though. I've been paid by the Service. More as a consultant than as a rat, though. As a consultant in terms of national interest."

At the end of the 1980s, the marijuana business in Canada was going through a major transition, in the throes of changing from an import-dependent retail industry fed by overseas suppliers to a self-sufficient producer and big exporter. The cannabis arrived in a hundred different ways from Thailand or Pakistan—or anywhere, really. The west coast of Canada was a gateway to North America, and international syndicates had been landing huge quantities of dope since the 1960s.

Vancouver always has been an entry point into the continent for marijuana and hashish. Initially, the pot trade in Canada was a handful of affluent kids with the money to travel and the nerve to cut a deal and bring back a backpack or suitcase stuffed with bud or hash. Those kids quickly got bolder and bolder until they had international partners and were importing shiploads of dope and containers filled with hash.

The Brotherhood of Eternal Love, one of the first big importation groups based in California, started using the port as their primary portal in 1970. The Brotherhood drove vanloads of hash from Afghanistan across the border into

Pakistan to Karachi. It was loaded aboard ships that steamed to Vancouver. The Brotherhood was busted in 1972 by port police after the accidental seizure of 700 pounds of hash—a minuscule amount in terms of what was arriving.

Another international crime ring operating in Vancouver was headed by Emery pal Howard Marks, who consorted with the IRA, the CIA and the Mafia. The last authentic Thai stick of any quantity seen in the city came from one of his shipments back in 1983. He was busted by the Americans and served seven years of a twenty-five-year sentence before being released. He went on to write a best-selling autobiography and found the Mr. Nice Seed Bank.

There were also a dozen or so Canadians who got into the trade and quickly became players in the global cannabis and illicit drug importation business.

In the 1970s and 1980s, British Columbia became party central for international drug dealers. Initially, the liberal attitudes and social mores, if they didn't condone, at least tolerated drug use—cocaine for the fast set, marijuana for the old hippies. The lengthy, poorly patrolled coastline was an invitation. When Canadian drug laws were changed to eliminate mandatory jail sentences for trafficking, it was as if the country had thrown down the red carpet.

From 1980 on, getting caught with hundreds of pounds of marijuana meant little more than a fine and a day in jail if you were convicted in B.C. And the unscrupulous took advantage of the situation. On any given day, there were dozens of suitcases bursting with dirty money leaving the province for off-shore banks. When the Mounties conducted a sting operation on money laundering, more than four hundred Vancouver residents were identified.

Robert Hyde was the veritable local archetype of the international B.C. dealer. He had come in contact with most of those who were active in Vancouver's hippie era, if only through the mementoes, furniture, clothes, objets d'art and bric-a-brac he flogged from his travels in Asia and South America.

After graduating from North Vancouver's Delbrook High in 1964, Hyde spent a year at Simon Fraser University, then travelled for two years in Europe. From 1968 through 1969 he was at British Columbia Institute of Technology, taking a course in business administration. He worked for a year with CN as a brakeman/switchman, then on the production set of *McCabe & Mrs. Miller*, one of the first Hollywood movies shot in Vancouver. He continued to travel, first in South America, then in Europe and Asia.

Hyde's charm touched many. He was big, square-jawed, blond, sardonic, confident, challenging, flamboyant and boastful. A brash big-spender, Hyde liked to be known and seen — his ego demanded recognition, even if it was a dangerous desire for one of the most successful drug importers of his era. Boldness made the game more interesting.

In 1972, he opened the English Bay Trading Company, and later, the Strawberry Experiment. He was a travelling representative and the goods he imported filled the shelves of stores in Vancouver, Calgary and Victoria. The next year, he bought a home at Whaletown on Cortes Island. In the end, Hyde's true métier may have been the party. His annual get-together was a luxe bacchanal, held everywhere from Belcarra Park to Cortes Island — wherever Hyde happened to be on the coast. The events introduced boomers to mind-altering substances and sometimes served as sumptuous backdrops for his business meetings.

Former director of film development for British Columbia Diane Neufeld remembered him as "one of the exciting and dangerous people we watched; one of those who lived a little harder and faster, drinking and smoking dope with flamboyance in 1965. Robert came to be something of a legend. Not many people have the courage to live on that fine edge."

Hyde, along with Philip Bradley, Richard Sifton and several associates formed a mesmerizing group.

Bradley, a marine engineer, was a friend from Hyde's high school days and locally celebrated for beating a charge of opium possession. In November 1969, Judge Alfred Watts dismissed the charge, after police failed to identify the neatly dressed Bradley as the accused from a crowd of bearded hippies who later cheered the decision.

Sifton was the photographer who documented the World Habitat Forum in Vancouver and filmed a documentary on orcas with whale activist Paul Spong.

Hyde was one of the top three importers working in British Columbia through the seventies. He often had several deals going on at once, and it didn't matter when he lost a shipment, such as one that was seized in the Panama Canal. Business was that good.

In Thailand in those days, marijuana cost $50 to $75 a pound; in the United States it was fetching US$1,400; in Vancouver $2,500 to $3,000. Smugglers could afford to have a load caught now and then. Police confiscated as much as $10 million worth of pot and other drugs and various assets from Hyde and his partners over the years, but that was less than 10 per cent of their revenue during the period.

Hyde and his various partners brought in two or three shipments a year. Nothing came out of Bangkok that he didn't know about. Undercover cops watched for twelve years, but they were always two weeks behind.

Police started a file on Bradley in December 1980 and followed him to Bangkok three times in early 1981 when he visited Hyde. In November 1981, they seized $2.6 million worth of pot in caches found in Sidney, Alert Bay, Surrey and Coquitlam—some in heat-sealed plastic bags printed with red-and-blue three-elephant brand labels (Hyde's idea). They found the broken printing plates at his house in Thailand.

Hyde, Bradley, Sifton and others were ultimately caught with more than half a ton of Thai stick marijuana. The bust also pulled down eight others, including Hyde's brother Spencer, Michael Berry, a friend of Spong's at Alert Bay, and George Dyson, the son of the noted American physicist Freeman Dyson.

Berry was fined $5,000 for 120 pounds, Dyson $1,500 for 30 pounds. Hyde paid their legal costs and fines. He, Sifton and Bradley were fined $30,000 each and given three months to pay. Hours later, they were crossing into the United States. Hyde headed for Bangkok, the others for Los Angeles and Amsterdam.

Less than three years after the bust, on May 6, 1984, Hyde was found dead in his home in Pattaya City, Thailand. He was thirty-eight. A few weeks later his life was celebrated at a memorial in the Vancouver Buddhist Church at Powell and Jackson streets. He didn't leave much: a house on Cortes Island, a collection of Studebakers, small properties in Thailand, a promissory note from an accountant for $230,000, a string of failed investments.

In the marijuana industry in which he had been a baron, a sea change was occurring. Satellite surveillance made it more difficult to land bulky cargo on even the remotest shores; packing containers made more sense, especially with U.S. President Reagan's linking of military and police resources in the war on drugs. The RCMP drug branch had also changed its focus. Instead of rounding up low-level distributors, they were targeting those dealing in multi-ton loads. The proceeds-of-crime squad had grown from twelve to sixty officers. And it had an effect.

In August 1996, each entrance to the San Francisco Federal Building, a twin of the tower destroyed in the Oklahoma bombing, was protected by an airport metal detector and a handful of armed U.S. marshals. On the seventeenth

floor, under the barrelled ceiling of Federal District Courtroom No. 6, Judge Eugene Lynch presiding, Michael
Medjuck stood impassively, staring intently at the nine
women and three men who decided his fate. He nodded in
resignation. After several hours deliberation, they had convicted Medjuck of smuggling humungous quantities of hash.
Not that he denied it.

There were hundreds of 8-by-10 glossy surveillance photographs, some enlarged to poster size and placed against
the court's wood-panelled walls. There was testimony from
dozens of police officers, customs agents, Mounties, G-Men,
undercover narcs and stool pigeons. The physical evidence
ranged from de-bugging devices secreted in hollowed books
to myriad telephone and financial records. Nothing was left to
the imagination.

Looking every inch the well-heeled businessman in a con-
servatively cut grey suit, the 46-year-old former Vancouver resi-
dent listened to the verdict and mulled his appeal. His defense
team included, at one time or another, Alan Dershowitz, of
O.J. Simpson fame, and Abraham Sofar, whose legal acumen
the White House relied on to justify bombing Libya.
Medjuck acknowledged being a hash dealer. His lawyers
argued that the U.S. government had no authority to prosecute him since the dope had been confiscated in international waters and he did not intend to sell or distribute
drugs in the U.S. But Medjuck was not just another Sixties
time-traveller caught bootlegging narcotics: he had been
nabbed with what was then the largest cache of controlled
substances ever incinerated by North American police. Like
Hyde, his was the story of a particular generation and a
particular era that will remain forever in the social memory
as one of the defining moments in Vancouver's history.
Some made their mark and earned their money selling stocks
that were little more than blue sky and moose pasture, some

such as Hyde, Medjuck and at least a dozen others, by importing cannabis.

Medjuck was one of the most successful of Vancouver's importers for twenty years. Using a combination of dead-eyed nerve, smuggler's horseshoes and a skein of dummy companies, he rose from selling lids of pot to brokering containers of hashish. He made his first real dope connection in 1972, but soon he was making regular trips across the continent ferrying kilos between the coasts. There were no X-ray machines in those days so you could just carry it onto a plane. Or he'd drive to Florida and connect with Central American dealers and drive back to B.C. in a car stuffed with Columbian pot. Medjuck preferred the Mercury Marquis because you could stuff 400 to 500 pounds in back. He was busted once on the way back to Canada in a station wagon with the side-panels jammed with dope. Later he switched to Winnebagos.

Medjuck made millions and was a prominent member of the ostentatious nouveau riche of the Me Decade. In 1991, though, because police had been surprisingly lucky in staunching imports, a hash shortage in Central Canada had driven up the wholesale price by hundreds of dollars—about the same differential that had tempted Medjuck back in 1972. In 1990, a kilo of hash was selling for between $3,000 and $4,000 wholesale; in 1991, the price had risen to between $4,800 and $6,000 a kilo. He decided to capitalize on the situation.

The deal was typical.

It began with two Dutch nationals, who purportedly paid a Pakistani general some $20 million for the hashish. A shady Sausolito-based middleman orchestrated the delivery of the product in Pakistan and its transportation across the Pacific. He was to hand over the load to Medjuck, whose job it was to arrange the mid-ocean transfer and the delivery of the hash to a secluded bay on the B.C. coast. From there, he would have it transported by tractor-trailer to Montreal for distribution. The drivers were to be paid $150,000 for the four-day haul, the man who provided a parking spot for the trailers was to receive $1,000 a month and a $30,000 bonus.

In Montreal, the trucks would be unloaded at a fortified, two-storey, 12,400 square-foot warehouse with a conveyor belt connecting the loading dock to the second floor. On the top floor, the slabs of hashish would be cut and re-packaged into thousands of retail sales bundles. They would then be trucked to safe houses throughout the city.

Medjuck put up no money. He was to pay the cost of the off-load and to get the hash to Montreal--an investment of between $800,000 and $1 million, according to trial testimony. In exchange, a third of the load was his. He stood to make $30 million on a deal worth as much as $1 billion retail on the street.

But Medjuck turned to the wrong person to help arrange the pickup.

Guarded by Pakistani tribesmen armed with Kalishikovs and grenade launchers, the hash began its journey in the northern wilds bordering Afghanistan. Rough, kilo-sized slabs of the clay-like intoxicant were wrapped in red cellophane, covered in tan plastic and packed inside green sacks. The 3,100 duffel backs, each containing about fifty pounds of hash, were packed onto more than three hundred camels—a train nearly five miles long. It was then loaded onto small skiffs on the shores of the Arabian Sea and ferried to a motorboat waiting beyond the surf.

About 100 miles off the coast, the motorboat rendezvoused with a cargo ship called the Saratoga Express and transferred the initial load—about 30 tonnes. Another 40 tonnes was put in a second ship, the Lucky Star. When the Saratoga Express foundered in a Philippine typhoon, its load was taken on by the Lucky Star. The off-load was set to happen about seven days due north of Hawaii.

Just after dawn on June 23, choppy seas hampered the transfer, and the captain, getting nervous, decided to head back to Asia after unloading about 100 bags (2.4 tonnes). Two American destroyers suddenly appeared and threatened to open fire. The defiant captain refused to be boarded because the 450-foot cargo vessel was on the high seas—the no man's land of international waters. It was brief and futile gesture of resistance.

Medjuck was arrested by the FBI on Sept. 9, 1991, as he headed to San Francisco for a business meeting. What had been a life of adventure, of love, of affluence, of joy, of parenthood, of friendship, of success, was instantly transformed into a nightmare. He became a pariah not because he was wrong, but because he was caught. His life as a free man ended. He was sentenced to twenty-five years in prison and would not regain his freedom until late 2004.

His last deal was perhaps the final attempt to land a load of illicit foreign cannabis on the Canadian west coast. It marked the end of an era. The days of the hash and pot ships was over for good.

President Reagan's so-called War On Drugs aimed not just to combat the problem within American borders but to eradicate the underground market in controlled substances. The policy allied American law-enforcement agencies, the military and prosecutors and created a framework for them to work together. It allowed them to follow Medjuck's deal on military satellite—the pictures captivated the court. High technology surveillance of the world's oceans by spy satellites and the U.S. military ensures nothing travels between continents unnoticed. Unless it's in containers. The west coast of Canada is no longer the porous border it once was.

In the 1980s, importers started moving their resources to cocaine, real estate, the restaurant business and horticulture.

By the time Hyde died, police already had discovered the first big indoor grow operation in the province, in Nanaimo. By the time Medjuck was caught, grow-ops were already an epidemic.

———

Charles Scott had an insider's view of the evolution of the domestic Canadian pot industry. In the beginning, he said, it was very different from what it is today.

"You got $3,750 at the door and it was still wet," he laughed. "You said, take it or leave it. The American buyers were few and far between then. The domestic market just sucked it all up."

The pot was a higher quality, too, he believed, because the gardeners cultivated strains that had a longer growing period. The extra growing time produced pot with better psychotropic qualities and bumper yields. Those were the days when B.C. Bud made its reputation, between 1989 and 1993. Today, most commercial growers use strains that mature in six to seven weeks.

"Nowadays the growers wouldn't take those old strains if you offered them, because they take ten to twelve weeks to flower, and there is stuff out there now like 40-Day Wonder," Scott said. "As a seed seller, my number one customers in the U.S. and Europe buy the stuff that's really great pot—our Vietnamese strains and stuff that is unique and killer, but you have to wait a while if you are growing them. All the commercial growers are growing the same average swag. B.C. Bud isn't what it used to be."

The Internet chat rooms were simmering with such debate.

"I'm saying it's not even close to what it used to be," Scott insisted. "We don't get paid enough to grow it the way we used to—because you are talking about a double-time factor. Even if you tell people you are going to get double yields if you do it right over the extended period of time, they'll tell you the risk factor has doubled because they could get two harvests in that time period with other strains."

Scott is a marijuana Mendel. The original draft-dodger growers in the Kootenays and elsewhere in B.C., Scott said, grew what were called "tips" between 1969 and 1973—weed that came from Mexico via California.

"One of my strains here is bred out of their stuff," he said. "It's the first stuff Marc Emery bought from me, called Flaxseed. They called it 'tips' because they couldn't get a bud forming. They sold leaf and they sold tips back in those days because that is what they could actually achieve."

Over time, the growers got better, and in 1978 and 1979, developed Kootenay Gold and Kootenay Green, the first strains commercial enough for the American market in any bulk back. In every way, these first pot farmers lived off the grid, in the hollows and isolated valleys of the corduroy mountain ranges in the Interior. They were radical people into self-sufficiency and minimal government intervention. Out in the middle of nowhere, nobody cared or was around to complain. Until pot became big business in the 1990s.

"Now it's a seedy business," Scott intoned. "There are a lot of shysters in this whole thing. It's sad. You name it, it has happened to me. I've been ripped, robbed at gunpoint, had some of my people kidnapped and held for ransom. I've been imprisoned, I've been beaten, you name it."

In his mind, he is a persecuted farmer who would like to be left alone to rear his family. "Who am I to say that I'm guilty of being who I am—a reclusive pot grower? Our kids, man, are our main focus outside of my work. And my work is in the garden. I just don't quite understand it, so I really feel quite angry and bitter that I was thrown in a cage with other people and deprived of my civil liberties for growing a plant. I don't do anything else that is illegal—well, maybe I do since I trip out on some other shit, but I don't steal. I pay my taxes, I even pay taxes on seed sales. I mean, you know, I give Caesar what Caesar is due."

And the money is huge.

"Back when we started doing it, it was worth more money per pound," he explained. "There weren't very many people doing it. It's widespread now and the Americans are consuming most of it. It's a lot of coin Canada will lose if they shut it down. So why would they really want to shut it down?"

He said he thought the fiscal reality should drive public policy. "We keep people off welfare," he said. "I put $100,000 into this community just in clipping and labour wages. At least. That's conservative. It has to be more because I sell. When you factor the seed value, what it costs me to grow it, the whole thing, there's at least that."

If pot were legal or if he could get a government licence to grow a commercial crop, Scott would immediately need forty full-time employees. "That's unskilled," he emphasized. "I'm able to employ a sector of the community that otherwise is unemployable. The economics just make total sense."

A scruffy farmhand wandered into the room.

"How are you doing, Kevin?" Scott asked.

"I've got thirty holes filled," he replied.

"What have you been doing, man!" Scott said in mock horror.

They both chuckled.

Scott suggested a tour of the plantation—"The Cannabis Reserve," as he dubbed it.

"We've learned to use the climate here," he explained as we headed outdoors. "I'm so grateful for it. We harvest plants out of our greenhouses in the winter when everyone else is completely indoors. I don't like growing indoors. We do, but I essentially far prefer growing under natural light, although it's not an easy plant to grow, especially when you're talking about growing it on guerrilla terms."

He pointed to the surrounding bush. Every 3 to 5 metres, the scrub was infiltrated by a marijuana plant, invisible to the untrained eye against the camouflage screen of alder, poplar, spruce, pine, roses and blackberry hedges. Some were 4 to 5 metres tall with colas as thick as a forearm. Each breath of breeze was perfumed—heavy with citrus and skunk.

"You have to hide it and conceal it from everyone—from your neighbours to the police who are flying over your house in helicopters."

Although Scott was pretty brazen. His place looked like a pot farm. A cement mixer stood in the yard for combining the chemicals and manure.

"I'm so happy with my compost this year," Scott bragged. "I went back to the old Kootenay recipe using nothing but horseshit. I'm using horseshit, peat, a gelling agent and a little bit of perlite, some dolomite lime to adjust the pH and it's just awesome."

Scott is the ultimate pot snob. If you're not into the plant or interested in the minutiae of marijuana horticulture, he'll bore you to tears or drive you to smoke pot till you're stupefied. As he strolled through the light forest, Scott pointed to specific plants, each sitting in a camouflage plastic bag so that, if need be, it could be picked up and moved. At the moment, most were about 2 metres high; some were shorter, bent over like a bush or a creeper.

"That's Brazilian," Scott said, "the Lambada Strain. We're going to do Panama Red."

Around the globe, marijuana is ubiquitous, like real grass. For obvious reasons, it was among the first plants cultivated. Filled with sugars, albumen and a host of chemicals, marijuana is nutritious, useful and fun. The plant produces a strong, versatile fibre for making everything from paper to clothing to canvas to rope to concrete. Seeds contain a pale, jade-coloured oil, rich in the unsaturated fatty acids that are useful in making fuel, soap, varnish, paint . . .

Some believe the plant originated in Central Asia, near Mongolia and the Siberian lowlands. Others suggest it could as easily have come from China, the Himalayas or the Hindu Kush. More than one pot fancier believes a case can be made that the *sativa* strains naturally love the tropics, *indicas* are more altitude-inclined and the *ruderalis*, with its hardy, hemp-like traits, is a steppe-dweller. Scott is of the opinion that the plant first appeared in Cambodia, because his research shows that's where the *indica* and *sativa* strains meet. He believes the early references in Cambodian culture suggest that as well.

"I think it was carried from Cambodia to India and around the globe," he theorized. "I don't think it came from Central Asia or the Kush. *Sativa* seems to definitely originate in Cambodia. Nepalese is like the missing link. It has characteristics of both plants. It flowers like an *indica* but it smokes and grows like a *sativa* in a lot of ways."

He pointed to new releases that had been crossed with Nepalese: Panama Red, Acapulco Gold, Colombian Gold.

"It maintains a *sativa* high, gives a firmer bud and reduces the flowering time drastically. Although some of the Afghanis will do that too." He looked my way. "That will be a big yielder," he said, pulling my face out of the dank lemony cola of a big, gold Colombian plant to show me something truly exotic for B.C. "This is Lebanese," he said. "We have the seeds for North Indian but I don't have any growing at the moment."

He stopped and sparked a spliff in the glade. We stood in the diffuse green light of the hollow surrounded by a half-dozen plants, their colas bushy, plump and laden, fully gone to seed.

"Damn," he said. "This one has mould. I knew we should have harvested it the other day. It rained yesterday."

You could see the dark purple stain of the fungus like a bruise on the plant and, if you bent close, you could smell the earthy pungency of the rot. Ruined.

Two other potted plants nearby were entwined like a pair of mating serpents in flagrante delicto.

"Male and female—best way to pollinate," Scott said. "If there isn't much pollen, I use a cornstarch solution, add the harvested pollen and apply it to the plants myself with a paintbrush."

"Don't you worry about them seeding the other plants?"

"It's too heavy. Unless we have a hurricane, the pollen won't travel very far—a few feet maybe. The environment will screen it out."

We continued down the trail for another hundred metres or so.

"My dad called it the Ho Chi Minh Trail when he was here," Scott joked.

The path opened up to a field of tall hay with a large white greenhouse. Inside were dozens of verdant plants in various stages of growth. You could see the different strains easily. Some had thin narrow leaves, like the Acapulco, others broad dark green, like the Congolese. Some had colas heavy with crystal structures, rich with purplish-black resin and stinking of pine tar; others were delicate shades of green speckled with red hairs smelling of sandalwood and Juicy Fruit.

"This is sort of Research and Development," Scott said. "Full, there will be sixty plants in here. You're never going to get me for too much. My other grows are licensed by Health Canada. Right now it's not that profitable to grow indoors— why bother, my overhead is killing me. It's not as lucrative as it used to be because we're not talking about $3,500 a pound any more."

The Canadian pot market was flooded by the U.S. border clampdown following September 11, 2001. As well, the Mexicans started producing better pot, called Pretendica, that's pouring into Arizona and eroding U.S. and Canadian homegrown prices. Mexico exported more than one hundred times as much marijuana north into the United States as Canada sent south. If you can buy Mexican that gets you high for $35 a quarter, why pay $80 for B.C. Bud?

"We are probably fuelling the fire by selling them seeds," Scott said.

As we walked back to the house, he explained the economic facts of growing. "When I'm growing *sativa*—first of all the shit takes twelve to fourteen weeks to mature and even then it doesn't yield anything," he said. "It's so wispy and the buds are less defined, so my clipping crews are way more expensive. It costs me 600 bucks a pound to clean it. So when I tell somebody I want $3,500 for a pound of Vietnamese, it's actually a good deal because it has cost me twelve weeks of flowering time, which means so many kilowatts of light, to produce a half-pound instead of a pound that I'd get with an *indica*.

"With the glut," he said, rolling his eyes for emphasis, "growers are lucky to get $2,000 a pound unless they are selling to an elite market. It's really tough and I'm not BS-ing or poor-mouthing. I make good money because of my seed company, but if it weren't for that I would be really worried."

Some Americans, he acknowledged, would pay whatever it costs to get what they want because they are shopping for the rich and famous. That's his main market these days: selling to those who want a globally recognized, brand-name product prized by hipsters everywhere.

"I also charge ridiculous amounts of money for things I grow that take a long period of time. Either the local market, Marc and that type of crew, will consume it, or last year a certain celebrity buyer bought all our organic greenhouse pot at $500 more a pound over market. Our whole outdoor crop last year went to Laredo, Texas. To Willie Nelson. That's the one variety I have here with his name and it was done with his blessing, as it says in our seed catalogue. He told me that himself over the telephone. Then there's Dennis Rodman and a whole group of elite potheads."

Up until even the late 1980s, you could find Mexican brick-weed in Vancouver. No more. If you don't want to pay the price for the best, triple-A B.C. Bud, Vietnamese growers are pumping out a B-grade pot that sells for almost half the price. They're into the export trade in a big way, too, with their own market primarily in San Francisco. They've been so successful, police estimate they've grabbed 30 per cent of the market share.

"It's obviously theirs—big, orange, hard buds," Scott said. "The first time I saw it I was impressed. But it has very little smoke quality. They use a lot of plant growth regulators and it tastes very chemically. They use massive dehumidifiers to dry the pot, to keep it hard. They have a very different kind of product and certain American buyers will work with it because you can offer it to them for a fair price. L.A. is really heavy into the lime-green thing. If you want to get triple-A prices it must be lime green and it has to be crystally, because California already produces so much of its own good pot, especially from the medical co-ops that are extensive across the state. For it to go into the L.A. or into the Southern California market it has to be pretty damn good."

Scott figured any legal and regulatory regime would be good for him. "I'll make more money," he said. "Bottom line. I know how to farm anything and it frustrates me and somewhat depresses me that I can't operate at the level I need to be profitable. Which is being able to do things on a mass scale without the prohibition bastards looking over my shoulder.

I just want to go where I can work. I don't want to grow fifty of one type to select the mother from, I want to grow five hundred."

Scott said he could produce nearly 2 tons of smokable bud a month, almost immediately, if it were legal.

"With those economies of scale, I don't need to make very much profit per pound and I can produce a higher quality product. There are not a lot of people ready to tackle commercial cultivation. I have tackled it to a certain degree and I'm willing to tackle it on a massive scale. I would, the first year, be willing to plant between 4 and 5 hectares. I'd be talking specifically about hash plants that would be grown for trichome production so we could make dry-sieve and water-extracted hashes and resins. That's where the market is going to be. Clone sales, too, will be huge.

"I will have my seeds in every retail outlet from here to Timbuktu when I can. For me, the seed prices are not going to drop. They are not so disproportionate right now for what you are actually getting. They will stay around $50 for a packet of quality cannabis seeds in a legal market. I'm not worried about a drop-off. You might see 10 per cent or 15 per cent. But not much. Brokers like Emery already take that much at least."

He predicted a change in the pot market in terms of the products and strains available. "When the prohibition ends, nobody is going to give a flying fuck about how long it's going to take to flower. They are not going to care what colour it is. All they're going to care about is how good it is."

There's always going to be profit in direct dried cannabis sales, Scott agreed. It'll cost $5 a gram, with some selling at $7.50 a gram—which would cover the costs and a reasonable margin.

"Somebody's going to rise above the rest and there is going to be one brand that will rise above the rest," he said.

"I intend to be it. I'm not being cocky. I'm being practical. Just as a lot of Canadian-based alcohol companies rose to the top during Prohibition, I fully intend to do the same. I'm going to be in Art Knapp [Garden Centres]. I'm going to make more money because I'm not being middled and the consumer is going to see a more reasonable price. That's how I plan to dominate—offering top-quality cannabis strains from around the world. Nobody else can do it. Seriously, because I've been doing this for fifteen years now—collecting, buying, holding, multiplying."

He bent to check the progress on a four-foot Romulan.

"I want to be the Seagram's of the pot business, that's what I aspire to. That's my aspiration. I often use the word *corporatizing* cannabis. There are ten big companies right now. We are dominating the genetic market—Canadians."

He said Dutch companies were buying seeds from people like him, relabelling them and selling them as Dutch seeds. Most of the Dutch growers had moved away, leaving the Netherlands for Switzerland first, then Spain because of recent clampdowns by police.

"Canadians like me have multiplied their stock for them under prohibition because there are less serious consequences here than there are in Holland for cultivation. I'm well on the way to dominating, to literally dominating. I have more stock than anybody else and I'm acquiring more all the time. I just pay for it, it doesn't matter what it costs me. This year, I'll probably spend $10,000 American buying stock—seeds from anywhere in the world. It's worth it."

He had plans. Big plans. "I have the largest thesaurus of cannabis seeds perhaps anywhere. I have every strain. I have Panama Red. I have Colombian Red. I have Acapulco Gold, and that's just my Central Americans. I have hash plants from Turkey, Lebanon, Egypt, North India, Afghanistan. From all over the earth. I have *sativas* from everywhere. I've got them from all over Southeast Asia, China. We just have a massive number. It's a compulsion. Sometimes I will spend excessive amounts to obtain these at auction. You can multiply them, but I often don't want to sell them. I have a huge genetic bank to play with."

He told me he hoped the laws on growing soon would be eased to allow him to become more legitimate.

"I think we're the biggest, the largest seed producer now," he said of his Reeferman collective. "We have as many strains as Sensi Seeds and Dutch Passion combined on our site right now. There are companies with one or two strains and they're just sidelines, but there are probably ten major suppliers. Reeferman is being talked about, we're being compared to the old-time breeders like Ben Dronkers, which is an honour."

Starting around 1974, after a trip to the Indian subcontinent, Dronkers became a disciple of the plant. He later opened a coffee house, was arrested more than eighty times, founded Sensi Seeds (one of the first offering a wide variety of strains) and thirty years later is a multi-millionaire. Today, he runs a commercial empire that embraces hemp fields, a cannabis museum, coffee shops and a Thai resort.

"Sensi Seeds is the most lucrative seed company—they make a lot of money, millions a year," Scott said enviously. "We have more than them, but they are making more money than us. We're literally able to offer an international cannabis menu. Nobody has really done this since the 1970s."

Scott wanted to create a corporate entity to capitalize on his knowledge and genetic assets. He knew there was investment out there, had been offered it, but hadn't yet determined the best way of using and profiting from it.

"I need about $2 million to set up," he said. "That would turn over about $18 to $20 million a year in revenue. Especially when you are talking about capital holdings in terms of seed production. With seed production, it can get massive. I think we could start a cannabis bio-company and go public."

Instead of looking for capital in Canada, however, Scott was looking overseas. We returned to the house and he flopped back down on his recliner.

"We have an offer right now from a guy in Switzerland that wants to get involved," he said. "I'm being cautious. There's a lot of market speculator types with real interesting contracts combing through the people who are semi-legitimizing cannabis."

Scott thought Europe held out hope. But Spanish police in Madrid had thrown his closest connection to the Dutch coffee-house industry in prison two days earlier.

Nol van Schaik owned the Willie Wortel's coffee-shop chain and the Global Hemp Museum in Haarlem, just outside of Amsterdam. At the time, he was being held on an old French warrant for escaping custody in 1989. Spain was threatening to send the true-life cannabis action-hero back to France, where he had been convicted in absentia and sentenced to five years' imprisonment.

Scott said van Schaik was using some of his genetics but what worried him was that he himself was headed to Spain hoping to cut his own deal.

"I'm packing up my suitcase full of seeds and buying new clothes when I get to Spain," he said with a glance at his moth-eaten sweats. "I was just thinking of that song from Woodstock: '*Coming into Los Angeles, / Bringing in a couple of keys, / Don't touch my bags if you please, / Mister Customs Man . . .*' I'm thinking, fuck, isn't that a cliché given what I'm about to do." He got lost in the reverie.

"There isn't a doubt in my mind," he said after a moment. "I will make $1 million in the next three years. I'm a quarter of the way there when I sell the seed stocks. The idea is to take that sale and the work I've been able to do without getting busted and reinvest it outside of this country. Which is sad because that money could stay here and I could probably get—I bet I could get $1.5 million in the next six to eight weeks out of Europe to do what I want to do here."

The trip to Europe, however, produced more illumination than investment. The next time I saw him, Scott said his first stop in Amsterdam had been an eye-opener.

"There are huge payoffs if you're willing to go there and grow commercial herb, because they're getting 5,500 euros a kilo," he explained. "If you hooked up with someone in England—and I was approached by guys in England—they'll pay 8,000 [euros] for top-notch stuff in the United Kingdom. There's huge money. We're talking about that all over Europe. The pot is worth three times as much."

Switzerland had changed its liberal attitude toward pot growing, Scott said, so "the Dutch market is starving, France is starving, the German market, that whole area. They're massive consumers—just like America—especially now you have these free-flowing borders. The struggle in Holland is to keep the coffee shops stocked and get people to grow something other than Power Plant, which is just like our Jamaican. Basically, it's illegal to grow there just like here now. So I went there and learned the dynamics of the economy."

Scott said he realized while in Europe the value of his genetic pool. "In terms of what my collection was worth, my thesaurus of seeds, in terms of the global market, I had no idea. Nobody has it. I had no idea. I expected to go to Holland and be able to pick up seeds. Instead I was hustled into trying to sell seeds, my own breeding stock. So I realized, whoa!"

Scott also received job offers. "I had offers to go work there for Popeye's coffee shop. They called again this morning, as soon as I got back, and for good money—200,000 euros a year. Greenhouse Seeds called me on the last day and gave me the royal treatment. But I don't want to leave here now."

Scott had abandoned his hope of commercial cannabis cultivation in Spain. "I've been here since the beginning," he said. "My wife and I have been in the scene since the beginning. Whether we were popular or not, we've been breeding and slinging weed and everybody knows us. I've done time in this country for this shit. And I don't have any intention not to [continue to] do it. I didn't realize what we were doing was so unique. I honestly didn't."

Scott said he had changed his strategy and was about to start selling direct to the public. The last time he did that, in 1998, he was busted shortly afterward. He was in Saskatchewan, supposedly operating a hog farm, but the barns were stuffed with grow-lights and dozens of lush, pungent pot—120 pounds every nine weeks. Revenue of roughly $1.7 million a year.

He picked up a bag of grass and began to roll a spliff. He saw few options. "Most of the hydroponic industry is owned by organized crime," Scott said. "Especially in B.C. and Quebec. I mean the Hells Angels actually came out with their own nutrient and put their own symbol on it—a drag bike with a devil chick. They came into our stores and said, 'Sell this. It's good.'"

He sparked the reefer. "I mean it's entirely disgusting. We need legalization, we don't need decriminalization. We need total legalization to get rid of the bikers and criminal stakeholders like them.

"I met some cool people in Europe but overall it was big stress," Scott continued. "This business is cutthroat and lowlife. That's just the way it is globally because of the prohibition.

Especially the seed business, when you do the work we're doing. We're coming out with brand-new stuff and other people are threatened by it. Even Marc and me are touchy because now I have begun to sell direct. Marc is no longer my exclusive distributor. So he sees probably all of this coming directly out of his budget." He gestured at the myriad glassine seed packages and pre-labelled envelopes lying around the floor ready for mailing. "And I guess essentially it is. He was my main distributor. But I'm going retail."

He nodded toward his assistant at the computer. "I just got off the phone with *High Times*—I'm placing my first full-page ad in their next issue," Scott said, pointing to the computer screen displaying a long seed and price catalogue.

"We have to have the text to them by tonight," he added. "They are really where it's at in terms of cannabis advertising. There's more money generated through them by advertising because of their distribution than in any other way. Kind Seed downtown, they don't advertise anywhere but there and they do $1 million a year, mostly mail order. For all these hicks in the sticks in the U.S., *High Times* is like apple-fucking-pie to them."

On top of marketing his seeds direct, Scott was considering a Reeferman store—right across the street from Emery's HQ—offering gelato, espresso and pot. He said he had woken up to his market advantage. His European trip had underscored that. Scott had gone to the Netherlands a little in awe of the reputation and history of continental breeders; he had returned with a different perspective. He planned to exploit his expertise.

WHOLESALE

big mike

May 22, 2004

MICHAEL STRAUMIETIS, all six foot eight of him, climbed out of the glistening black-and-chrome Hummer—licence plate BUDS1—and strode toward me extending a beefy paw.

"You got a cellphone?" he asked.

"Sure," I replied, thinking he needed to make a quick call.

"Pull out the battery." He acted as if the phone were alive. "They can switch them on and listen."

"Of course." I nodded, unplugging the power unit.

"I'm not giving them anything," the big man quipped with a smile, softening now that the potential for danger had passed. "Good to meet you. You know they busted us in 2001 and charged us with conspiracy over 200 pounds of pot in Washington State. They stayed the charges and we're suing them. My lawyer thinks it's a slam dunk."

We strolled through a light sun-shower toward Starbucks. He stopped, scanned the café, decided there were too many customers. The hulking Straumietis could be a double for actor Michael Madsen, who played the scary Mr. Blonde in *Reservoir Dogs*. It's no surprise police paint him as some kind of Tony Soprano. ("I always thought it was because of my name," his wife Carmella tells people.) He's a strapping guy who could easily be perceived as menacing.

"You know a hundred armed cops stormed into our offices," Straumietis continued, swivelling toward Milestones. "I don't know how many were DEA — but I'm sure they were there. There's 150 of them operating here now."

It was a Saturday morning in Langley, a bucolic town in the picturesque Fraser Valley. Bright shafts of sunlight lanced through grey rain squalls marching east toward the cordillera; snow-capped mountains hemmed the northern horizon; the metropolis lay invisible to the west, sprawled across the fertile delta; the U.S. border was a few kilometres to the south.

Truckloads of marijuana move across the forty-ninth parallel daily—only a fraction of them detected by customs officers, the same as with alcohol in the twenties. You could walk across, swim across, canoe across, drive across, fly across. The summer armada of recreational boats, caravans, campers and other vehicles all cruising the coastal waters and West Coast highways from Mexico to British Columbia made stemming the flow of contraband impossible. Then there was commercial traffic—fishing boats, logging trucks, transport trailers, tanker trucks with bladders, school buses . . . not to mention the swarms of private aircraft. Interdiction had worse odds than roulette.

Langley and this part of the fertile Fraser Valley are full of used car dealerships, late-model malls and cookie-cutter bedroom neighbourhoods home to commuters seeking a coun-trified lifestyle. There are a dozen or so stunning, high-end nouveau riche hobby farms and vineyards. The surrounding fields are peppered with immigrants, turbaned farm workers stooped amid the various crops.

"They seized our planes, too, but we got them back," Straumietis added indignantly, referring to what happened after the drug-trafficking charges were stayed. "You know what it did? It turned me from a businessman into an activist."

Straumietis was one of three principals in Advanced Nutrients, the main firm in a skein of businesses that at one time included a flight school, eight laboratories, a lobbyist, an image archive, a genetics bank, a newspaper, a documentary unit, more than one hundred different products designed for cannabis cultivation and the largest network of medical marijuana grow operations in Canada. His partners were Robert Higgins, a former flight instructor and commercial pilot, and Eugene Yordanov.

The towering man stopped in the middle of a parking lot. "They put my secretary on the floor with a gun to her head. Can you believe it? You know what they wanted? My records." He paused. "Hello! All they had to do was knock on the door and ask."

He set off again.

Finally ensconced in the empty Milestones, he washed down a bacon-and-egg Atkins plate with a root beer while reminiscing about his years on the lam.

"A different phone booth every week," the forty-four-year-old laughed. "That's always how they get you. Your family. They just sit on them. Everyone needs to connect with their family." He was currently embroiled in another major legal battle to stay in the country.

The gregarious Oregon-born Straumietis has grown pot across the United States. He is a proud member of Mensa, the group for people with confirmed genius-level scores on the IQ test, and a Mason. Like Emery, he spins a well-honed narrative when asked about himself that sounds like it could have been written by Horatio Alger—the 19th-century author who invented the rags-to-riches yarn. And just about as probable. In Big Mike's case, he said he built a multi-million-dollar international company after coming to B.C. with only $25,000 in his jeans and a green thumb.

Straumietis, who did a year of pre-med before embarking on his illicit agricultural career a quarter-century ago, was a born entrepreneur and salesman. But he was running from a Wisconsin marijuana-manufacturing charge when he arrived as a fugitive from the United States in 1996. Upon coming to Canada, he initially marketed his expertise in growing marijuana, especially his knowledge of plant nutrients to maximize yield and potency. Pressed by a supplier about the amount of chemicals he was buying, Straumietis saw what he thought was an opportunity to go legit and decided to start a business.

He got together with Higgins, who was teaching him to be a pilot, and Yordanov, a Bulgarian immigrant turned Fraser Valley businessman. The three opened a hydroponics shop and began creating their own gardening empire. Straumietis had realized that when you moved growing from outdoors to indoors, you could control the environment and make production predictable. As long as you were farming outdoors, there were innumerable variables. Move indoors, follow the advice of the experts and voila— regulated production.

Emery and his organization revelled in pot culture—the zany, carnival-like current of hedonism that ran through the 19th-century Paris salons to the fields of Woodstock to some of Amsterdam's coffee shops. The principals of Advanced Nutrients exploited a business opportunity—selling specialty fertilizers to specialty gardeners. They were selling sugar to bootleggers, if you will, riding a commercial wave as familiar to the businessmen of prohibition as to Bill Gates—*There is a need and I will fill it.*

Through Canadian Soiless Ltd., Straumietis initially distributed chemicals and then offered to supply his customers with the ancillary equipment they needed. He and his partners created Polar Bear Manufacturing Ltd. in 1998 to provide heat exchangers, fans, blowers, CO_2 units, monitoring systems and other necessary hardware for indoor growing.

The more successful they became, the more they branched out. People who bought chemicals or fans from them began asking about lights, and a year later, Advanced Nutrients formed a company to distribute high-energy bulbs and ballasts. They also expanded into doing their own research and developing proprietary feed-solutions specifically for marijuana. To that end, they employed five PhD researchers, who have since helped produce more than one hundred specific proprietary products for growing marijuana. In 2004, Advanced Nutrients and its related firms had sixty-five employees and estimated revenues of $30 million.

Advanced Nutrients has been one of the biggest beneficiaries of the booming marijuana industry and has nurtured a clientele of patient-growers, medical pot producers and guerrilla farmers. The company employs doctors and chemists, spends about $500,000 a year on R & D and advertises in a dozen trade publications, including *Heads, High Times, Weed World, Soft Secrets, High Life, Cannabis Culture* and *Cannabis Health.* Locally, Advanced Nutrients has been all over the radio, on CFOX and Rock 101—thirty-one slots a week, a $250,000 campaign. There was also a weekly calendar girl in the *Buy And Sell,* another $250,000.

More than seven hundred retail distributors in Canada, the United States, Australia, the U.K., the Netherlands, Germany, Italy, Spain and France carry their wares. With short-term sales projections topping $50 million within five years, *Forbes* magazine touted the potential of their anticipated initial public offering. A mainstream U.S. firm wanted an equity interest; Advanced Nutrients held off.

There are similar firms in Australia and the United States, but unlike Advanced, they do not flaunt their sales to marijuana growers. They fear prosecution under the kind of broad U.S. drug statutes that allowed the arrest and imprisonment of Tommy Chong. The Canadian comedian was jailed for nine months because his company sold innocuous glass pipes designed for smoking cannabis. Who knows what Washington would do to those whose clients were illegal growers, primarily organized criminals buying in bulk to fuel their commercial operations.

Advanced Nutrients emphasizes the medicinal properties and medical applications of cannabis and the scope of the current medical program in Canada. But fewer than one thousand people have exemptions from Health Canada that allow them to possess or grow marijuana. To supply them with all the pot they could smoke would require only a few thousand dollars' worth of fertilizer and feed annually

Advanced Nutrients has made far more money feeding the major growers, selling them on its research and plant supplements. That's where big money was to be made. At that level, marijuana is a commodity exactly like tomatoes. It just so happens their commodity is hot. Big Mike and his partners—each an imposing physical presence—are as high up the pot-industry food chain as you can get.

"I knew I could make better fertilizers than what was then being made by all the other companies in the industry," Straumietis said. "I was treated extremely badly by a wholesaler based in Langley, B.C. I said to myself, 'If she is treating me like this, she must be treating other people just the same, or even worse.' So I knew there would be a need for courteous and kind wholesalers in the marketplace. Rob, Eugene and I created Advanced Nutrients, and we have proven that courteous wholesalers who sell quality product are welcome in the marketplace. Indeed, if it was not for that wholesaler being so impolite, there probably would not be an Advanced Nutrients today."

Straumietis sees himself as akin to the distillery owners who supplied the underground U.S. market during Prohibition. They lived in a chiaroscuro world that handed some a jail sentence, others extravagant wealth as the light dawned and alcohol became legal. Straumietis was betting on the wealth part. He'd already spent ten years living underground on the run from U.S. law enforcement, he said, talking to his family via a different phone booth every Sunday and calling prearranged and random locations.

Next month, he said, he hoped to open an office in China, which would become a supplier of tables, light stands and the miscellany of electrical and plumbing odds-and-ends needed to operate a grow-op efficiently. "The industrial revolution is happening there, man," Straumietis said in awe. "It's unbelievable."

He said he and his partners are cashing in on the changing attitude toward the herb.

"I spent a year in isolation growing marijuana," Straumietis said. "That was the hardest. Didn't talk to my family for a year. But I made $40,000, gave some to my brother as a holdback and came to Canada. I think I had about $25,000, and I started growing here. I've had grow-ops with two thousand lights. So when I talk to people about nutrients, I know what it means to be depending on that crop. But look at me now—a multi-millionaire."

Albeit one currently fighting deportation and struggling to establish his legitimacy.

Documents obtained from the Wisconsin Circuit Court in Vernon County tell quite a story about Straumietis, also known as Michael A. Remington, a.k.a. Micheal A. Paulson, a.k.a. Tom Newman. Jerry Fredrickson, under-sheriff for Vernon County, swore out the warrant for the arrest, stating that during the summer of 1993 Straumietis was the brains behind a large outdoor marijuana farm in Liberty Township.

On September 10, 1993, Vernon County sheriff's investigator Thomas Johnson and Wisconsin conservation warden Richard Wallin found the farm surrounded by a four-strand electrical fence. Inside, row upon row of lush marijuana plants flourished, fed by an elaborate sprinkler and fertilizing system. The two law enforcement officers returned to town for a search warrant. The next day, sheriffs descended on the field and hauled away 1,869 pot plants.

Later they arrested a man named Jonathon Williams, a.k.a. Michael Lawson. He told them he rented the property in November 1992, especially to grow pot. He said Straumietis arrived on May 29, 1993, with a U-Haul containing numerous plants. That day, he estimated, they planted about 1,450 plants. On June 22, Straumietis arrived in a Jeep Grand Cherokee with another 750 plants. Lawson said Straumietis delivered an additional 900 plants on July 1.

According to Lawson, Straumietis also provided fertilizer and a timer so Lawson would know when to apply particular chemicals. When he heard about the bust, Straumietis fled. He did not immediately run to Canada; he obtained a phony identity—Thomas Scott Newman, a real person born in Texas on January 6, 1965, but who died as a fifteen-day-old infant. He hid in the United States under the moniker Texas Tom Newman, at one point producing adult entertainment films. He came to Canada for vacation on August 4, 1996.

Shortly afterward, he met Cynthia Falconer, a single mom with two daughters. They fell in love and began living together, and Straumietis stayed. He and Cynthia were married on the inauspicious date of September 11, 1999, at a time when his future looked bright and his wealth was multiplying daily. About a year after they were married, he applied for Canadian citizenship, using Cynthia as his sponsor.

Straumietis was a fugitive from U.S. law enforcement, yet he lived openly, building a commercial empire in the marijuana industry without police or Canadian authorities saying boo. Straumietis was even the host of a popular growing-tips show on Emery's Pot TV.

He also was already under surveillance—one of some two score men and women caught in a net by law enforcement agencies on both sides of the border. Still, it would take authorities another eight or nine months to actually identify Straumietis by his real name. It was a matter of happenstance that they targeted him. No, not happenstance even, but the result of the underground nature of the cannabis cultivation industry and its role as a revenue stream for organized crime.

In the summer of 2000, the RCMP were still investigating the 1996 disappearance of a young couple from a home in the Fraser Valley. The remains of the forty-three-year-old husband had been discovered in a shallow grave on a remote logging road after they were dug up by bears, but his wife was still missing. They had been murdered over a drug debt.

After nearly five years, the Mounties believed they were closing in on the murderers and they were running an undercover operation in hopes of finally solving the case. That's when they bumped into a man who had nothing to do with the killings but who was a linchpin in the continental marijuana trade—Gerard Majella Morin. Police began following him and tapping his phone calls.

Morin was an underworld broker who moved between criminal organizations such as the Hells Angels and smaller smuggling rings and gangs with equal ease. He put buyers in touch with sellers and arranged cross-border deals—business he'd handled for more than a decade, whatever the commodity. He was one of about a dozen men performing this service in B.C. There are a similar number at least in Ontario and Quebec.

Back on July 5, 1994, Morin was sentenced to eighteen months in jail for breaching a firearms prohibition, the second time in a year he had been caught with illegal weapons. At his trial, it was said that Morin's expertise in making silencers and converting semi-automatic weapons to fully automatic had earned him the underworld nickname "The Wizard." But his lawyer shrugged that off, saying Morin was a misunderstood "gun nut."

Indeed, the Quebec-born Morin was a champion marksman with the B.C. Snipers Association, a former firearms officer with the Canadian military and an experienced gun technician. When arrested, he had a personal grocery store of weapons. Found in the trunk of Morin's car was a .22-calibre AR-7 automatic rifle that had been chopped to the size of a pistol and fitted with a silencer. In his home, they found a gun shop and seized the following:

- a MAC-10 semi-automatic 9mm pistol tooled to take a silencer
- a J-15 automatic military assault rifle
- a TEC-22 semi-automatic assault pistol fitted to take a silencer
- magazines for semi-automatic and automatic weapons that carry more bullets than are allowed in Canada
- 6,000 rounds of ammunition, including hundreds of

rounds of police-issue rifle ammunition probably
stolen from an RCMP vault
- more than 3 kilograms of gunpowder putatively used
to manufacture custom bullets
- a power hacksaw and a lathe, with a metre-high pile
of metal shavings

All of these indicated a thriving business.

Morin had been caught a year earlier trying to smuggle a
trunkload of semi-automatic pistols, high-tech laser sights
and a large quantity of ammunition into British Columbia
from the United States. The judge in that case sentenced
Morin to a nine-month jail term, which was reduced to four
months on appeal, and banned Morin from possessing any
weapons for five years.

Provincial Court Judge Norm Collingwood later
imposed the eighteen-month jail sentence on Morin for
breaching the prohibition. The judge said he would have
sentenced Morin to more than two years in prison, but took
into account that he had served five and a half months in
custody.

Collingwood also imposed a concurrent eighteen-month
jail sentence for nine counts of possession of prohibited
weapons, banned Morin from possessing firearms and ammunition for ten years and set a three-year probation term.

Police said Morin sold to gangs and anyone else who had
the money to purchase one of his guns or homemade
silencers. One of his close friends in those days was Michael
Vukelich, then twenty-nine, who was sentenced in June 1994
to sixteen years in prison and fined $140,000 for conspiracy to
import $12.3 million worth of cocaine (123 kilos) from Seattle.
B.C. Supreme Court Justice John Hall described Vukelich as
a "chief executive officer" of a major drug-trafficking ring
and one of Canada's largest cocaine dealers.

Morin served his stint and went back to work. But he kept himself out of police sights until the summer of 2000. The forty-seven-year-old subsequently led investigators to Advanced Nutrients and a host of other "individuals of interest," including two separate and humongous smuggling rings. One was supplying most of Eastern Canada—reportedly nearly all of the pot sold in Newfoundland and Labrador—and the Eastern Seaboard.

Hash used to be the smoke of choice in Atlantic Canada, the Mounties said, but the favourite had become B.C. Bud. They said the dope was shipped across the country by train to Halifax—typically in 40- to 60-pound loads that would wholesale for as much as $150,000. The pot was then taken by car and truck via ferry to St. John's.

The other group, with ties to the Angels, was running massive quantities of marijuana into the United States and bringing cocaine and guns back. The scope of the smuggling was immense, the scale staggering, with multiple cross-border helicopter flights daily in even the most harrowing of weather. And never far from the surface was violence or its intimation. The young couple executed over a debt connected with a grow operation were not the only casualties. In the Vancouver metro area, more than a hundred young men and a handful of women had been shot, set alight, tortured or killed in less than a decade, all in the struggle for dominance of the street-level trade. Across the continent—in Toronto, Montreal, L.A., New York—marijuana and murder were often connected.

Police said Morin was facilitating cross-border drug deals of huge proportions—brokering hundreds of pounds in association with at least three dozen people across the continent capable of financing and distributing that kind of weight. Those people were also capable of protecting their investments, which is what created the nexus of cash, commodity and guns. When you can't call the cops and you're dealing with a lot of cash, you'd better be prepared to deal with potential robbers yourself. Therein lies the nub of the problem with organized crime and pot.

The pot prohibition inflates the price of cannabis and makes large quantities of it not only extremely valuable, but also extremely easy to turn into cash. Avoiding being ripped off and protecting large amounts requires muscle and that means people who are willing to resort to violence, which in an underground economy means gangsters. On the big deals, the truly commercial-scale purchases, organized crime is dominant. The Angels' drug dealing in Quebec earned them more than $100 million before police and the bloody internecine warfare with their competitors led to so many being jailed. In British Columbia, they have made hundreds of millions and diversified into high-tech stock market plays, real estate development, retail sales and trucking.

That would all change if marijuana were legal.

As a result of their interest in Morin, police began following Big Mike and his partners in the summer of 2000. Optics is everything: Is someone who provides the equipment, the fertilizer, the expertise and the support for illicit growers to thrive part of a criminal conspiracy? Law enforcement agencies believed they were and said so in the documents they filed with the court to obtain search warrants.

Police claimed they had reliable informants who said Straumietis and his partners operated an organization known as "the Company." On June 6, 2000, the Mounties said an informant told them that the Company operated out of the Garden Supercentre and that Straumietis was the boss.

The Company supposedly maintained some four hundred grow-ops in the Lower Mainland, each with a minimum of five hundred plants. Some of the grows used soil but most were hydroponic, and all the equipment was supplied by the Garden Supercentre. Police believed the Company was a sophisticated criminal organization in which everyone had a specified role—supervisors, set-up crews, growers, clippers and staff for collection and transportation.

Different crews were responsible for setting up the grows—some handled construction, some the electrical work, some the planting; others were the growers, clippers and landscapers. According to the police informants: "There was also a 'hydro guy' that would hook up directly to the pole and upgrade the transformer so it did not 'melt off the service.' This cost $40,000 and this guy showed up with the hydro truck, bucket and all, to do the job."

The investigators maintained, "Tom (a.k.a. Big Mike) got 50 per cent of every grow the company controlled, the grower got 25 per cent and the sponsor 25 per cent. To become part of the company you had to be sponsored . . . Yordanov is believed to be an 'enforcer' for the Company who deals with discipline and security problems . . . he was the muscle of the partnership . . . Higgins is believed to be directing the collection of marijuana from producers which investigators believe is for exportation . . . [Andrew John] Ivany is believed to be involved with the Company as the helicopter pilot who transports the marijuana into the U.S."

The investigators said there was a coded language—for instance, "pizza topping" referred to psilocybin mushrooms, "children, kids, little guys and kitties" meant marijuana clones, "elbow" a pound, "sugar candy" cocaine, and "Ben, benji, and benzi" meant U.S. currency.

Seven of the grows were taken down in 2000 without affecting the business, the informants said. And demand for dope was so high that the Company would also buy from freelance growers, sometimes paying as much as $3,200 a pound. At a meeting of between fifty and sixty of the growers and clippers in January 2001, Big Mike told them that they were looking to double production that year and that there was going to be "lots of money and lots of work for everyone." The meeting took place at a warehouse run by a guy named "Meat" Sinclair, a.k.a. Norm Contis, whom police described as "a very mean guy who carries a 9mm handgun and had two bad dogs at the site."

A helicopter from Advanced Nutrients–linked Chinook Air, investigators said, would "usually make one or two trips a day [into the U.S.] but had made as many as three or four. It would fly three days a week and the trip was about two hours round trip . . . the product was exchanged for cocaine, cash and guns . . . They were also into meth labs and guns."

The informants said Big Mike had a list of rules for the employees: "No drugs; tested for cocaine; fines for using cocaine; no visitors to the grows without permission, cellphones destroyed if pulled over by police . . . if an employee decided to quit the company there were no problems when he left. Eugene would just tell him that if anyone asked about them, 'they had never met' . . . Newman and Eugene were associated to the Hells Angels."

Clippers were getting $20 an hour and did not use their real names, according to the informants. They were picked up in white vans, usually a windowless Dodge that had a partition behind the front seats so the clippers did not know where they were being taken. All the residential grows had garages that the van pulled into; the door closed and the clippers were let out.

"Crew bosses still pick up numbered envelopes with cash in them to pay their crews . . . the funds are always U.S. funds. The Company is sending 300 pounds a week south [that's $600,000 wholesale at $2,000 a pound] and will buy marijuana from anyone as well as their own growers.

"The Company owns all the grow houses and will offer some people free rent to stay there if they want someone there for full-time but the rules are that you can't have a hard line or cable hook-up. The Company sets up the hydro account but whoever is in charge of the grow must pay the hydro at the Money Mart or something and then they get reimbursed. All the hydro accounts are in fictitious names. Several of the large grows have had transformers replaced by actual hydro employees who would do the work under the table."

A plausible story was hidden somewhere in the illiterate mess of information the police provided for their warrants, but little against Advanced Nutrients and its principals would ultimately stand the test of a trial. Especially after the helicopter pilot died in a car accident.

On March 27, 2001, the police ended each of the investigations that had begun with their interest in Morin after arresting him in Seattle delivering 98 pounds of marijuana to an undercover RCMP officer. Subsequently, the Mounties raided marijuana grow-ops in Chilliwack, Rosedale and Mission, seizing nearly ten thousand plants and more than $100,000 in cash.

Three days later, special police observation units were in place to follow the helicopter pilot Ivany from his home in Chilliwack to a ranch about 58 kilometres northeast of Penticton. The RCMP conducted aerial surveillance as a helicopter took off from the ranch and headed toward the U.S. border. A U.S. Customs Service surveillance aircraft was waiting to track it into U.S. airspace and Washington State.

At about 2:45 p.m., Rodney Weekes, U.S. Customs Service special agent in Spokane, said customs service pilots and DEA agents covertly intercepted and followed the helicopter across the border near Oroville, Washington. It landed at about 3:30 p.m.

Canadian Travis X. Ranger, who was driving a grey and black Ford pickup truck with a black camper shell, met the pilot. The two transferred several large hockey bags and a couple of smaller white bags from the helicopter into the back of the pickup.

The helicopter, worth an estimated US$500,000, took off and headed back to Canada. The truck drove toward the US-97 near Okanogan, Washington. U.S. law enforcement officers tailed it to a house at 40 Utke Lane, Omak. Inside, police found the hockey bags stuffed with 91 kilograms of B.C. Bud. They found GPS units and satellite cellular phones. They also discovered other empty bags redolent of marijuana. In the pickup truck, police found a 9mm Browning semi-automatic handgun with thirteen rounds in the magazine.

Facing a lengthy prison sentence, the twenty-nine-year-old Ranger pleaded guilty, saying he was "just a mule." His lawyer called him another "gullible sucker." The total load, Ranger said, was worth $374,000, but his potential profit was only $2,000. He did not at any time name who was behind it all. Ranger was sentenced to fifty-seven months' imprisonment. After his release, set for August 18, 2005, he was to serve parole for three years.

The helicopter was seized by the RCMP about a week after it returned to Canada, but police did not move in on Advanced Nutrients until a month after Ranger's arrest because they were still not sure how everyone was connected.

On June 18, at about eight a.m., the RCMP along with Canada Immigration officers arrested Straumietis. They raided Advanced Nutrients, his home and the homes of his partners. In his, they found false driver's licences and other fake ID—he claimed the documents were only for anonymously obtaining post office boxes.

Then, on June 21, Straumietis admitted he was not Tom Newman.

A week later, the police charged Yordanov, Straumietis, Higgins, the helicopter pilot Ivany and others, alleging that between January 16, 2001, and June 2001, in Abbotsford, Chilliwack, Princeton and elsewhere in B.C. and the United States, they conspired with Ranger to traffic and smuggle marijuana. Yordanov and Higgins were also charged on June 28 in Surrey with possessing more than 3 kilograms for the purpose of trafficking.

A month later, more arrests occurred in the United States and Canada. The RCMP, the DEA and the U.S. Customs Service confiscated 250 kilograms of marijuana, 24,000 plants, and 35 kilograms of cocaine. Grow-ops in Kelowna, Nelson, Langley and Chilliwack were shut down. Authorities also confiscated massive amounts of personal property—more than four hundred items, including airplanes, vehicles, boats, furniture and recreational equipment. It was the largest seizure of assets in Canadian legal history.

"I knew they were bugging my calls from jail," Straumietis recalled with relish, "so I used to do these fabulous rants . . . marijuana is harmless, how can they go home to their wife and kids having any pride in the job? I went on and on. It was a laugh."

He was released on bail after three months, and he and his partners prepared an aggressive, strident defence—the Crown stayed the charges. The federal justice department refused to speak about the case or the return of their assets.

Higgins also retrieved his target pistols—a Glock .40-calibre semi-auto, a Para Ordnance P16–40 Limited and a Browning .22 semi-auto pistol—his weights and the veritable cornucopia of syringes, vials, ampoules and boxes of bodybuilding supplies and health supplements police seized. All the drugs were prescribed for his health problems. But he was forced to surrender an unlawful U.S. Customs Service border sticker, California ID and social security cards bearing his picture and an ASP baton (police truncheon).

Yordanov even got back his throwing knives, bulletproof vests, listening devices and ERT helmet. What he was forced to surrender to police, because they were unlawful, were a tactical knife, court studies on grow operations, a fake security enforcement badge, a list of police and border patrol radio frequencies and a file labelled OURANUS containing information on the RCMP Air Section. He also forfeited a small stash of marijuana, a chunk of hash, a bag of dried mushrooms, a box of shotgun shells and a box of .22-calibre hollow-point bullets. A Ruger .22 was confiscated and sold, the money returned to him.

Straumietis ridiculed the entire operation. "You know, a criminal case usually means they have to get to ten on some imaginary scale, say," he said. "These guys didn't even get to three."

He won another victory too. The man who had ratted him out in 1993 recanted. Nevertheless, Straumietis was snookered. Cynthia left him, he faced huge legal bills and he was told to get out of Canada. He refused to give up.

With a new wife and a child on the way, he told me he was again forging ahead. Like every other testosterone-pumped successful CEO, Straumietis wanted nothing so much as to end up on the right end of a long-shot bet.

"If they throw you out of the country, they want you to fill in this form telling them where you're going and all that," he said of the Canadian government's deportation rules. "Forget it," he snarled. "If I have to go, I'm gone. I'll show up at some Canadian embassy, say, 'See I'm out of the country,' take a Polaroid or whatever to prove it, and I'm out the door and I'm going to disappear. I'm going to do it on my own terms."

Straumietis was convinced he was part of a revolution that was about to occur with the decriminalization and eventual legalization of marijuana.

"You know Russian president Putin just signed a law that lets people carry up to 20 grams of pot and 1.5 grams of cocaine? Of course it's coming. Legalization is just a question of time and regulatory issues, no longer *if*. Only the United States' anti-drug policy and its influence are slowing the process."

Advanced Nutrients, he predicted, would be at the forefront. "Right now our nutrient knowledge is cannabis specific—do you know anything about plants?" asked Straumietis, pausing only briefly before launching into a fascinatingly detailed lesson in botany.

Marijuana is its Mexican name. *Cannabis* comes from the Greek *kannabis*, from the earlier Sanskrit *cana*. The Assyrians called it *qunubu*, the Jews *qanneb*, the Arabs *qannob*, the Persians *quonnab*, the Iberians *cañamo*, the Celts *quannab*. *Kan* was common in many tongues as the word for *cane*, but *bis* was more likely a derivative of the Hebrew *bosm*, or Aramaic *busma*, or "aromatic"—the "aromatic cane."

"Listen," Straumietis added, "you want the story on all that ancient stuff, talk to Chris Bennett—he knows it all." He laughed.

The mulberry tree. Marijuana, marihuana, pot, grass, weed, dope, reefer, hop, Mary Warner, Mary Jane—call it what you will, Big Mike knew all about it. And he loved to talk about it. Carolus Linnaeus, a Swede considered the first botanist, dubbed it *Cannabis sativa* (or "cultivated"

Cannabis) back in 1753. Later, a French naturalist, Jean-Baptiste Lamarck, noticed the European plant differed from the weed found in India and he designated the latter *Cannabis indica*, that is, from India.

Nearly two centuries later, Russians studying *Cannabis* grown in central Asia identified a third species they called *Cannabis ruderalis*. But not much was really known about the plant, Straumietis said, and for the last century, research was fettered by the Prohibition. Advanced Nutrients changed that.

"If you're growing *indica* or *sativa*, we can tell you what to give it at what time to produce exactly what you want. Soon we'll be strain specific. If you're growing Blueberry, this is what you give it at this time."

The nutrient king said the plant was actually misclassified originally and that *Cannabacae* now are considered a separate and distinct plant group that includes only one related species, *Humulus lupulus*. Hops. So, he said with a shrug, Advanced Nutrients was starting research into hops, which has the same two-stage, up-and-flower growing cycle. A business opportunity. Hops are the key ingredient in beer and being able to manipulate their characteristics would be a boon.

"Why not improve beer while we're at it?" he said with a grin. "We can do the same to optimize the hops production, too, we think."

At that time Advanced was the key player in the pot-nutrient market and Straumietis had one of the best vantage points from which to gauge the breadth of the industry. Yellow, brown, white or biker, if you were growing the best bud, you were probably buying chemicals from Advanced. Big Mike could extrapolate pretty quickly to figure out what kind of operation you had. Contrary to media reports, Straumietis said, the cop estimates weren't far off.

In the latest Organized Crime Agency report, law enforcement specialists pegged the annual wholesale value of

B.C. Bud at $6 billion. That's about 5 per cent of the total economy—or about the same amount generated by the province's public sector, topping legal exports of sawmill products ($4.6 billion) and oil and gas ($2.5 billion). Up to 150,000 people were putatively involved—making Bud Inc. one of the province's biggest employers, well ahead of construction.

Straumietis estimated that 30 per cent of the money in B.C. banks was related to marijuana production. "It's all mortgage helpers and to-get-stuff-for-the-kids money. Let's face it, BC Hydro (get it, nudge-nudge, wink-wink) is a long-standing pun. There may be a few people ripping them off for power, but I bet a lot of their profits are due to grow-ops who are happily paying their bill."

In the Interior, where hard economic times had pushed unemployment into double digits, marijuana profits kept entire communities alive. Nowhere else in North America was a single illegal industry this important—although the rest of Canada, the United States and Mexico produced plenty as well.

While Straumietis thought the cops had a handle on the scope of the business, he disagreed with their spin and parsing, which posited organized crime, led by outlaw biker gangs, as ascendant.

"The Angels have 1 per cent of the market," Straumietis insisted. "The Angels just aren't very good growers. Some of them have done well, some haven't. The Angels are just the most evil face the police can put on marijuana and it has everything to do with their funding. The East Indians and the Asians have 2 to 3 per cent. Mostly it is well-organized, middle-aged, middle-class white people that look just like you and me."

In my view, he was doing the opposite of the cops and minimizing the involvement of the gangs. But the number and size of the busts the police were making belied his picture as much as the size of the market ridiculed theirs.

Nevertheless, unlike Emery, Straumietis said pass the sunglasses—he saw nothing but profit in the future.

"There's the pharmaceutical end as well," he noted. "GW Pharmaceuticals [in England] is synthesizing the cannabinoids [the active ingredients in the mature plant]. We're there too. We're coming at it from either end with our research. The market is huge."

Just look at all the ancillary industries, he added: The music, fashion, film, food and other sectors all have significant pot components.

"The trade fair is this weekend," he said. "You've got to come. We've got eleven booths, I think—we wanted to own the show this year. We've hired all these great girls who'll walk around wearing airbrushed pictures and nothing else. Pasties on their nipples. We're even going to let people watch the artists airbrushing them. It's going to be wild."

Since many pot growers are young males who spend too much time alone, a puerile frat-house ethos is a predominant feature of small-c cannabis culture. Emery and his business reflected and embodied it. Straumietis and the big boys monitored and exploited it; Advanced Nutrients literally knew where the underground growers lived.

"That night," Straumietis continued enthusiastically, "we've got a great party at Sugar on Sugar's. We tried to get Bryan Adams to play but he wanted $500,000. But it will be someone with a big name—make sure you're there."

He pushed back his chair as if to go. "Actually, you know what this business has taught me," he said as an afterthought. "How much profit there is in the chemical business. I want to get into spa things. Those creams and unguents, you know? Now that I know what some of them actually are. They're no different than some of the salt solutions we're making now. They're dirt cheap to make. I could offer them at 50 per cent of what the designer-label guys are doing.

That's another market that's going to go through the roof. Baby boomers pampering themselves."

You could see the wheels turning. He grinned. Another business opportunity.

"I'm actually a very lucky guy," he said, heading for his Hummer. "Don't forget to come to the show."

The Vancouver Convention & Exhibition Centre on Burrard Inlet is a landmark. The white ship-shaped structure, called Canada Place, is a remnant of Expo '86 , as spectacular as the Sydney Opera House, which it slightly resembles with its Teflon-coated sails. On this bright spring weekend, the exhibition hall is filled with the cream of the hydroponics industry. Sponsored by *Maximum Yield*, a B.C.-based trade magazine about getting the most from your indoor crops, the massive display moves to San Diego in August, Montreal in October. In the spring, there are trade fairs in Chicago, Florida, Europe . . .

Jim Jesson, the man behind this show, was vainly attempting to maintain the fiction that those involved were selling equipment for the home tomato cultivator. That illusion was shattered by the extravagant, in-your-face marijuana display by Advanced Nutrients. "This is for legal gardening, and that's all I'm going to say," Jesson insisted when goaded by journalists pointing to the pot smoke swirling into the hall from the smoking area.

The exhibitors came from around the globe—Airtech, Bin Nova, Canna Canada, Atami B'Cuzz, General Hydroponics, Max-Air, BioBizz, Dutch Master, PlasmaponiX, Grow Tec, Hanna Instruments, Can Gro . . . and many more

There were exotic growing machines such as the Bonzai Garden or the Omega Garden, devices that rotated plants to maximize the yield via gravity. A ready-to-go garden capable of bringing 240 plants to maturity cost about US$5,500. If the plants produced the promised 3 pounds each, it was a steal.

In the most advanced grow-rooms, a computer regulated temperature, humidity, airflow, light cycle, venting and watering. At the same time, Internet video cameras allowed surveillance of the garden from a separate condo, mansion or yacht. There were also items such as electronic scissors, some with their own power supplies and names like Testarossa or Bonsai Hero—professional-grade cutting tools ranging in price from $410 to $735 that clean buds up to three times faster than can be done by hand.

Straumietis and Advanced pulled out all the stops, including offering a free bar with specialized martinis named after some of their more popular products, such as Tarantula Juice. They won the best booth award.

Body-painted women and bikini-clad models strolled among identical, gleaming black-and-silver Hummers and displays of multicoloured packages of chemicals, all for growing dope. One of the company's products was Organic Iguana Juice, a vitamin formula. Another was Piranha Beneficial Fungi, a root-mass builder and yield enhancer.

Staff handed out free baseball caps, T-shirts emblazoned with the company logo, yo-yos and hemp tote bags. Researchers were available to provide growing tips and explain how best to use the variety of proprietary solutions.

One of the experts was Dr. Paul Hornby, a ponytailed marijuana alchemist whose concoctions were guaranteed to boost your buds and whose caricature appeared on several of the company's products, particularly Big Bud. Hornby's passion for his work, the promotional material claimed, "produced unparalleled products that supercharge resin production and substantially increase yield. Big Bud has been extensively researched, developed and field-tested. Big Bud is extremely plant specific. Guaranteed or your money back!"

Hornby sipped a juice and enjoyed the show. He and American grow king Ed Rosenthal (who also was on Advanced's payroll with his own line of products) were among the most sought-after of celebrity endorsements in the marijuana cultivation industry.

Rosenthal was part of the indoor grow-revolution that happened in America in the late 1970s. His how-to manuals were among the first and the best. In the late seventies and early eighties, the indoor techniques and genetics he and others pioneered were exported to Holland and British Columbia. The first seed producers were based in California, but Sensi Seeds and other firms established themselves in Amsterdam during the 1980s.

Genetic development leapt ahead in the Netherlands because the Dutch looked the other way if you were growing to produce seeds. That's why Holland was so important until the mid-1990s, when Emery opened up shop, putting B.C. growers on an equal footing, and U.S. domestic production began to take off too. Advanced Nutrients was cashing in on the changes that the hydroponic revolution had caused in the industrialized world's marijuana industry.

That night, Sugar on Sugar's was wall-to-wall people and the music was loud, loud, loud. In one room, the air was thick and a hazy slate colour from smoke. Throughout, bartenders poured drinks as fast as they could—wine, liquor, beer, highballs, name your fancy, Advanced Nutrients was picking up the tab. It was saturnalia.

Straumietis played host with a very pregnant woman on his arm demurely sipping soda. Everyone took the time to come and say hello. Big Mike was everyone's favourite guy. He grinned, shook hands and slapped backs all night long.

It was hard to believe he had been arrested and held without bail three years earlier as one of British Columbia's major crime figures.

"Glad you could come," Big Mike greeted me warmly.

He was in his element.

———

Quietly and without fanfare, Big Mike's lawyer informed the Canadian immigration department on October 4, 2004 that he had driven across the border, back into the United States, and was no longer on Canadian soil.

Straumietis was forced to leave the country and his $30-million-a-year pot-based empire because he came to Canada under an assumed name. "I came here under an assumed name, Tom Newman—get it, New Man," he chuckled. "But I owned up to all that." Although lawyers were able to deep-six the serious criminal charges, they could not evade the charge of fraudulent personation when he entered the country illegally in 1996. What sunk Straumietis was the refusal of Provincial Court Judge C.J. Rounthwaite to grant him a discharge.

Though she had been told that anything short of a discharge would prevent him from staying in Canada under the Immigration Act, the judge refused to consider his crime a misdemeanour. She did not think operating under false pretenses benign. She pointed out in an April Fool's Day ruling that Straumietis had been accused in 1993 of growing a massive field of marijuana, some two thousand plants, behind electrified wire fencing. The operation was sophisticated and well-run, especially for that era, she said, less than swayed by Straumietis's protestations of innocence and the retraction from his original accuser.

"If the allegations had been true I would have simply continued to run in my own name," Straumietis futilely insisted.

"I decided to take a false name because the allegations were not true and I expected that the authorities would pursue these allegations forever and that I would have to create a new identity to avoid them for the rest of my life."

He pleaded with Rounthwaite to give him a second chance. "I do not want to run away any more," he said, stating that even the man who was the key witness against him in Wisconsin now supported him.

In a deposition from his current home in Virginia Beach, Virginia, Michael Lawson explained that when he was arrested in September 1993, he was intoxicated and addicted to cocaine. He said police threatened him with forty-five years in prison and that he implicated Straumietis to reduce his own sentence and to get back at him for stealing his girlfriend. He said that although he had plenty of time to change his story, he repeated the lies during a taped interview, with his lawyer present.

"Again," he swore, "the taped interview on November 4, 1993 [with his lawyer, the prosecutor and police present] concerning Michael Straumietis was completely false concerning involvement in my marijuana-growing activities."

Lawson was sentenced to ten years in February 1994 and had served his time by the time of Big Mike's arrest in 2001.

Rounthwaite remained concerned. Straumietis came to Canada and lived under a false identity, she said, filed numerous phony immigration forms, denied he had a criminal record and submitted fingerprints that belonged to someone else. "Remarkably, while in Canada, the accused has established successful businesses," the judge said, referring to the glowing *Forbes* article that was provided to the court.

"From the community, the defence has filed thirty letters of support from medical marijuana users, employees, distributors, researchers, scientists. They all speak of affection, respect and high regard for the accused."

But Rounthwaite said a discharge would be suitable only if Straumietis was of good character, had no previous conviction or discharge, and didn't require any personal deterrence or rehabilitation. "The accused has a criminal record from twenty years ago including obstruction, theft, possession of stolen property and driving under suspension," she decided. "When he was arrested in 2001, he possessed a quantity of other false identification documents: for example, driver's licences with his photograph in five other names and American social security cards in three other names. Notwithstanding the glowing testimonials of his supporters, Mr. Straumietis cannot be described as a person of previous good character. His dishonesty has spanned two decades."

His personation, she said, was premeditated and required repeated and persistent acts of deception over a long period of time.

"Sentencing principles of general deterrence and denunciation required not just that a conviction be recorded, but a sentence that reflects jail," the judge said. "I recognize that this conviction will render Mr. Straumietis inadmissible for immigration purposes. That should not be considered as an indirect consequence of the conviction, but rather a direct and natural consequence flowing from the facts of the offence . . . He has only himself to blame."

Given that he had already served the equivalent of five months in prison awaiting trial, Straumietis was sentenced to one day in jail—paper time only. He was not taken into custody.

His real sentence was leaving the country he loved, the country that had made him rich.

———

Robert Higgins arrived at Cardero's, a seaside restaurant, still steamed about the entire affair. Higgins was running the show.

A new bottling plant was about to come on-line, the Australian market was heating up, and those goddamn lawyers.

He picked up the wine list. "What year is the Dominus?" asked the short, straw-haired bodybuilder with a blunt, square jaw.

"I'll find out, sir."

"Maybe we should try the Opus One," I suggested.

He wrinkled his nose. There wasn't much else in the $300 price range. Higgins, a stunt pilot in his spare time, has a cellar of eight thousand bottles and loves exceptional wine.

"You know those bastards even took my weights!" he replied.

I nodded. Like Straumietis, Higgins remained absolutely outraged that the police raided his home and office. He held out his wrist. "They even took my watch. The art off the walls. My wine cellar."

The RCMP took his computer, his top-of-the-line stereo components, a collection of nature-scene prints by Carl Brenders and Robert Bateman, his boat, his Land Rover, his dirt bike, his Tag Heuer, his sweetheart's $8,000 Movado, a ton of jewellery, his barbecue . . . his dining room suite, for crying out loud!

"My Breitling!" he said, shaking his wrist, the watch now back in place.

The waitress returned with a bottle of the pricey Californian. Higgins brightened. It was a 1998.

"Yes," he told her, "decant that, please."

Though raised as a poor kid on welfare, Higgins liked the good life. He had just bought his mom a new house next door to his in British Columbia; his dad still lived in Ontario.

"And don't mention the flight school," he said, sniffing the proffered cork.

As a result of the raid on the businesses connected with Advanced Nutrients, nearly sixty flying students lost their training and the money they invested in lessons. Though they got the planes back, the school folded. It was a ridiculous waste of everyone's time and resources, Higgins said.

He ordered the sea bass and mussels.

Higgins had lived on his own since he was fifteen, and had been flying since he was seventeen—that's all he wanted to do. Until he met Straumietis, who came for flying lessons. They were soon partners in the hydroponic business and neither looked back.

"But let's talk about the business—it's going great." He grinned.

He had just returned from the Montreal trade show and Advanced Nutrients was a hit again. "Compared with us, most booths were just getting mercy-fuck attendance," he quipped.

From a folder, he pulled pictures of near-naked women airbrushed with colourful tarantulas and piranhas. "We gave away Metallica tickets for this one," he said. "Front-row seats and a huge party. It was incredible."

The sun glinted off the Grouse Mountain gondola as it made its way to the summit on the other side of Burrard Inlet. The white sails of Canada Place dazzled. A dozen yachts motored toward the harbour and Lions Gate Bridge.

"What we have over our competition is, we are researching cannabis," Higgins said. "We have the largest facility anywhere in the world. We have doctors, chemists, with a long history researching cannabis, trying to unlock the mysteries. We talk about cannabis, we talk about marijuana, and we do hard research." He paused.

"Think about this: Health Canada has issued licences to exemptees. These licensees are now sent out onto the street to find cannabis. Take those cannabis plants or seeds home with them and, 'Hey, figure it out yourselves, kids, grow your own medicine.'"

The waitress returned and poured the wine. He took a whiff of the bouquet, sipped and seemed disappointed. "Maybe it will open up."

I swirled the luscious varietal.

"Hey, the cops accused me of having three hundred grow-ops. I said, Come on, what do you think I am, small time? It's got to be well over seven hundred!" He laughed.

Higgins likes to joke about his own pot growing as a teen and how his plants were always better than his mom's roses. But it is easy to understand why police, or anyone for that matter, would be scratching their heads about Advanced Nutrients and the lucrative market niche it has created from a nondescript industrial building in Abbotsford.

The government was doing no research. Advanced Nutrients was forging ahead at breakneck speed.

"With all the varied strains," Higgins said, "we've been able to break down the different cannabinoid profiles of the various strains. We have determined that some components of that plant work very, very well for pain management, for appetite stimulation, some are excellent for MS patients— but which components, which plants at which level are ideal for which person with a given condition?

"We are the absolute leaders in medical marijuana research," he continued, "and we are going to maintain that position by employing the best people we can. It's opening up and in the very near future—we can see it every day—doors are opening up as people's minds are opening up. A lot of states have compassion clubs now. They have medical marijuana laws in place and large facilities that manufacture medical marijuana. Even with the suppression, as it stands right now, it's not hindering us as much as people think. If it becomes legal, our company will explode."

Its researchers have created products that allow growers to increase the yield per 1,000-watt light to roughly 1 kilogram of pot (more, even, if they're punctilious) from the 340 grams they harvested not so long ago. As well, the feeding and fertilizing regimes they have pioneered allow gardeners to increase the levels of THC and other substances in the plant to produce higher-potency pot and designer strains of marijuana.

The University of Mississippi—which grows pot, tests pot and provides all the research for the U.S. government—tested Advanced Nutrients' suggested feeding system. It produced buds that were 20-per-cent larger in terms of biomass, and THC levels that were three times higher.

Advanced Nutrients was providing anyone with a medical licence from Health Canada with the equipment, expertise, nutrients and clones to grow their own supply of marijuana; it gave medical marijuana to those who could not afford their own; it offered in-home help and it had a toll-free hotline for growers, dispensing free trouble-shooting advice.

In turn, patients provided the company with "tissue samples" of their plants. During the growing season, that allowed the experts to determine what nutrients the plant needed. At harvest time, Advanced received the finished product to test and could determine the results of that particular feed regime.

"The people we employ are doing a lot of testing on cannabis—our products are designed and built for the medical marijuana user and it's an absolutely massive market," Higgins said. "People are only beginning to realize the overwhelming size of the industry and that is why laws are changing and people's views are changing."

Yet to police and prosecutors, Advanced Nutrients was boosting the profits and fuelling an illegal underground industry dominated by organized criminals. That's why the Mounties used proceeds-of-crime legislation to freeze bank accounts, seize assets, confiscate records and completely disrupt the business and personal finances of the company and its principals.

"It's a vicious industry and that's one of the challenges we're facing: defamation, business libel, people trying to narc on our company," Higgins complained. "That's what happened three years ago when we got raided."

With the backing of both the U.S. and Canadian governments, law enforcement and regulatory agencies continued to harass Advanced Nutrients. Its products were seized at the border by regulators who queried the legality of some of the ingredients, and U.S. Homeland Security officers questioned its employees.

All of the legal trouble, Higgins insisted, was primarily the result of law-enforcement animus toward marijuana and those who would legalize it. I believe he is right—Advanced Nutrients is a case study in what happens when a criminal law can no longer be enforced. Advanced Nutrients is akin to a distillery in the waning years of the Prohibition, a firm legally profiting mightily from an illegal trade and poised to dominate if the laws are liberalized.

"We make nutrients for medical marijuana growers," Higgins insisted. "Unfortunately, all the big commercial growers buy all the nutrients too, and have turned this tiny little Abbotsford company into a multi-million-dollar corporation."

But changing the law would take time. The movement for legalization was too factious, he said. "Everyone's voice must be heard in unison, then the government would listen. But right now there's a lot of infighting, a lot of problems. There are thousands of very frustrated citizens. But there's no system in place to bring everybody together collectively so there is one voice heard by the government."

Higgins believes 99.9 per cent of hydroponic customers the world over are growing cannabis. "We deal with hundreds of stores, some seven hundred in Canada, four hundred in the U.S., and they are there to cater to the marijuana grower," he insists. "I know there are only eight hundred exemptions in the entire country. Maybe a lot of these people are waiting for their exemptions. Maybe they don't speak bureaucratese. Maybe they're too sick to wait."

He shrugged. "This industry is not dominated by large organizations. It's not the Hells Angels, it's not the Big Circle Boys, it's not the Vietnamese. It's people like you and me. Hopefully the U.S. will snap out of it and there will be some social change."

In the meantime, he is still open for business. "It just keeps getting better and better for us all the time," he says, indicating to the waiter that it was time for the bill. "We have interest now from other parts of the world to distribute through Asia and in the Middle East. And all the research we've done—we could apply that technology to the world's food situation to give bigger yields."

Advanced Plant Sciences was an envisioned spinoff company focused on food production, golf courses and a line of products for the professional rose and orchid gardener. It might not do anything for the Boston fern in your living room, but if you were into competition-class gardening, Advanced wanted to help.

"We expect to continue to grow the company until we hit sales of about $100 million," Higgins said. "We started with one container, one label, one lid going on it. It grew from that and it didn't just grow on its own. Three guys with tenacious attitudes getting their asses out of bed every day, wanting to go out there and conquer this industry."

Sales were skyrocketing, but Higgins still had trouble believing Big Mike was gone. "A man comes here, he's living here for seven years, maybe he was under an assumed name," Higgins lamented. "But he got himself married here, he had two beautiful stepdaughters. At the time they threw him out of the country he had created jobs for almost two hundred individuals. They really had no basis or foundation for not granting him at least some kind of status to stay here in Canada. It's absolutely ludicrous." He shook his head.

"Anyway." He drained his wine. "Have you been over to Da Kine Café? Have you met Don Briere?"

I nodded. The experiment in open cannabis sales in a trendy part of Vancouver was drawing international attention. It was impossible to miss.

"That's the future," Higgins said. "That's the future of marijuana retail sales in Canada."

RETAIL

the budder king & watermelon

DON BRIERE REMAINED on parole in June 2004 from being busted as one of British Columbia's biggest marijuana dealers. He sat in the back of the Da Kine Café rolling joints. The café name was Hawaiian slang for "the best" as in "*the* kind." Briere's hair was bleached flaxen, his blue eyes pools in an otherwise red-lined road map. On the wall was a picture of Emery, Straumietis and Briere in sartorial splendour, arms around one another's shoulders, grinning like they'd just shared the finest reefer: The Three Amigos.

"Can you believe it?" he said from behind the oversized desk piled with paperwork, pounds of pot, assorted rolling papers and a healthy sprinkling of discarded bud. "I'm telling you, Amsterdam has nothing on Vancouver now."

The office was a mess, its walls filled with a collection of posters and a big picture of Allen Ginsberg emblazoned with his message "*Pot is a reality kick.*" A chalkboard for inspirational quotes bore Jim Morrison's lyric "*No eternal reward will forgive us now for wasting the dawn.*" The board also noted that Mark Twain, Van Gogh and Rembrandt all worked on hemp paper.

The storefront space was located on Commercial Drive, or "the Drive," as Yuppies now call the street that once was the heart of Canada's most vibrant and radical neighbourhood. From about January to April 2004, Briere and a handful of friends renovated the dilapidated store. He chose parchment-and-bone base colours overlaid with an Egyptian motif. Archeologists have found numerous references and connections between pot and the ancient Egyptians. Framed archival papyri hung on walls adorned with rainbow hieroglyphics. One wall was a desert mural of Thebes, the ceiling a *trompe l'oeil* of a baby blue summer sky with wispy, cotton-batting clouds. A seven-foot replica of an idol from Cleopatra's palace stood in the corner. There were a few oak tables and a score of chairs.

The shop opened May 4, 2004, with a range of Advanced Nutrients products, soft drinks, munchies and the usual array of head-shop fare. Large well-lighted glass cabinets displayed pipes, sixteen types of rolling paper, scales, bongs, pouches, grinders, various smoking appurtenances and even T-shirts featuring the original Canucks logo with a joint in place of the hockey stick.

In a ventilated smoking room the *carte du jour* featured two *indicas* (Cameo Hash Plant and organic Hash Plant), a *sativa* (Jamaican) and four crosses (Pineapple, Juicy Fruit, Bongo and Skunk). The menu also bore a note on strains for the uninitiated: "*Sativa*—Primarily the effects of sativa are on the mind and emotions (uplifting, creativity enhancing, great for migraines, increases focus of creativity); *indica*—effects are predominantly physical or sedating (pain-reducing, muscle relaxing, aids in sleep, anti-convulsion aid); crosses contain qualities of both."

The bill of fare also offered organic kif, or dry-screen hash, doobies pre-rolled from the house blend, and specialty products such as Budder, cookies, brownies and granola bars.

"We didn't go to city hall and say, 'Hi, this is what we'd like to do,'" Briere explained. "We went in and said, 'Hi, this is what we are going to do.' We'd still be waiting for permission, I'm sure. We went to the community police station, the drug and alcohol committee and made a one-hour presentation along the harm-reduction lines. Marijuana is a good medication; it's a good stress reliever. People use it like a beer or a cocktail after work. It's a lot safer."

He talked as if opening a marijuana café and selling cannabis products over the counter was the most natural thing in the world. Indeed, he was pushing franchises. Norm Siefken, a burly bearded medical technician who was the Western Canada leader of the Marijuana Party of Canada, a federal version of Emery's organization, made notes. He was hoping to open a similar coffee shop in the Fraser Valley. If Amsterdam could do it, why not Vancouver?

"The police have been here five times," Briere continued. "They have been very polite. We have given them the tour. We told them what we were doing beforehand."

The café had been open several weeks and that day a constant stream of people came, purchased and consumed. Others pocketed their score and headed back out the door. The joint was a roaring success. In it, a lot of people glimpsed the future.

Carol Gwilt, thirty-eight, and Briere had been lovers almost since he got out of jail; now they were business partners as well. The round-faced and friendly Gwilt described herself as the store manager, and she smoked pot daily for relief of a chronic vertigo condition: "I'm able to live each day and get out of my bed because of marijuana."

She, too, thought marijuana an essential part of the global pharmacy and depriving people of its medicinal properties wrong. Over her desk and computer, a video security monitor displayed the front of the café and the cash-register area.

"The store requires my attention fifteen hours a day, seven days a week." She beamed like a beatific nun engrossed in the Lord's work.

The café was exactly what many Canadians would like to see across the country. Access to marijuana without any fuss or muss. There were a handful of similar but much more discreet, bud-friendly cafés in Eastern Canada. It was what they had in the Netherlands and in some parts of California. You could add as much regulation as you wanted.

The rules at Da Kine were simple. Unlike the more conservative compassion clubs, Briere's Canadian Sanctuary Society sold "medical marijuana" to anyone who signed a form that said they wanted it for a headache, arthritis, glaucoma, multiple sclerosis, hepatitis C, stress, a broken heart . . . oops . . .

Well, that was just it. The form was pretty meaningless because no one actually cared what you filled in. It was little more than a smokescreen, a process to muddy the waters for the courts should the police change their mind and come crashing through the door. That's what many so-called "medical marijuana activists" were doing across the country—using the green cross as a front for retail sales. Sound similar to those doctors' prescriptions during the Prohibition?

"We're putting the onus on you—that you want to use this. Pot helps alleviate a lot of things. I use it to relieve stress," Briere said with a smile.

With the tip of a knife, he dug a small gob of a crumbly yellow paste out of a vial and propped the blade against a large ashtray. He picked up a thin, flat, discoloured spatula and an acetylene torch that sparked to life with the flick of a switch. He stood up, heating the spatula. As it glowed, red, yellow, white, he put down the torch and again took up the knife, rubbing the buttery wad onto the incandescent metal.

An explosion of smoke occurred and Briere bent over, hoovering it into his lungs.

"Mmm—this is the best," he croaked while holding the toke. "Budder."

Two young women—cutting, weighing and packaging pot from football-sized bags—giggled as Briere exhaled a steady stream of smoke while moaning with bliss.

Budder is 99.3 per cent pure trichome paste (the plant's oily resin). "Tested at UBC and with Dr. Paul Hornby." Briere grinned. "No heavy metals. Nothing. Totally, totally pure. It is deadly. You cannot get any higher."

He offered Siefken, the prospective franchisee, and the women a toke.

"It is the most pure. All kinds of people have endorsed it saying it is the most wonderful high you can have. Clean, clean, clean. You take a gram of this stuff—which we sell for $75 as opposed to $10 for a gram of pot—you probably get fifty hits out of it. That means fifty less joints, fifty less papers . . ."

The first woman took a hit.

"It's better with Budder," Briere said with a chuckle, doling out the second toke. "If you work here, you have to smoke."

The girls swooned with delight. "Thanks," they said in unison.

Siefken took a big hit. Briere laughed and put down his tools.

"I've consulted on Da Kine and basically assisted in layout and design," Briere explained. "I was in the alcohol business before, and construction—I built and designed alcohol bars. It's not dissimilar to set up something in this area. I'm just sort of volunteering my services because I feel—between me and you—I'm volunteering to help this establishment get going and anybody else who wants to set up and get the legalization of marijuana going because the laws are not only wrong and disgusting, they are based on lies."

They bought locally where possible. "Some of the hash doesn't cross more than two streets to get here," he said. "We're purchasing off all local people. The only thing that is imported is the Afghani hash. Other than that, we make our own hash—our own bubble. Well, not us, local people are producing this stuff. The Brownie Man comes in and sells us brownies, Watermelon sells us cookies, we buy kif from someone else, we get different strains of marijuana—ten different strains on the menu, ten different people growing pot, ten different moms and dads." He paused.

"I think there are more varieties of pot than alcohol— some stronger than others, some weaker strains. Just like there is beer at 4 per cent, beer at 5 per cent and beer at 6.5 per cent."

Born and reared in New Westminster, B.C., the fifty-three-year-old, twice-married Briere was busted in March 1999 for what was considered the most sophisticated and extensive marijuana grow operation in Western Canada. "I was raided by about fifty cops," he said. "I believe they hit eleven locations and arrested twenty-two of us. I had thirty-four locations and probably sixty people directly involved."

To the RCMP and the DEA, Briere was a drug kingpin, an organized crime boss, a godfather of misery. He had small private planes flitting back and forth across the border carrying duffle bags stuffed with B.C. Bud and returning with bags of cash. Millions a month sometimes. Briere was convicted of growing and possessing marijuana for the purpose of trafficking, unlawful storage of ammunition and possessing a prohibited weapon.

During a raid on his warehouse, police seized 260,000 rounds of ammunition, a 12-gauge Winchester, a 12-gauge Springfield, a Husqvarna 9mm handgun, a MAK-90 Sporter

7.62 rifle, an Intratec 9mm machine gun. They also found an estimated $625,000 in pot and $50,000 in growing equipment.

It took two years for authorities to trace Briere's profits to a nondescript office in Burns Lake, a tiny lumber town north of Vancouver. Through a numbered company, Briere's brother-in-law and partners operated a quasi-bank for people in the town. They offered 12 per cent interest on deposits and charged in the neighbourhood of 17 to 18 per cent on loans. The books showed they putatively received $40 million from four hundred to five hundred "investors" over the course of a decade—whether those names were real or aliases, who knew? Briere paid a 15-per-cent commission for the cash they cleaned for him using four bank accounts and the fictitious firms GH Video and WR Import Export, supposedly located in Surrey and in Blaine, Washington. The money laundering kept the small municipality afloat during tough times.

Dubbed "the Burns Lake Laundry," the firm pumped money into a community economically ravaged by forest industry cutbacks and a soft lumber market. If you needed to borrow, they provided cash without a real financial institution's rigorous application process or any pressure to repay. As many as 1,400 people got loans to stay afloat, have a dirty weekend, invest in llama farming or post bond for a heavy-equipment contract. Sometimes they didn't even sign a promissory note.

The bank was well loved.

Originally charged with more than fifteen counts, Briere pleaded guilty to five (in part to save his brother-in-law from testifying against him), including production of marijuana for the purposes of trafficking, the unsafe storage of a firearm and $2.3 million in money laundering. As part of his sentence, he was to pay the tax man some $2 million. While he had been generating prodigious profits, Briere had filed tax returns declaring annual income ranging from $22,000 to $59,000.

Those arrested with him received modest penalties for their roles. One high-living partner got three years in jail and forfeited a Harley-Davidson Softail motorcycle, a Porsche 911, $250,000 worth of furniture, art from his lavish home in South Surrey, a Jeep, three speedboats, a $50,000 wine cellar and a lakefront home in Osoyoos. He said one of his pilots was out and already back in business.

Briere wrinkled his face in contempt at the memory. "They investigated me for six months. They had Special O [the undercover observation specialists], seven to nine people follow me around for six months. Huge amounts of money were spent . . . not just on the investigation, there were fifty days in court, so chock up another half-million."

While he was waiting to be sentenced as a drug lord, Briere ran for Emery's Marijuana Party (he got 385 votes) and helped manage other candidates' campaigns. He formed the Canadian Sanctuary Society, his own compassion club, the day before going to jail. Released from prison after fourteen months in January 2003, he began scheduling medical marijuana information nights in hotels across the province.

Within weeks of his release, he addressed a standing-room-only crowd at the Sheraton Guildford Hotel in Surrey, boasting to reporters he would hold another talk soon for those who couldn't get in. Contemporaneously, he was seeking investors for a franchised chain of medical marijuana cafés. Da Kine was the prototype, a knock-off of the better cafés found in Amsterdam and a step above the Pot Block's funkiness. That's when he met Gwilt—he showed her how to bake with pot.

Briere's business model assumed sales would plateau at about $10,000 a day. Within a fortnight, though, he was doing $13,000-plus, he said. There were lineups in the morning waiting for the café to open at ten a.m. and people clamouring to get in long after it closed at eleven p.m.

Sitting in the rear office of the bustling business, Briere relished being back in the thick of it. He was a devil-may-care entrepreneur at heart—pot just happened to have attracted his obsessive attention. Like most, Briere had his first toke as a teenager and middled marijuana to cut the cost of his own habit. "We didn't have any trouble getting it. We bought it off my friend's brother." He laughed at the memory.

"A few years later when I decided I wanted to get involved a little more I had a friend I knew who was buying it off someone who had runners bring it up from Mexico," he explained, sparking a cigar-sized joint.

"They had kilos, bricks of them. The guy had a big butcher knife and he would cut off what you wanted and weigh it up. You got the sticks, the seeds, the works. We would clean it up—we'd get a record album, or a shoe-box top, break it up and roll off some of the seeds, pull out the stick and then we'd sell it. We'd buy it for between $160 and $200 a pound and we sold ounces only—$20 an ounce. It was pretty decent stuff, you could smoke it day and night pretty much."

He quit school at sixteen, got married and went logging in Williams Lake and Port Hardy to support his family. Later came the bar business. "I owned a nightclub and ran bars for about ten years throughout the 1980s . . . I had Rocky's in Coquitlam, [was] part owner of that nightclub with two other partners. From there I worked at other different liquor establishments."

Briere tried growing marijuana in 1980, but the seeds he planted died and it was 1990 before he had the opportunity to get involved again. "I started with two bulbs in a friend's place. I supplied the equipment; he supplied the room. One bulb was mine and one bulb was his and away we went. In 1999, when I was arrested, I had hundreds of 1,000-watt bulbs burning in thirty-four locations."

The two young women stopped cutting and weighing, agog at the size of his operation.

"It's true," he insisted, reaching under his desk and pulling out a phone-book-thick scrapbook. He flipped it open to headlines announcing his arrest that were of a type-size usually reserved for such gravitas as "War Declared."

"I saved all my clippings," he boasted, turning to page after page of stories about a man reporters described as a polite, likeable, middle-aged imp but police vilified as a veritable Mafia don.

From the perspective of law enforcement, Briere's operation epitomized the organized crime that made marijuana so insidious. He was, in their minds, the personification of the evil that lurked behind the thin veneer of mom-and-dad grow-ops. Briere argued his business was as benign as any that sells goods or services on a cash-only basis and doesn't report income to the tax man.

Here's how it worked. Briere rented the space and set up the growing equipment (an investment of $15,000 to $20,000). Then he found a couple—usually on welfare or out of work—who wanted cheap rent and a share in the profits. "People would beg me to set them up in business," he said.

The standard show, he said, was a sixteen-light operation in two rooms—eight lights to the average-sized bedroom and a little bit of workspace. Marijuana grows best receiving regular cycles of light and darkness timed to the plant's development. Each light requires a control switch, or ballast, but Briere's electricians quickly figured out how to wire ballasts so that they would power two lights each: eight lights for twelve hours, then flip over and power another set of lights during the next cycle.

"You could run the ballast for twenty-four hours and have sixteen lights on eight ballasts," he explained. "We mounted the ballasts on two-by-six boards. Everything was what we call plug-and-play. We would have four ballasts on a board, and though really heavy, we had them mobile so we could move them from one operation to another. Everything was unpluggable."

Some guys would take two months to build a grow; Briere's crew could have it up in a week. Tear-down in a blink. "We had eight to ten guys go in there and you could be eating off the floor in about two to three hours," he said. "It was gone. I have lots of references from landlords. It was amazing. I had a crew of carpet layers, drywallers and carpenters working. So we would fix up these places so they were better than when we moved in. We left places in pristine shape." The lawns were always cut, the houses were always tidy. The homes, condominiums and apartments were well lived-in.

"I would get the newspaper in the morning, and in the early 1990s when it was easier, I would circle the three best properties—you know, an acre, large house, full basement, da, da, da, for rent," he explained.

By the late 1990s, however, he said finding a suitable property—something in the $1,500 to $2,000 per month range—was a challenge: there were so many people looking for grow space. More than a dozen organizations like Briere's were operating.

And it would only get tighter. A few weeks earlier, the watchdog Financial Institutions Commission had seized the files of a mortgage company at the core of a large Vietnamese grow business that had employed two real estate agents to buy houses financed via phony employment records. More than nine hundred properties were involved.

With as much as a half-ton of bud to move every two months, Briere's operation generated millions—nearly $1 million per month regular cash flow. And it was labour intensive.

"If you picture this like building a house," he said, "there are guys that exclusively sell houses. There are guys that just do the wiring. There are guys that just do the roof. There are guys that just do the landscaping. In this industry, there are guys that are just clippers, there are guys that are just electricians, there are guys who are just growers, there are guys who just make the babies—the cloners with mother houses [gardeners who breed a strong potent plant and then make cuttings from it], and there are guys who are shippers, who just middle the stuff, brokers and that sort of thing."

The trimmers got $25-plus an hour. So did the carpenters, the electrician, anyone doing labour. Like sailors guaranteed a daily quota of grog, they usually got a supply of dope too. Aside from producing pot, Briere said he and his partners also produced clones for other growers.

"We took care of securing the locations, we took care of building the locations, we took care of bringing the clones to maturity, drying, curing and packaging the pot. We sold it on the open market to the highest bidder—the middlers or brokers."

Like Morin. He had eighty people working directly on the payroll, another one hundred indirectly. "We created a lot of jobs and we brought a lot of money into the country. We spent our money, we put our money back into the economy. It was spent on gas, clothing, shelter—it went directly into the economy. Imagine if we didn't have this industry here. We pay the bills. We drive the economy."

Think about it. Someone paid $25 an hour could work a forty-hour week: that's $4,000 a month—take-home. Where could someone get an unskilled job paying that these days? The 7-Eleven didn't pay it. Neither did McDonald's.

"If you or I were making $25 an hour legally, which is a way-above-average working wage," Briere emphasized, "and trying to raise two kids and support a wife, by the time you've paid your income taxes, 30 per cent, you're looking at $2,800 a month take-home. Which are *you* going to choose?"

Briere said his truth was staring everyone—including politicians and policy-makers—in the face.

Marijuana had evolved into a multifaceted industry solely because there were so many jobs and so much money in it.

After his arrest, Briere more than embraced the cause of legalized pot. He became a zealot. "We really felt like the laws were wrong," he maintained. "We weren't doing criminal things, we were outlaws living outside the law because the laws were wrong."

Such was a common theme in the marijuana industry: We're pirates, just like Robin Hood, Bonnie and Clyde, Sundance and Butch, Che and Castro—the romantic outlaw was a potent image. It made being bent sound like a moral imperative. Of course, the money had something to do with it.

His eyes welled. Briere's son had developed a heroin addiction and overdosed.

"Instead of supporting this drug war, to create wages for police, to create wages for lawyers and judges, to create wages for people who jail our citizens and who are putting people in concrete and steel cages . . . I think it's time to end this drug war. Decriminalization isn't even close. All it does is again create a fine system, a money system, another tax system for the police. Legalize it. Put it under the tax department: tax it, regulate it, create jobs and do all these things. But stop this drug war."

He stopped, still not out of breath, as a thin, wire-haired man came into the office.

"Hey, how are you doing, Andrew?" Briere said.

He gestured to the empty chair; Gwilt had slipped out during his rant.

Andrew put down a big box and unpacked four half-pound packages of pot, each the size of a small roast.

"I really think we have won," Briere said. "I think [Da Kine] is the beginning of the end. I think [the end of the prohibition] is going to happen fairly quickly. In the Netherlands, they didn't really change the laws, they just stopped enforcing them. That's basically what has happened in Vancouver. Everything here that's sold in this store is taxed—PST and GST—and the wages have income tax taken off. The shares and dividends in this company will also be taxed. So we have brought this out into the legitimate world. We are contributing to society, we are creating jobs and this is a great place to work. This is way, way, way better than alcohol."

He envisioned a string of similar cafés across the country, especially in areas close to the U.S. border. He had four other locations picked out in the city—one at Tenth and Alma, another on the trendy stretch of affluent Fourth Avenue . . .

"We're still scouting locations," Briere added. "I really do believe we're on the front line right here. We're on the front line."

He picked up one of Andrew's plastic bags, opened it and stuck his face into the pot, inhaling deeply. "Great. Same as before?"

"Yep."

Briere pulled out cash and counted off a stack of bills. He handed over $4,000. Andrew grinned.

"Anyway, I do think it's a wonderful service that we're pro-viding," Briere said. "If you want to take something away from organized crime, end prohibition. Prohibition corrupts. Prohi-bition corrupts all kinds of people. If you want to take the money away from organized crime, legalize it. Legalization is one of the first steps to healing this society."

Andrew nodded. "I got to run, though, Don," he said, ris-ing and heading for the door.

Seifken, now a very stoned prospective franchisee, got up to go too. The Budder had rendered him mute.

"Pot's going to be legalized, and when it is, I'm going to be in this business," Briere said adamantly as he shook Seifken's hand. "I don't want to go into any other business."

A few blocks from the Da Kine Café, on Victoria Drive at Grant, a small, square, grey stucco building is home to Watermelon's Saturday-night cabaret. Mary Jean Dunsdon, a.k.a. Watermelon, is Vancouver's pot diva. Every week she holds a private party—$15 at the door, which includes free pot edibles, or beer if you prefer.

Watermelon is a blue-eyed, blonde thirty-two-year-old with a taste for burlesque. Her bar rested atop female mannequin legs dressed in racy lingerie, garter belts and frilly undies. Adorning the walls were posters of Watermelon in skimpy dominatrix gear or in little more than a mask, amid a hothouse of verdant pot plants: Crops and Robbers. The pictures were by her oft-time collaborator, artist-photographer Maria Coletis. This was Watermelon's parlour.

On any given Saturday, local comic Richard Lett or the Wet Spots would take the tiny stage, entertaining a hipster crowd of maybe thirty on a good night—some of them engaged in an ongoing poker game using Monopoly money. Sometimes the lady herself would entertain, doing stand-up. Tonight, the Tall Brothers were moving through a set of marijuana-inspired jazz.

Watermelon had graced the cover of *High Times*, acted as a celebrity judge at the annual Cannabis Cup in Amsterdam, and been at the forefront of the Legalize It movement since the mid-1990s. Watermelon could be the Betty Crocker of the marijuana industry. For a decade now, she had made a living selling marijuana edibles and entertaining the troops on the front lines who were risking their lunch. Everybody watched Emery or the talking heads with their fact-function-fact spiel about marijuana; Watermelon reached millions subversively with humour and sex.

She sparked a reefer as the band took a break.

"They sent Marilyn Monroe to Korea to entertain the troops," she said. "Potheads need to be inspired too, to keep up the good work." She gestured around the room. "Here, I don't really make any money but I try not to lose any money. I know so many artists in this neighbourhood. I just bring them all in here, everybody in the neighbourhood gets high, nobody in the neighbourhood complains."

She was right. A handful of drug houses within a few blocks' radius had operated for years, cars coming and going, busier than a Safeway parking lot. In and out, all day long. But it's just weed, so no one appeared to bother and no one got busted. Malmo-Levine, in fact, was selling pot up the block until the previous week.

"My client base is loyal," Watermelon explained. "I haven't had a job for years. I sell pot cookies to rich gay men, mostly down in the West End. It fluctuates from a peak of eight dozen a day [$480 gross] to four dozen a week. At Christmas it hops back up."

She has a mailing list of about sixty, mostly elderly men suffering from AIDS who don't want to smoke but want the anti-nausea effects of pot. Okay, some of them also want to get high. She's putting together her sixth Christmas catalogue with erotic pictures of marijuana pin-up girls. Very funny, very campy: *Hope you've been naughty and nice!*

She has specialty orders for those with food allergies or intolerances and customers who want something special for a particular occasion. "I provide a 100-per-cent money-back guarantee — nobody is ever disappointed with my product, ever."

For Watermelon, the prohibition is wrong because it handicaps a wide range of beneficial economic activity and erodes everyone's faith in the political-legal system. It permeates every aspect of society.

"We do not want to refer to cops as 'the other team,'" she explained. "Clearly no one is getting rich in the neighbourhood. For starters, we all still live in East Van—hello! And why would anyone want to shut down something that brings cash into their neighbourhood? That's stupid, unless it's undesirable. Like money from crack. That's undesirable. Neighbourhoods want that out. But who wants a stoner out? The whole neighbourhood would have to move."

Watermelon is the daughter of a former fighter pilot who retired and became a ginseng farmer in the B.C. Interior. Her dad is a staunch conservative who adamantly dislikes his daughter's politics. She told him to "fuck off" the other day when he was giving her a hard time. Now she'll have to mend the bridge so she can get her other drugs—wild meats. He supplies her with moose meat and fresh halibut. Watermelon is a practical girl.

Her mom runs a wellness clinic in Kamloops. So Watermelon is also very much into holistic health, which is part of her charm and image. "I'm a baker," she said, "not a criminal."

Sitting at a table covered in worn green felt, fingering the cigarillo-sized doobie, she was persuasive. "I bake more than I do comedy, for sure," she said. "Cookies pay my rent and pay for the schooling I'm doing now. Cookies pay for everything. Comedy buys me new shoes."

If she models, say, for *High Times*, she gets a windfall of $2,000, for her "a huge amount of fucking money but which the rest of the world can sneeze out over lunch.

"I pull in $130 on a Saturday night, God forbid the government finds out—I didn't give them their cut. Meanwhile some guy is pissing away $130,000 in the sponsorship scandal? It goes back to the undermining of our institutions," she said. "How long can you keep up the facade? We're stupid, but some of us aren't that stupid."

Watermelon said she believed the government would amend the law sooner rather than later because of pressure from patients who want access to marijuana for its medicinal properties. She wanted to be ready to profit.

"I do want to be Betty Crocker," she insisted.

And why not?

In 19th-century Paris, physician Jacques-Joseph Moreau, Baudelaire, Honoré de Balzac and Victor Hugo gathered with their pals as Le Club des Hachichins to consume hashish-laced delicacies. In the Middle East, more often than not, people will eat cannabis rather than smoke it. Up until the popularity of tobacco following the discovery of the New World, some scholars believe, *most* cannabis was probably ingested. Given the aging of the baby-boomer consumers and knowledge of the stress smoking puts on the lungs, it's only natural that more people will drift toward edibles if they have an alternative.

Watermelon is enrolled in an entrepreneur and small business management program with 25 per cent of her course work tied to completing a successful marketing plan for her company. She wants to improve her marketing and management skills because her pot business is not a snicker or a pipe dream. Watermelon tells everyone in the industry: Put together a business plan.

"My new plan is fairly humble—I'd like to eventually just have a bakery," she explained. "Like in the Kootenays, somewhere off in the Slocan, a mystical place with nice clean water and small bearded men with pointed hats baking cookies." She laughed. "No, a wood bakery near good water, and I bake pot cookies that I distribute internationally. You know, move over Mr. Christie, I'm the Diva of Pot Cookies. 'My business is rolling in dough'—that's my slogan. I feel within three years I will be legally selling marijuana cookies."

But putting together an investment prospectus was tough, she said. She can't compare her sales to regular cookie sales because pot cookies are aimed at a different consumer than are Oreos. "Besides, I don't want to serve the masses. I don't want to be shooting out the proverbial dime bags."

If the world doesn't change, she has faith she can eventually make a million off her own pot-loving community. "I'm fine with that. It's what you want in life. We're trying to free the weed here. I'm in this business because I find it enjoyable. Every once in a while I get busted or tripped up or something."

Or tripped up or something . . . the primary risk of the marijuana business. As Emery, Malmo-Levine, Big Mike, Don Briere, Watermelon and everyone associated with it can attest, it's still against the law.

Watermelon's main place of business once was Wreck Beach, the nudist hangout a half-hour's drive from the city centre. The beach is at the base of cliffs and difficult to reach. Watermelon went there to meditate, to indulge her own naturalist predilections and to sell cookies. She was not alone in catering to beach-goers. Vendors peppered the beach selling pizza, coffee, ice-cold pop, beer, frozen margaritas, shots of tequila, bud, chocolates laced with psilocybin and assorted fruit.

The RCMP stationed at the University of British Columbia must have tired of issuing traffic tickets and harassing students. They decided to target Watermelon. In what could be filmed as a *Saturday Night Live* parody, Canada's national police force launched a covert operation on the nudist beach. Two officers—a man and a woman—set up on the beach to trap the perp, Watermelon, to catch her redhanded. The Mounties asked an illegal vendor to point her out. She wasn't hard to spot, strolling starkers between frolicking naked adults, chanting: "Krazy Kannabis Kookies, Krazy Kannabis Kookies—ginger snaps with an extra snap."

She approached the "undercover" officers, a man and woman both in swimsuits, who purchased three cookies, each with a sugar flower in the centre, for $20. Dramatically, they announced who they were and told Watermelon she was under arrest. They nearly got torn apart by the usually sedate sunbathers. In a display of chivalry reminiscent of the Middle Ages, everyone on the beach sprang to the damsel's defence. While the crowd was non-violent, it sure made the cops think twice.

Next time (you couldn't make this up), they came with a hovercraft and backup.

Ironically, every time the cops busted Watermelon, they gave her undreamed-of exposure (even for a nudist) and publicity—for an enterprise like hers, it was wonderful free advertising and great branding.

Today she took a long drag on the joint and talked about the way she had been forced to think about politics, and why she found herself in conflict with larger forces. Her second bust was surreal. Imagine sitting on a log in your birthday suit enjoying good company, the ocean lapping at your feet, stars afire, someone singing a few songs . . . then, searchlights. Searchlights! And *thud-thud-thud*—the sound of a helicopter somewhere above in the night sky. A searchlight sweeping the beach, a hovercraft racing to land, men with bullhorns. Everyone diving into the bushes.

Watermelon was astounded. "I can't believe I'm hiding in the bushes with Captain Bob [another Wreck Beach regular] because there is a chopper with a spotlight and the hovercraft is on the beach," she said, eyes wide. "There were four RCMP officers running around. After they left, the ten people who had been hiding in the rocks came out. There were twelve of us in total, I guess. Twelve people for a hovercraft, a chopper and four RCMPs."

As part of her bail conditions, the court said Watermelon couldn't return to the local nudist Mecca.

Forget about going to jail—banishment from her community was cruel and unusual punishment. She began to feel like some scapegoat driven into the wilderness carrying sins she didn't commit. Watermelon drove to the RCMP detachment at the university and pleaded with them to lift the area restriction, assuring them she wouldn't sell pot or crazy cookies. She just wanted a little dispensation to go down and catch a few rays and celebrate the planet.

They arrested her for coming to the detachment and breaching her bail conditions. She spent the night in jail.

Watermelon is a nudist, and Wreck Beach is her temple. There is a Wreck Beach Society, and the regulars stage annual meetings and interact with other organizations, and she's a part of that. They have an annual bun run, a polar bear swim, weddings and all sorts of things.

"Wreck Beach was my place of recreation, my place of worship," Watermelon fumed, still incensed. "It is gorgeous, and that's my religion, essentially, know what I mean? The moon, the fire, the ocean . . . I'm done, you know?"

Watermelon found herself in the crosshairs of law enforcement without really understanding why she had drawn so much animosity. Watermelon's refusal to accept a plea bargain brought the edibles issue to the fore and the science used to support the charge would be scrutinized and found not just wanting, but absent.

"I was charged with trafficking in cannabis resin," Watermelon said. "But everyone agrees that was the one thing they could not find in the cookies: resin. They could find THC, other cannabinoids, whatever, but there was certainly no resin. They can't prove I baked my cookies with cannabis or cannabis resin. If I win this, it will be a huge loophole for anyone making marijuana blended into something."

She held out a bag of cookies. "I'm going to get off because of *CSI: Crime Scene Investigation*," she laughed.

Watermelon had drawn a line in the sand, and as far as she was concerned, the marijuana laws had violated the social contract. She was not going to allow that.

"To get the cookie girl, the cops are going to have to come in and stare me in the face and give their evidence sticking it to me," she said. "Crown counsel will have to run around collecting evidence and he'll have to stare at me and stick it to me, you know? The judge is going to stare me right in the face and pass judgment on me."

She wanted her day in court. Watermelon stopped and fixed me with her gaze so that I knew exactly what she meant.

"They will all have to look me in the eye," she said. "I'm going to make them do it. It may end up being the most expensive satirical play I've ever produced—and I've produced a lot of fringe theatre around town. It's me, Lenny Bruce and Voltaire hanging out in the courtroom."

She was mad.

"They want to establish marijuana cookies as some kind of evil commodity [linked to] gangs," she said. "Here I am, the cookie girl, as sweet as can be. I often serve the firemen's annual golf tournament and stuff. Like, people at city hall. Someone was joking the other day that I have my own Heidi Fleiss list."

As if, her eyes said, going for the roof.

"I'm not afraid," she continued. "I hope to become a trusted stoner household name. Right? And the second marijuana is legal, to launch my cookie empire and just really take good care and produce a product that sends out that whole message, that spiritual connection."

She grinned. "I can do it. I know it."

A few days later, Watermelon wheeled her aged flaming-pink, flower-power VW van into the tiny parking lot of the ranch-style suburban courthouse. Her blonde hair was pulled back in a ponytail and when she took off her white faux fur, she was dressed in a knee-length blue-pleated suede dress and a black long-sleeved button-down sweater. Mind you, it was a tad tight.

I thought of her strategy: *I'm going make them look me in the eye.* At least she wasn't naked.

She carried a red-and-white plastic bag covered with smiling watermelon-faces filled with apples, a Thermos of coffee and a bag of cookies. The hearing didn't last long enough for the snacks to be eaten.

In Canada, drug offences are parsed according to the substance and circumstance. Cannabis and its derivatives, in natural and synthetic forms, are all included—cannabis, marijuana, cannabis resin, cannabinoids . . . Some things are exempted, such as non-viable seeds or stalks, to provide legal space for the hemp industry.

In 1997, Ottawa also decided in terms of cannabis that the offence of possession should be split for those caught with more than 30 grams of marijuana and more than 1 gram of resin or hashish. In its wisdom, the Liberal government cleaved trafficking offences into those that involved more than 3 kilos, with a maximum penalty of life imprisonment, and those that involved lesser amounts, with a maximum of five years less a day.

The reason it's five years less a day is that anyone facing a longer stretch of imprisonment is constitutionally guaranteed a jury trial; under five years and you keep the scoundrels in front of a judge. If you traffic in cocaine or heroin, you have the right to a jury trial.

For good reason, the government and legal bureaucrats wanted to keep cannabis sellers away from juries—jurors might be surreptitious tokers and might balk at sending the accused off to jail. And in Watermelon's case, who would convict her for her small business?

There was little question Watermelon was guilty. It seemed the government had an open-and-shut case. Two police officers testified they went to Wreck Beach and bought from "the target," Watermelon, three Krazy Kookies guaranteed to get them high for $20. She was charged with trafficking in cannabis resin. Which brings up the question—how do you prove there is "cannabis resin" in a cookie?

In Canadian courts, prosecutors normally establish legal proof that the substance at issue is cannabis or some other drug by filing a certificate of analysis. The laboratory analyst is not required to attend court. The certificate of analysis for Watermelon's cookies said the substance submitted did indeed contain cannabis resin. How was that possible? Her lawyer, John Conroy, summoned the analyst to the small oak-panelled courtroom.

Jenny Luk, a slight, studious-looking woman with a BSc in chemistry, said she'd been analyzing substances for Health Canada for five years. The department did work for various police agencies. She described receiving the foil package containing the evidence of Watermelon's crime. She opened it. Inside, she testified, she found what appeared to be a cookie.

"What did you do?" Conroy prodded.

"I began my examinations," she said.

The first step for any good *CSI*-type lab worker is what is known in the business as "the macroscopic examination." She looked at the evidence.

"It appeared to be a cookie and smelled slightly of ginger," she said.

No cannabis, no stalks, no stems, no seeds, no fragments of leaves, no plant characteristics. No resin. She proceeded to the next step—"the microscopic examination." She broke off a piece of the cookie-like substance, crushed it and placed the debris under the microscope.

"I saw what appeared to be cookie crumbs," she told the court.

She took a few of the crumbs and applied a solution that produced a chemical flag for the presence of cannabinoids. Aha! Her chemical quarry spotted, she proceeded to the final step—the mass spectrometer and thin-layer chromatography, a process in which the tiny particles of what appeared to be cookie crumbs would be separated into their atomic constituents and the culprits identified. Sure enough, the machine detected a half-dozen or so cannabinoids; ergo it was cannabis resin, commonly known as hash.

"So I signed the certificate saying the sample contained cannabis resin," Luk said.

Silence filled the room.

"Wait a minute," Conroy said. "You didn't find any resin. You found cannabinoids."

"Right," she said nonplussed. "That's what we do."

"What?"

Luk told the court that in Canada, if legal analysts find no physical evidence of plant matter (even a microscopic piece of leaf, stalk, stem or seed is enough to declare a substance "cannabis") but instead find chemical evidence of at least a handful of cannabinoids, they declare the substance "cannabis resin." Even if it is a cookie.

The judge wrinkled his brow. "Really?"

Luk assured him that was the procedure under the government's guidelines. If you couldn't find some microscopic bit of the plant, some "plant characteristic," if you could only find the presence of cannabinoids, the evidence (a cookie, a chunk of hash, a vial of hash oil, a pound of mouldy decomposed pot or a jar of Budder) was declared "cannabis resin."

The Crown supported her.

Conroy proceeded to call as an expert witness Dr. David Pate, the grey-bearded, grey-ponytailed researcher with HortaPharm. The Dutch company was set up by U.S. dope growers with a dream of cashing in on the medical uses of pot. One of the only licensed-marijuana producers on the planet, HortaPharm was currently conducting research and development in Holland for GW Pharmaceuticals.

HortaPharm provided the marijuana used in the British firm's sublingual spray, which was undergoing final testing. U.K. regulators had said they wanted more evidence about the benefits of its drug, Sativex, delaying its approval and battering GW's shares a few weeks earlier. Canada, though, had confirmed that Sativex qualified for approval—a first for a true prescription cannabis medicine anywhere—and shares in the firm rebounded as much as 9.5 per cent. Pate had also helped write the federal government white paper on hemp production. He held Canadian patents-pending on a vaporizer and believed the only danger in cannabis was inhaling incinerated plant matter (THC was benign). Pate, who was recognized by the court dealing with Watermelon's case as an expert on cannabis and the processes used to conduct chemical analysis, said the government's claim in this case was ridiculous and represented such an assault on the language as to be Orwellian double-speak.

He gave the court a quick lesson on the differences between hemp and cannabis. One's a pinhead-sized seed, the other fat and more like a lentil; they have different growing patterns, and the central distinguishing feature is their chemistry. Cannabis contains more than four hundred chemical compounds, sixty-plus cannabinoids. "In reality, there are only small quantities of, at most, a few dozen terpenes and only three or four cannabinoids present in significant quantities in any one plant—the big four: delta-9-

tetrahydrocannabinol [THC]; cannabidiol, which may have anticonvulsant, anxiolytic and analgesic effects; cannabichromene, and cannabigerol."

Pate said THC, as well as being the most potent psychoactive component of the plant, is probably responsible or a catalyst for many of the other pharmacological actions. One of the properties of cannabinoids, he added, was their lipophilicity—they are insoluble in water and must be transformed first to be consumed. That was why Watermelon first boiled butter and pot together before baking. That was also why the oral preparation of the synthetic THC dronabinol (marketed as Marinol) is formulated in sesame oil for use as an anti-emetic and appetite stimulant. But the way ahead probably lies in developing other methods of administration, Pate said, such as cannabis aerosols and metered-dose inhalers.

Resin, he said, incorrectly called "pollen" in some countries, is the THC-rich, oily material held in the glandular structures of the plant. He described several methods for isolating the resin and turning it into consumable products such as kif, hashish, oil or even more purified preparations of THC. There was no resin by any ordinary understanding of the word present in Watermelon's cookies, he emphasized.

"That would be impossible." He said the resin was destroyed in the baking process. All that was left were the chemicals. And, as far as the chemicals were concerned, Pate said, there was no way of knowing whether the baker started with cannabis, hash, synthetic products or legal non-viable seeds that are usually covered with dust containing THC and cannabinoids from the plant.

Conroy told the judge the case should be dismissed.

Watermelon had been charged with trafficking in cannabis resin—an amount was even specified so that her process rights were restricted. But the Crown could neither prove the presence of cannabis resin nor provide the court with a weight.

"They can't prove there was any resin there at all, much less how much resin was in the substance," Pate said.

Judge E.D. Schmidt took only a few moments to rule:

> In creating these different offences for those two substances, resin and marihuana [the legal spelling], Parliament has ascribed different weights of those substances that will attract, not only different penalties, but different court process. The analyst who gave evidence in this case said they cannot quantify cannabis resin when it is in the form of a baked product, such as a cookie. It therefore becomes impossible to place it in one of these categories that the Parliament has created, because it cannot be seen and it cannot be quantified.

He acquitted Watermelon.

She was stunned. "That is just so great!" she said after a moment. She turned and gave Pate a squeeze, Conroy a kiss and me a hug.

As we walked out, she said, "So, John, what's it all mean?"

He shrugged. "They should have charged you with selling cannabinoids. That's what they'll do next time. They'll just rethink how they analyze cannabis resin, how they analyze edibles, or they will simply charge for a specific cannabinoid or cannabinoids—but appreciate then that people could opt for jury trials."

It wasn't a huge victory but it continued the relentless attack on a law whose purpose could not survive scrutiny and whose usefulness was becoming increasingly difficult to support.

The pot diva pulled an apple from her bag and bit into it.

"It's just another little thing," Conroy continued, "a little hurdle thrown in the way of the federal government to make it more difficult for them to prosecute, to complicate their ways and means of doing it, and they may change the law again. It's always amazing how quick they are at changing the law in order to further prosecutions and convictions. And how slow they are to do it in order to remove them, in order to come to the realization that maybe this is a waste of the tax-payer's dollars, that there are greater priorities in terms of the expenditure of police, court and criminal justice resources."

The prosecutor said the Crown would file an appeal say-ing the judge had erred. The case could be in the courts for years.

"You know, it's a business," Conroy said to Watermelon as the crown attorney walked away. "The Marijuana Party has its motto: 'Overgrow the government.' You just have to make [the law] too difficult to enforce. We'll get there."

"Right, John," she said paternalistically, and rolled her eyes.

Then Watermelon said she had to run. She had to get her Christmas catalogue in the mail and there were cookies to bake. Her own present would come later—when the gov-ernment abandoned all its appeals.

———

A crowd clotted the entrance and clustered around the counter area of Da Kine. In the office at the back, Briere waved from amid the clutter and commotion. An employee named Charlie stood to one side trimming and weighing buds, handing them to a slim, twenty-something woman who put them into tiny see-through envelopes. Briere was grinning from ear to ear. It was August and the café was booming.

"I do know that in the 105, 106 days we have been open, we've had a huge, huge number of Americans come up here," he was telling a burly man in a natty conservative pin-striped suit.

He waved me to a nearby chair, and continued speaking to the men.

"People from New Jersey said they saw us on the Internet. They had been to Amsterdam ten times and were going to go there, but diverted here. They couldn't believe how good it was. They were here for eight days. They spent literally several thousand dollars, tourist dollars that would have gone to Amsterdam, and they'll tell all their friends. I think it's a really good thing for everybody."

I had to admit, Briere was a great salesman.

"It's not a difficult industry or business to work in," he went on. "I think it's a real good thing for everybody. I was in the alcohol industry for a good dozen years. People should have an alternative. Marijuana, THC, hash, hemp, whatever you want to call it, has been around for thousands of years. The only reason it is banned now is because of the Americans, *Reefer Madness* and Harry Anslinger, or whatever his name is, the first guy who wanted to keep his job and did a job-creation project for himself. He didn't like blacks and Americans. It was a racist thing."

When the well-dressed man mentioned organized crime, Briere scoffed. "I was growing some pot—we were not organized crime," he said. He gave me a wink and reached for a canister of Budder.

A young chubby man in a camouflage jacket carrying a large cardboard box interrupted him. He put the box on the desk and Briere opened it.

"Let's see, what have we here?" he said giving the burly man a grin. He turned back to me. "We support a lot of people in the local community. Local growers. We have local bakers doing THC cookies and baked goods, K-Nanaimo bars. This is all money going into the community. We're paying income tax on everything. We're paying tax on everything."

He pulled out a half-dozen, 1-pound bags of pot. "This is

some of the material that is out there right now," he said. "There are a lot of entrepreneurs in B.C. They all know that the laws are all based on major, major lies."

He took a bud from one of the bags, ground it and stuffed it into the Volcano sitting on his desk. A green cone-shaped vaporizer made by Storz & Bickel in Germany, the Volcano was unique, patented technology. It permeated the herb with hot air, causing the psychotropic elements and flavours to vaporize and inflate a large, tube-shaped balloon-like bag that was linked to the heater via a detachable valve. He flicked the on switch. The marijuana was heated to the point where the sought-after chemicals were released, but not to the temperature at which plant matter ignites. You could get high without inhaling the toxic tars, harmful plant carbons and carcinogens that came with combustion. The bag inflated quickly.

"Yes, this is an amazing little utensil—I can't believe what this thing does," Briere said. He unhooked the bag, took a toke and passed it.

"Anyway, it's a public attack thing. What happened is when I went to court, they had seized everything I had. Pretty much. Before I had what would be called a thriving business, that's my side of it. From their side, we were what they called organized pot growers, low-life murdering bastards." He laughed, then was interrupted by one of the front-counter staff.

"Do you have any more chairs, Don?"

He shook his head. "Go across the street and buy some," he said, digging into his pocket and pulling out bills. "The antique place has chairs." He peeled off a handful of twenties.

"I can't believe we're running out of chairs. Isn't that a great problem to have?" he said to me.

He took a long hit on the bag. "This is really tasty," he said, passing it to Gwilt, who had arrived from the front of the store. She looked weary.

"Charlie, my dear," she said, "want to bounce the door for me? We have a lot of dope but we can't have this many people."

"Excuse me, it's not dope—it's medication," Briere quipped.

"Is this a full day of work for me, Don?" she asked acidly.

"Carol is in charge of the hourly scheduling," he said to the burly man, who looked dazed.

"If you came in here on any given day, there would be a number of tourists here," she told him. "We get calls from all over North America because for the past four months, we've been in *Cannabis Culture* and on Pot TV, so people that are looking for cannabis when they're thinking of coming to Vancouver find us, and that seals their trip for them . . . There are so many people that used to go to Amsterdam, and now they're coming to Vancouver for this. People are moving to the area because they think it's just fabulous and so progressive."

A middle-aged man in tweed stuck his head in the door. "Can Herb come in?"

"Yeah." Don nodded. "Good to see you."

Herb was an old grower and film-industry set designer who had helped Briere renovate Da Kine in the spring. "Can I smoke a joint?" he said, finding room in the now crowded office to perch on a corner of the desk. "The floor turned out really nice." He examined the Volcano. "These cost lots of dough."

"We bought two," Briere replied.

"You must be hitting the big time now," Herb said, and laughed. "Did you ever think we would be seeing this in our time? Bang, it happened. Amazing, totally amazing. There's a real zoo going on here, Don. Can you control this beast?"

"Absolutely," Briere enthused. "I used to have a nightclub in Coquitlam and I actually had to put my arm in front of me and use it to part the sea of people it was so crowded."

Herb said he heard Briere had partners to open one in Whistler.

"Actually," Briere replied, "we've got four or five stores coming up here really quick."

"Awesome. If we can do that, I'll give you a wholesale price to decorate all five."

"They'll all be themed," Briere added.

"So," Herb said, "no opposition or problems?"

"No," Briere said as if the question had never occurred to him. "No. We need a larger, a much larger warehouse now."

The café was selling more than 4.5 kilograms a day, not counting edibles or hash. The lineups had caught the media's attention and a veritable feeding frenzy had begun, with reporters referring to the café as "the now-famous Da Kine." They had also highlighted the other pot-friendly spots in the neighbourhood.

At the Spirit Within, which featured a large chalkboard price list by its front counter, staff refused to speak to reporters. Almost directly across the street from Da Kine, it sold pot, books and paraphernalia. No one was asked to fill in a form saying they wanted the dope for medical purposes. Owner Ken Hayes was a Californian refugee who, like Straumietis, arrived as a fugitive from U.S. cultivation charges. He had been a major grower in California.

Vancouver Police spokeswoman Constable Sarah Bloor faced a barrage of questions at her daily summer briefing. Why had police failed to shut down this café? She said police were aware various stores in the city openly sold cannabis. She insisted police had expressed concern to the city's licensing department when Da Kine applied for a business licence in January, but said the city issued one on May 4, 2004, anyway.

"We were aware of what the situation was, but we have to prioritize our responsibilities and the way our resources are deployed," she maintained. "When you don't have enough resources, it's hard to take action. We can only do so much with what we have."

The department was more interested in cracking down on serious criminals and large crime organizations, she said. It was exactly the kind of situation Stephen Easton had predicted—overtaxed police able to spend infinite resources battling marijuana and a seemingly insatiable demand feeding an unslakable desire to get into the market.

"Our priority is to investigate [marijuana] grow-ops and organized crime," said Bloor, pointing to a recent seizure of about 450 kilograms of pot, worth about $2.5 million, from three Vancouver residences. But then she emphasized, "We haven't received any complaints . . . You just can't walk in and shut down an operation. If we can work with the city to have [Da Kine's] licence pulled, we'll do that."

At city hall, though, all hell was breaking loose.

Residents of the neighbourhood around the café were dealing with a flood of cars and no parking—the popularity of Da Kine was affecting their quality of life. Neighbours of Da Kine phoned Twelfth and Cambie.

Pia Tofini-Johnson, of the 225-member Commercial Drive Business Improvement Association, was absolutely livid that neither police nor the city had curtailed Da Kine. The long-time owner of Turistano International Travel brandished minutes to show that two police constables had attended a July BIA meeting at which Da Kine's dealing was discussed.

"Whether they told anybody, who knows," Johnson fumed. "The BIA is totally against that place. They should never have been allowed to open in the first place. What they're doing is against the law and it should be stopped. You can't have selective enforcement of the law."

The BIA president, Carmen D'Onofrio Jr., a wine merchant and shoe-store owner, said he was baffled that Da Kine managed to get its licence approved, especially since the café is located a block away from an elementary school, a high school and a community centre. "We're not trying to be exclusive," D'Onofrio said. "All we're asking is for businesses to be responsible and viable members of the community. This is a family-oriented neighbourhood."

The licensing department denied it ever sanctioned Da Kine. Paul Teichroeb, the chief licence inspector, insisted there was no suggestion marijuana might be sold when Da Kine was granted a business licence. In the face of the furor, the department scheduled a hearing where Da Kine would be called to task. Tsk-tsk.

The loony left who controlled city council played to their constituents, many of whom lived near the Drive. Committee of Progressive Electors councillors Tim Louis and Anne Roberts said they didn't think shutting down Da Kine should be a priority. Mayor Larry Campbell, a former RCMP officer and ex–chief coroner, shrugged. He did not condone it, but said, "Where's the impact? What's the big deal?"

He agreed with his fellow councillors that there were "higher" priorities. He was long out of the closet on pot and joked with reporters: "I was a Mountie—when you guys were out getting stoned, I was upholding the law." He'd rather have a good glass of Amarone but he had friends who were pot smokers.

"And they aren't bad people for it," said the mayor, who moonlighted as a scriptwriter and was the inspiration for *Da Vinci's Inquest*, the weekly crusading-coroner television program.

Mayor Campbell wanted marijuana legalized, taxed and subject to the same regulation as other business. He blamed the controversy on Gwilt, who gave an interview to a local television station in which she admitted selling marijuana over the counter.

"Frankly, I'm amazed they've been selling for four months," he said. "And if I was running that café, there'd never have been media allowed in. I have no idea why they feel they can be that open. Still, the one thing that just amazes me was that for four months, on one of our busiest streets in the city, there was nothing—no complaints, nothing. People went about their business. It's just amazing. In all that time, we never had a call or an e-mail of complaint. Not one. Not one. Clearly, there was no public disorder."

He told the media that in his view, Vancouver had a different value set than many places in Canada, and possibly the world: "We're much, much more tolerant."

Campbell said the mail to his office on the subject had been three-to-one in favour of allowing the café to remain open. He said a large proportion of that response had been from Americans telling him they were impressed that in Vancouver they could go to an Amsterdam-style pot café.

"You know, even when I was on the drug squad," he added, "marijuana was never a big deal to me because there was so much of it around. We'd concentrate on the big stuff, the organized operations where they'd ship it in bales."

Councillor Jim Green, his closest ally, also pooh-poohed the uproar. "I checked throughout the city and with other councillors and there have been absolutely no complaints about this store. We get complaints about everything—I've got five or six e-mails today about a guy parking a truck by a construction site."

———

At Emery's store, by the end of the summer, staff were directing tourists to the Drive. The queue at Da Kine was out the door and down the street now from morning to night. Truth be told, they couldn't sell their product fast enough. Da Kine was so busy, they ran out of cheap swag.

Since the smoking room was always filled, customers bought and then strolled over to the Melting Point to sit, smoke and dream about buying $800 Volcanoes.

"I got flow," owner Marc Richardson crowed, looking over the motley capacity crowd in his store.

Richardson left the hemp-growing business in Manitoba to procure marijuana for the BC Compassion Club Society up the Drive. He quit about eighteen months ago to open "Canada's only inhalation station." The Melting Point stocked artistic glass bongs priced up to $2,625, gems, artwork, bubblebags, clothing and paraphernalia.

With the recent business that had been generated by Da Kine—$100,000 worth of Volcanoes alone—Richardson joked that he would pay enough in tax this year to fund the salaries of four police officers: "We're not an organized syndicate that needs to launder funds. Just check my income-tax statements." He figured that so far Da Kine's customers had pumped another $100,000 at least into the four dozen or so nearby boutiques and food joints.

But local community police volunteer Eileen Mosca, a mural painter, couldn't complain loudly enough. "We have a whole lot of high people with car keys in their hands," she said. "The only parking is on our streets."

She was steamed that marijuana businesses were moving from the Pot Precinct—which is "a tad too seedy," she told reporters—to the more upmarket Commercial district. "They want to make this a mainstream business, so they're moving it."

Which in part was true.

Insisting she was not on an anti-marijuana crusade, Mosca said she only opposed the "nudge, nudge, wink, wink" attitude of city hall. "The level of naïveté among city officials is just incredible," she told TV reporters. "Our city government has decided that the laws of Canada don't apply to the Republic of Vancouver. It's very hard to get a cold beer and wine store in Vancouver. It appears that anyone can open a marijuana retail in the city without residents having anything to say about it."

She said the media attention on Da Kine was "the most brilliant for-free advertising gimmick." She was soon on the most popular talk-radio station in the province debating David Malmo-Levine, who was described as a marijuana educator and agitator.

Mosca lost badly.

Still, the mainstream tourist industry and the Vancouver Board of Trade—the city's most conservative business lobby— were quick to join Mosca. Pointing to the national and international attention Da Kine was receiving, they feared the city was earning a reputation as a lawless place where visitors would not feel safe. More than two million Americans flood the city every year on holiday or for business.

The Board, of course, was mixing apples and oranges. What tourists didn't like to see in Vancouver as they they travelled around looking for a cannabis café were junkies and crackheads "using" on the street.

In Victoria, at the provincial legislature, Solicitor General Rich Coleman was outraged. The pudgy former Mountie was infuriated at the audacity and the lack of police response in the province's largest city. If the mayor and left-wing council didn't know the Criminal Code was supposed to be enforced, the law-and-order cabinet minister was about to inform them.

"You can't take a soft attitude towards the fact that somebody wants to sell an illegal drug in a store under a business licence in that city," Coleman said.

Although he did not and could not legally direct police operations or investigations, he insisted the law be enforced. "I don't think we need a ho-hum attitude to anything [associated] with drugs," Coleman added. "You've got people driving into a neighbourhood, buying marijuana, smoking it and driving away in their cars . . . That, to me, is unacceptable. It is still against the law in this country [for marijuana] to be sold and we have to deal with it. It's not something we want popping up on every corner because somebody thinks they can break the law."

Coleman said he found it ironic the city was blocking beer and wine stores from selling hard liquor but was willing to ignore the sale of marijuana.

"There are some people who actually think it's okay to mollycoddle with regard to drugs," the Liberal minister intoned. "I don't buy that. I don't know whether the city councillors or people in Vancouver are not going down to the Downtown Eastside and seeing the impact of these types of things on people in that community, but the fact of the matter is that if someone is breaking the law, my expectation is that the law will be enforced."

The Vancouver police were under siege.

"We're aware of Rich Coleman's comments and the chief has already indicated he does not support criminal behaviour from business," spokesperson Bloor told the clamouring media. "There will be an investigation, and we are in the process of investigating those businesses that conduct themselves in an illegal manner. We're aware of them, and we prioritize them as to how we can get to them in relation to other investigations that we have ongoing. We're aware of public concerns and we're addressing those."

Police Chief Jamie Graham exploded. The situation was completely out of control. Every time he turned around someone was asking him about Da Kine; every time he picked up a newspaper he was being attacked for permitting it.

"I'm being baited," he said. "We told them [City Hall] this was going to happen and they went ahead and let it."

John Conroy stepped through the back door of Da Kine.

"It's a great argument, John—I think you should look into what he's saying," Malmo-Levine said, following him in.

"Yeah, he probably wants me to do it for free," he quipped. "I can't do all of them for free."

He took off his jacket, looked around the room and shook his silver-haired head like a disappointed teacher. The staff, Gwilt, Briere, former Marijuana Party candidate and grower Tim Felger, Norm (who made the great herb granola and K-Nanaimo bars) and a handful of other supporters lounged glumly.

"What have I told you?" Conroy said. "I told you to watch what you were doing."

He looked over at Felger. "I saw you on camera talking about your thousand plants, how you weren't scared of the cops," Conroy groaned.

Around the room, there were giggles.

"And you." He smiled at Gwilt as he shook his head. "You're on camera admitting to selling marijuana."

She squirmed.

"You just can't do that," Conroy said. "I can't stop them from going down to the television station and getting the uncut tape and there is—there is the case. They don't need to do anything else and the court says—no matter what the other arguments you might raise are—the law against trafficking in marijuana stands at the moment." He took a breath. "You've got to adopt and push the medical model," he said. "You just can't be dealing over the counter."

Conroy would be in the Pot Warriors Hall of Fame, if they had one. He formed the National Organization for the Reform of Marijuana Laws (NORML) in Canada in 1978 with the idea of creating a political lobby to change the laws. The group had been dormant for over a decade, but perhaps now, with a minority government, was the time to revive it. Maybe NORML could spark change.

"But that will require everyone who's sitting around dreaming about getting rich getting involved in grassroots politics," he said, scanning the room, "calling their MPs, getting ahold of their MLAs, bugging their alderpersons and councillors."

Heads nodded.

"It's especially important to get Americans to write saying they hope Canada legalizes it, because that will have impact."

He paused, and seemed to sense the staff's unease.

"If there's a bust, what about the employees?" Amy asked.

"I don't think they'll charge the staff—but who knows?"

"What about the suppliers?" Felger added.

"The courts have said if you're growing for the compassion club, an absolute discharge. Same as selling at the compassion club to the ill. The cops don't see busting them as worthwhile given that result. But for profit, selling pot across the counter is a different story. I think you have to stick to the medical model because the law is such a mess. I don't know what they might do."

Watermelon, the would-be Betty Crocker of the marijuana industry, stuck her head in the door. "Hi, everyone, just thought I'd stop by." She gave hugs and kisses all around.

"See you all tomorrow with eight dozen cookies," she said over her shoulder, giving a sexy wave as she left.

A cheer went up.

"You need to remember," Conroy continued, "last week in Hamilton, Ontario, police walked into a newly opened cannabis café and made their first arrest for possession of marijuana. They said they had no choice, the law was being flouted." He looked around the room seriously. "They charged a seventy-six-year-old woman in a wheelchair who had no Health Canada licence to possess cannabis," he said. "She was buying pot because she used it to alleviate the symptoms of her multiple sclerosis. She was so distraught by the incident that she had to be taken away in an ambulance."

Everyone in the room seemed to get the message.

You didn't have to read the writing on the wall. It was emblazoned across the front page of the *Vancouver Sun*: "Coleman slams open pot sales: Solicitor general condemns city politicians for not taking marijuana shops seriously enough."

Anyone who didn't know a raid was imminent didn't understand the concept of saving face. Such humiliating comments from the province's top cop stung like a lash on the back of the Vancouver Police Department.

Da Kine opened as usual, and within an hour the same daily crush was underway. In the mid-afternoon, the owner of the Bulldog chain, Henk de Vries, arrived. He was among the first Dutch coffee-shop owners and a legend among the marijuana cognoscenti. He sat at a table with a few friends from Blunt Bros. and enjoyed a reefer. De Vries had operated a Bulldog restaurant and bar in Vancouver for ten years but could never really make a go of it. Today he thought of sticking his business card on the wall with the others from around the globe. One of his pals said, "Don't. It might not turn out to be a good idea."

Gwilt arrived back from the gelato shop with an ice, hoping for a minute to herself. She had a chance to say hi to de Vries as he was leaving and that was about it. Sitting in the back office with the door closed, she luxuriated in the Italian dessert.

Briere was in the smoking room. He must have a sixth sense about such things, but something, a shadow in the late-afternoon sunshine, perhaps, caught the corner of his eye, something . . . He rose from the table, calmly walked to the door and was just stepping out onto the sidewalk to look outside . . . The SWAT officers nearly knocked him down hurtling past to get inside Da Kine.

Briere kept going until he was a safe distance down the street. He did not look back.

The commotion in the front of the store interrupted Gwilt's reverie. She glanced at the security monitors covering the front door and the cash-register area. Men in dark clothes wearing balaclavas were storming through the door. She thought it was a robbery.

Inside the café, the three dozen customers were stunned. SWAT officers screamed to get on the floor. Gwilt could hear a cacaphony of yells and shouts: "Search warrant, search warrant, search warrant."

She opened the office door to bolt. A man in a balaclava with a gun in his hand blocked her way.

"I'm Carol Gwilt and I own this place," she said. "What the hell is going on?"

"Sit down!" the officer commanded.

She sat down.

By now, other uniformed officers were pouring into the store. The counter staff were cordoned off from the thirty-odd customers sitting on the floor and standing against a wall. All were terrified.

Gwilt started to get up.

"Sit right there or you'll be in handcuffs right now," the cop said.

She sat down and shouted, "Hey, everybody! This is what your taxpayer's dollars are doing."

One of her staff yelled too: "This is what the cops are doing with your money."

Outside the café, the Drive was an armed camp. At roughly a quarter to six on a Thursday evening, at the height of rush hour, a parade of thirty squad cars had converged on Da Kine. The major Eastside artery was shut down. Dozens of uniformed and undercover officers sealed the blocks around Da Kine, causing traffic and business bedlam. The big-budget Hollywood movie *Fantastic Four* was being filmed in the neighbourhood. Production had to be halted.

Within minutes of the barricades going up, a crowd of more than two hundred people was taunting police. They cheered as the Peg General Store cranked up Bob Marley's songs "Get Up, Stand Up," and "I Shot the Sheriff." Dozens sparked spliffs and blew smoke at the cops.

Some shouted, "We support Da Kine." Some yelled, "Legalize marijuana." Others mocked the police: "It only took four months to figure it out." A few hurled profanities and abuse.

Pot activists from all over town rushed to the barricades.

Chris Bennett railed at the officers, tears in his eyes. Ken Hayes, from the Spirit Within, filmed it all on his camcorder. He was easily identifiable the next day on the front page of the *Province* sporting his vintage Beatles *Hard Day's Night* T-shirt.

The crowd cheered louder as Gwilt and six other staff from Da Kine were loaded into the paddy wagon.

"We love you, Carol," people called out.

Each of the thirty-three customers was quizzed and asked to produce a Health Canada medical exemption or a doctor's letter. None did.

Police seized $63,000 in cash ($27,000 of it in the till), US$1,700, 9.5 kilograms of marijuana and 450 grams of hash. Officers also carted away boxes containing three hundred edibles. Overhead, a media helicopter transmitted live images to the six-o'clock newscast.

Police spokesperson Bloor explained the department acted because Da Kine had been "very blatant" about selling marijuana over the counter. One undercover police officer bought marijuana for her testicular cancer, another for his premenstrual cramps. Community residents and businesses, including Britannia Secondary School and the Grandview Woodland Community Policing Centre, had complained, Bloor added.

"It was obvious they made this a public event by flaunting their activity," she insisted.

The raid was "not to react to politicians. This is a criminal activity." She did not say whether police would raid other shops that were selling marijuana. They would not.

"This was not a small, insignificant compassion club," Acting Deputy Chief Constable Bob Rolls added. He told the reporters the store averaged $30,000 a day in sales and had plans to establish different locations. Rolls said there was a "strong likelihood" money from sales at Da Kine filtered back to organized crime. "This was a drug house and a very significant operation."

Investigators counted more than 230 visitors to the café during their ninety-minute surveillance preceding the raid, said Inspector Dave Nelmes, head of the drug section. "We made a decision to do this last week," he said. "We had enough officers here to discourage activities or confrontations."

In Victoria, tracked down by reporters, Solicitor General Coleman smugly refused comment.

Gwilt was charged with possession of marijuana for trafficking purposes as well as possession of the proceeds of crime. Briere stood in the crowd watching as she was driven away.

Undaunted, he planned to re-open.

CURRENT LIABILITIES

the man & the law

THE DAY AFTER THE RAID, people were milling around out-side Da Kine smoking weed and muttering revolution. It had been open about a half-hour. One police cruiser sat a block away monitoring the situation and another made a slow drive-by occasionally. Inside was pandemonium. Photographers, news videographers and reporters jostled in the packed café. Dozens were lined up at the counter filling in forms to buy dope and sign a petition to protest the police action.

In the back office, I found Briere behind large plastic bags piled on his desk containing pounds and half-pounds of mari-juana. Tim Felger and two other men were rolling joints and packaging pot, which was flowing out the door as fast as they could weigh it. Briere brandished a sheaf of papers, his mouth going a mile a minute, surrounded by a thicket of microphones.

"My name is Don Kine," he told them. "Here, look at these, here." He held out the papers.

"This is the city hall correspondence and the inspection report which clearly states that back in January civic officials were told Da Kine intended to sell marijuana as a medicinal herb to those who required it," Briere said. "It's all in the documentation here. We have all the written material. Every single aspect of it was told to them January 19." He began to read from the report: "'When asked what they meant by compassion club, Carol Gwilt stated for the dispensing of medical marijuana.'"

"Is it possible to get a copy of that?" someone asked.

"Sooner or later but not at this very second," Briere replied. "We got all of it in writing. Dated and signed. Here's the paperwork. As you can see, they knew about this and they knew about it a long time ago. The City of Vancouver."

He glanced around the crowd. "This store here, it took drugs off the street. We've got people who say there are no pushers down by the school or in the park any more. They can walk there with their kids. We're paying taxes on this. We're community members. They said the day before they didn't have the resources. Now they've redirected their resources from murder and violence, sexual assaults, to pot people."

He was warming up.

"There is going to be lots of overtime here, thousands of cop hours, and then we'll be in the court system with a judge, the defence lawyer and the Crown attorney to be paid. How many months of wasted resources will we have?"

"How many people who come in the door here are actually in medical need of marijuana compared to those just wanting to get stoned?" a reporter asked.

"That's an irrelevant question," someone shouted.

"It's a truthful question, though—I don't have a medical need for it but I like to smoke pot," the reporter replied.

Briere ignored him.

"We have people waiting to get into hospitals, we have people with heart conditions being put in linen closets, our children need more school supplies, and more teachers. We do not live in a police state. The mayor said he wanted to see marijuana legalized and taxed to hell, and the bottom line is the police came in anyway."

The phone in the office rang.

"Don!" Felger yelled.

Briere abandoned the microphones.

"We're really, really busy," he told the caller. "Get as many people down here as you can . . . Get over here, we need as many people as we can get."

He racked the phone and turned to a man in a grey two-piece suit, Lorne McLeod. A former fathers' rights advocate and Conservative Party worker, McLeod was a gifted guitarist and money man. He played in the old Cheech and Chong band and was known as "the Kid," because he was too young to get into the bars and they had to sneak him onstage. That's where he learned to smoke dope. But he never saw music paying all his bills, so he earned a U.S. law degree, learned about finance and was soon involved in lots of offshore banking, especially in the 1980s when he lived in New York. He helped Briere set up the Burns Lake Laundry.

I hadn't seen him in more than a decade, since back when he gained national prominence debating dads' rights and the poisonous divorce laws on television with Judy Rebick. He had done short time in prison for money laundering. But that was years ago and he laughed easily about it these days. He remained one of Briere's silent partners; he had hoped to stay in the background—now he was pushed outside to be the on-camera spokesman for Da Kine. He shrugged and headed out the door.

"They've done their raid, here we are again," McLeod began, as a score of news cameras whirred. "If they raid us again, we'll open again. If someone wants to smoke a joint and it helps them, or it's their prerogative, more power to them and we will be here to supply it."

Whoops and shouts of approval erupted from the roughly forty or so on the sidewalk.

"This is a legislative issue," McLeod said. "We will deal with it politically. We want to get the bad drugs off the street. We do not support the use of cocaine or drug dealing or gangsters or criminals or organized crime."

Bemused tourists in backpacks snapped photographs.

McLeod excoriated the police. "They were acting as if we were gangsters or some threat. We are no threat, we are members of the community, we are taxpayers, we are citizens and we are tired of the terrorist tactics of the police," he said. "We are a non-profit society, the Canadian Sanctuary Society, incorporated in 2001. What we want to do is provide to the community a safe, secure environment where they can purchase a product of their choice, where they can utilize that product without having to worry about gangsters or street criminals."

In the past week, Da Kine staff had received more than seven thousand applications from people seeking to use marijuana for medicinal purposes, he said.

"We are not drug dealers, we are community activists," he said. "We're doing vast business, but not on a profit basis."

He read a statement from New Democratic Party MP Libby Davies, urging Prime Minister Paul Martin to act quickly to introduce marijuana reforms when Parliament convened. Davies, who represents Vancouver East, said, "These sorts of situations are going to continue if Paul Martin and the federal government refuse to face the issue, and as [a] result lives are ruined because of criminal convictions."

A few hours later, Provincial Court Judge William Kitchen rejected prosecutor Mark Sheardown's request to bar Gwilt and the staff members from meeting one another or returning to the 1000-block of Commercial Drive. He quoted B.C. Court of Appeal Justice Mary Southin, who said marijuana "appears to be of no greater danger to society than alcohol . . . [and marijuana smokers] are no better or worse, morally or physically, than people who like a martini."

Kitchen was a no-nonsense judge who saw a daily grind of real crime and real victims. I spent a night drinking scotch with him. He was no ideologue and saw things with a gimlet eye. "It seems pretty silly to be held in jail these days for possession of marijuana," Kitchen said.

But the law was the law. He released Gwilt and the staff from custody on condition they stay away from marijuana. All faced charges of trafficking. Gwilt was also charged with possessing proceeds from a crime. Kitchen emphasized they'd better not reoffend: "Next time, I'll hold you in jail."

Outside the court, lawyer John Conroy warned Da Kine to stop selling pot. "I would hope anyone else involved with Da Kine would see the consequences if they continue. They're just asking for further problems from police. My advice under the circumstances is that she [Gwilt] shouldn't allow that."

Conroy spent much of his time trying to make those in the marijuana reform movement understand that cannabis might be tolerated in lots of places, but it remained illegal and the state imprisoned those who broke the law. You had to pick your battles, in Conroy's view, and sometimes you had to retreat.

⁓

The following morning, I found Gwilt in the back office of Da Kine, steamed for that very reason. Briere sat behind his desk looking contrite, Felger was beside him rolling joints, eyes glued to the floor.

"I'm doing great," she said, obviously not. "It's going good. I'm just trying to strategize my way through the day right now."

She was in the midst of cleaning, trying to make her desk usable again after police broke the casters, jamming in the drawers. She re-hung the poster for Dr. Hornby's Voodoo Juice and a picture of two men playing tennis on the wing of an airborne biplane. The police had confiscated the picture of the Three Amigos—Emery, Straumietis and Briere. They had also removed the picture of Don shaking hands with Mayor Larry Campbell. Gwilt was angry at the newspaper articles about the booming business at the café while she was appearing in court. She stopped, picked up the newspaper on the desk and threw it down—the huge picture of Felger beside pounds of pot stared off the front page.

"That's a really nice picture of you, Tim, rolling a joint beside about three pounds of pot," she sniped.

"I was just rolling a joint," he said coyly. "I don't know nothing about that pot."

He kept his eyes lowered.

"It's okay, Tim," she said sarcastically, "I'll take the heat for you."

Gwilt was wired. She didn't want them selling pot in the store. The café was mobbed again and they had already run out of edibles.

One of her assistants arrived looking stressed too. "I have to take some time with my sister."

Gwilt nodded.

Briere was summoned to the front, and he returned a moment later saying a CBC crew wanted to interview Gwilt.

"No," she said emphatically.

"It's okay if you speak to the media," he told her in the wrong tone of voice.

"You mean you'll let me?" she snapped.

He lowered his eyes. "They were real nice to us," he mumbled.

"Of course they were real nice," she said. "They're the media, that's what they do."

Briere slunk away to tell the reporters no Gwilt.

Watermelon arrived looking like Janis Joplin circa 1969, in aviators, faded Levi's jacket, dress and sandals laced up her calves.

"Hey, why the long faces?" she said, putting down a big box of cookies. "Let's cheer up. More cookies."

"It's the media," Gwilt said.

"The media are like a bad smell," Watermelon replied. "Don't trust them. I was interviewed once, and after we were finished the girl and I were just sitting around talking after the interview. I said 'Oh, you know, my sister used to give me acid when I was twelve.' Guess what they put in the head-line—'Watermelon dropped acid at twelve.' Imagine what my mom thought."

She patted Gwilt on the back. "Weed isn't going any-where, we aren't going anywhere," Watermelon said. "Stay strong. We are winning. We are winning. Surely?"

Gwilt looked like she needed a day at the spa. "It's time to stop the drug war," she said with a sigh. "It's time."

She walked slowly to the front of the store to close up for the day.

People were lined up twenty-deep on Sunday morning out-side Da Kine. Across the street, Vancouver Mayor Larry Campbell was celebrating the local library's longer weekend hours and talking to reporters about the raid. Gwilt stood in the sunshine, off to one side, listening.

"I support the legalization of marijuana, but at the same time that doesn't mean they get to flout the law until the law is changed," Campbell said. "Certainly there is a big deal from the standpoint of legality. It's illegal, and there's nothing the city can do to change that. It's a federal law, and this idea that we can pass a bylaw that says coffee shops can sell marijuana is craziness. We can't do it; it's not a municipal responsibility."

He did not back down from his earlier position. "My answer is you legalize it and tax the living hell out of it. And every bit of the tax should go straight to health care, not the general fund," he said.

Suggestions that Da Kine had erased street dealing in the area by its presence, he swept aside. "They are peddlers themselves."

Gwilt bristled.

"The fact of the matter is that it is against the law; it is illegal; they are trafficking in a drug. Would it make any sense if they opened up and started selling heroin?"

As he turned to walk away, Gwilt stuck out her hand. "I'm Carol Gwilt," she said. "Mr. Campbell, it's a real pleasure to meet you."

Campbell flushed. "Hello there," he said.

She smiled, turned and walked away. It wasn't the time or place to confront him.

"He's almost on our side," she said later. "He's not on our side because he still lets the drug war continue from day to day."

Afterward, we strolled to the park and she sat in the sunshine about a block from the sizable crowd outside Da Kine. She sparked a large reefer.

"There's a safe-injection site in Vancouver, although heroin is illegal," she said. "Why? Because there's a need for it, because people are dying on the street. And our wonderful mayor has realized this and has come to the aid of his people, which is what any good mayor will do." She took a toke.

"Why can't people have safe access to cannabis? I'm not

organized crime and I don't deal with organized crime. I deal with good, honest, hard-working middle-class people who smoke cannabis and maybe grow cannabis. I see nothing wrong with that. This is everyone's issue. Women didn't have a vote. Now it's expected. To make change you have to do something different."

She finished the joint.

"If they come again it's just absolutely absurd, and if they got the balls enough to do that, I got the balls enough to open up again . . . This is war. It's war for us. We didn't call the war, the war was called on us. We're just going to defend ourselves until something gives. I realize doing this isn't going to legalize marijuana. But marijuana isn't legal in Amsterdam either."

Later that night, Briere was arrested. Police found several pounds of bud in his car when they stopped him. His parole was revoked and he was charged anew with trafficking. Briere suffered a heart attack. It was mild and he would quickly recover, but he would require hospital care—and more than the arrest, the attack panicked Gwilt.

The next day, I talked to her on the phone. She was frantic about Briere and the media coverage.

"People have to know he wasn't a bad guy," she sobbed. "I'm talking like he's not here any more. We're still in business as usual. There's media camped out on our door. I don't know. We're done with the media right now. I told Lorne, don't even go in front of a camera, stay away from everybody and don't talk for me." She managed a laugh.

Several hours later, Gwilt was rearrested in her car with an assistant, a pound of pot and $5,000. She was charged with breaching her bail conditions.

———

"*Reefer Madness*—I'm living it," McLeod told me as he walked along the Drive through the late fall rain.

He had spent too much time with the Da Kine accountant in the past week and had a parcel of ugly questions. It was a mess, and that was putting it lightly: rent for September and October was unpaid, hydro and phone bills unpaid, no records of employment or hours, no paperwork, nothing. He had asked Gwilt.

"That's Don's job," she said about paying the rent.

The whole thing was an absolute train wreck. He was convinced police were tailing him. The big question was, Where did all the money go? Briere told him he didn't know; so did Gwilt. He called the accountant and asked for another meeting. He didn't know what had happened either, and hadn't met with Briere or Gwilt since July.

McLeod had established bank accounts in the Bahamas and in Liechtenstein for the money generated by Da Kine. None ever was deposited. Gwilt's name wasn't even on the lease.

"What am I doing in the drug business?" McLeod mumbled. "Don doesn't get it. He's going to do a long time in jail and he'll be an old man coming out with a suitcase. It isn't just a bad dream." He walked along, eyes on the slick sidewalk, shaking his head in disbelief.

From August 1 to August 31, what went through the till, what they had a record of, was $978,320.63. That was just August. May and June were about $110,000 each. Half of July was $660,000—the cash-register tapes from July 18 to July 31 were missing or the till was turned off for those weeks. Half of September was almost $800,000. That was more than $2 million altogether.

Even counting the $150,000 or so the police seized in money

and product, taking away costs and every imaginable expense and probability, McLeod believed half a million was missing.

Over the past five days, he and the accountant had been crunching the numbers every which way to Sunday; the results were the same: the profits had vanished. The best-case scenario—assuming the worst expense possibilities—was that $180,000 had evaporated.

But the records were nowhere to be found. Even the lease was in the name of the man who was originally going to run the café but backed out. It was bizarre. And certainly there was no one to complain to or seek help from. As a man who lived in the legitimate financial world, McLeod worried about the provincial and federal tax inspectors and the fallout of their inquiries. Briere still had that $2 million tax bill from his last illegal enterprise.

McLeod went to the jail to see Briere and tell him. His blue eyes twinkled behind the thick security glass and he let out a laugh. "Welcome to the drug business."

McLeod shook his head. He would go to the wall for his friend, but not over Da Kine.

"I'm not going to jail because you're stupid," he told Briere. "I've never seen anything like this. The poor accountant is totally lost and he has legal responsibilities. This was street dealing with a pretty storefront. I'm not putting you down, that's the businessman talking. This is unbelievable."

Everything had gone south, it was over. Sitting in the North Fraser Pretrial Centre, Briere maintained the mien of a defiantly unbowed dyed-blond Buddha. Perhaps no one would ever find out where the money went. It took investigators two years last time to trace some of Briere's profits to the Burns Lake Laundry.

By this point, Gwilt was working at Advanced Nutrients and continuing to support Briere as he served his time. She was living at Tim Felger's farm. He too was in jail awaiting trial, arrested after police seized more than two thousand plants from his barns.

"I'll be back at it when I get out," Briere told McLeod. "Don't worry. We were millionaires once, we'll be millionaires again."

———

John Conroy's second-floor law office was decorated with Indian art and court sketches—one featuring two shark fins knifing through the courtroom floor, circling. He threw down his coat, undid his tie and sat behind a desk cluttered with legal briefs.

"Sometimes I just can't believe it," he said in exasperation.

Emery was in jail too, convicted of trafficking in Saskatoon for passing a joint to a university student. The small prairie city founded as a temperance colony was a very unfriendly place for pot smokers and it didn't take kindly to being a stop on Emery's 2003 Summer of Legalization tour.

The Prince of Pot had seen a phenomenal publicity opportunity when the Ontario Court of Appeal found the federal possession law invalid. He quickly lined up dates across the country to proselytize for marijuana—and was promptly busted in Edmonton, Calgary, Winnipeg, St. John's, Moncton *and* Regina.

After a March 22, 2004, speech at the University of Saskatoon, Emery was arrested by four police officers. They took him into custody when he admitted to having pot in his pocket, 2.3 grams precisely. He was charged with trafficking because one of the students accompanying him confessed Emery had passed him a joint.

Emery, who was put in leg irons, was released after four nights' imprisonment upon posting $3,500 bail, promising not to possess marijuana and agreeing to let police show up anytime and search his home, car or person. Prosecutors argued he should be held in jail until his trial—a draconian measure usually reserved for violent offenders or those expected to flee.

All the charges against Emery elsewhere in the country died because it was decided the Ontario court ruling truly did put the pot law in legal abeyance as of July. Emery took the situation much too casually. He told his lawyer he was obviously guilty and that's what the judge was told. Emery forgot to mention that he wanted to raise a few important constitutional issues. It would hamper his chance to appeal.

To add insult to injury, Emery was given a righteous tongue-lashing by Judge Albert Lavoie, who convicted him August 19 and said he wanted to "make an example" of Emery for violating the laws of a democratic society and endangering Western civilization.

Emery's successful defiance of prosecutors and judges, his ongoing flagrant marijuana use and his gadfly attitude drove prohibitionists nuts. Lavoie was finally able to exact some retribution: he gave Emery ninety-two days in prison for passing a joint.

Conroy was stunned not just at the sentence from the Dark Ages but at Emery's nonchalant approach to the law. He really had difficulty making marijuana advocates understand the risk of being busted.

"That's how it is," he said. "People don't understand that. And they don't understand that although [police] say they're not busting people for possession—they are."

Whether it happens depends how the police feel that day; what happens next depends on what judge you face.

For three decades, Conroy has been the lawyer to go to if you had a pot problem. Marc Emery, Big Mike, Don Briere, Watermelon, Carol Gwilt, heck, you name them—if they were in the pot industry, they consulted him.

"I think my colleagues on the defence bar, just like the police, are not too happy with these efforts to legalize," Conroy said. "The prohibition pays a lot of bills. Just like impaired driving used to be the bread-and-butter for lots of criminal lawyers, now it's grow-ops for a lot of them."

He was just off the plane from Toronto. He, Ontario lawyer Alan Young and others were now actively reviving the Canadian chapter of NORML.

"The civil disobedience, at Da Kine, not that I'm against that stuff," Conroy said, "it's all got its place. But there are all sorts of people out there who would like to see the law changed that need a viable legal organization that they can either become involved in or anonymously contribute to in order to try and do it without having to throw their bodies on the line or become public."

There are too many disparate activists doing their own thing, he said; the movement needed a more concerted, focused effort. "Until they do that, I think they're just pissing in the wind."

His main partner in the enterprise, Young, was a Canadian Alan Dershowitz—a legal rebel who used his academic post at York University as a redoubt from which to launch hit-and-run attacks on the system. He graduated from Osgoode Hall law school in 1981, started practising in 1983 and earned a master's from Harvard in 1986.

Like Conroy, Young's ties to marijuana run deep. Emery hired him back in 1990 when he was still a little-known Southwestern Ontario bookseller trying to tweak local noses by selling banned CDs containing dirty words and scandalous lyrics. Vulgar records like *As Nasty as They Wanna Be* by 2 Live Crew. Conroy was from the first generation of legal activists, Young the second. Their stridency reflected the difference in age and perspective.

"We have criminals, we have the system, but what we don't have is justice," Young said. "We should be protecting the potheads and perverts so that we can prevent serious crimes, and lawyers stand in the way of that. Indifference and elitism are rampant in the profession. I'm talking about stuff that makes me sick. I can't sleep at night."

He is a huge critic of the marijuana hypocrisy — studies indicate 85 per cent of law students and 60 per cent of lawyers smoke pot.

"I smoked pot with judges," Young liked to tell audiences in his many public appearances. "I smoked joints with prosecutors. How can they get up in the morning and look in the mirror when they know they are going to ruin someone's life for that very thing? I know judges that go to prostitutes and I know judges that go to [dominatrices]."

Conroy is less confrontational, more apt to say it's a marathon, not a sprint.

Born and reared in Africa, Conroy started the first community legal office in the Fraser Valley back in the early 1970s when the province made its first attempts at establishing a legal-aid system. He was among the first of Canada's pot legal-activists.

Along with Clayton Ruby, Q.C., the celebrated Toronto civil liberties specialist, Conroy had formed the Canadian branch of NORML as an outgrowth of his defence work. His hair is silver now, as is his neatly trimmed beard.

"The Africans smoked pot all the time, and if my father saw a pot plant growing in the fields he just pulled it up and thew it aside," Conroy recalled. "I started doing pot cases in Chilliwack. That's what I think really politicized me. People were going to jail for it."

His secretary appeared with a coffee.

"Sure I was at university in the sixties when [pot] was a factor, but it wasn't a big factor in my space. I was in phys. ed. I was a jock in those days."

It was his clients who pushed him into incorporating NORML — in particular, George Baker, whose real name was

George Faulkner, a dealer he defended. There were so many dealers to defend in the old days, including the man who supplied the Beatles.

"I incorporated NORML as a Canadian corporation to create a viable legal way for them to lobby as opposed to civil disobedience to try and change the law. George became the executive director. Clay Ruby and I were the original directors. Chapters rose up all over."

But Vancouver always has had a special place in the history of drug taking and drug legislation. This is where it all began. The country's first anti-drug law, the Opium Act, was introduced by the minister of labour in 1908 because of the situation here.

⁓⁓⁓⁓⁓⁓

Opium dens existed in Canada for some forty years—from 1860 until the turn of the century—with scant concern. There were factories in Vancouver, Victoria and New Westminster, and the customers were primarily Chinese labourers lured to North America by railway companies and others engaged in the huge construction projects across the West at the end of the 19th century. Asian workers were offered salaries that far exceeded what they could earn at home, but half what whites in North America were paid.

None of this was a problem during the *fin de siècle* boom years when there was a labour shortage. But in the lean years that followed, racial tensions flared. Immigration dramatically increased in the first decade of the 20th century and, with high unemployment, the immigrants were very much resented.

The growing anger toward the recent arrivals exploded in September 1907. The Vancouver Trades and Labour Council organized a meeting just a block or so from Gastown and thousands of people flooded the area. Fired by incendiary speeches about "the yellow peril," the crowd transmogrified and rampaged through the nearby Chinese and Japanese neighbourhoods.

Prime Minister Wilfrid Laurier dispatched the deputy minister of labour, Mackenzie King, future prime minister, to investgate. King arrived on the coast in the fall of 1907 to settle damage claims from the riot. At his claims inquiry in 1908, he received two applications from opium merchants for compensation. It was an eye-opener for King. Reports say gross receipts from one operation employing nineteen people indicated revenues of $180,000 for 1907. The other employed ten people and was reaping a similarly staggering amount.

King was taken aback. He was unaware of the opium trade. But who would be? There had been no general alarum about opium, no real concern. This was also the heyday of patent medicines. Marijuana, opium and cocaine were ingredients of innumerable tonics, elixirs and analgesics. Up until 1937 even, there were countless cannabis compounds, tinctures and oils available in the United States, approved by the Food and Drug Administration, produced by pharmaceutical companies.

In Canada at the turn of the century, the public had little interest in drug legislation (aside from alcohol prohibition) and most would have considered drugs a private indulgence of no concern to the government. There certainly was no "opium problem" in Vancouver when King arrived.

But the Protestant Chinese clergy assured the ambitious young man that opium was as pernicious as alcohol. Sobriety, frugality and industry—it was a motto King could recite by heart. He concluded: "I think it should be made impossible to manufacture this drug anywhere in the Dominion. We will get some good out of this riot yet."

Within three weeks, the making and selling of opium was illegal in Canada. Merchants were given six months to conduct going-out-of-business sales of existing stock. Ottawa moved swiftly even though there was no apparent impetus for the law. The Canadian Medical Association and the Canadian Pharmaceutical Association even asked why the law was being pushed through.

King was engaged in the "eradication of an evil which is not only a source of human degradation but a destructive factor in national life." He was not so much making public policy as he was social engineering. I think the anti-opium law was inspired by a widely held belief back then that government should strive to make men and women better, to remove the shackles on their self-improvement and the hurdles that kept them from holding down a job.

Like the contemporaneous attempts to curtail alcohol, I think you can view the anti-opium law as a public policy aimed at improving the labour pool, profit margins, the bottom line and the community. That's why the labour minister introduced the first law criminalizing a psychoactive substance in Canada.

In 1911, the government continued its moral mission by expanding the prohibition to include cocaine and morphine and broadening the spectrum of drug offences to include possession, distribution and smuggling. The government said cocaine was "the agent for the seduction of our daughters and the demoralization of our young men."

Who could disagree? Sir Mick Jagger? But is that any of the government's business?

El Paso was the first jurisdiction to ban the possession of marijuana in 1914. Canada followed suit, surprisingly, in 1923. With no debate in the House of Commons, the minister outlawed marijuana with only the simple assertion "There is a new drug in the schedule."

Emily Murphy, the country's first female magistrate, whose picture now adorns the $50 bill, appears responsible for a virulent campaign against marijuana that led to the legislation. She began demanding pot be banned almost as soon as the national alcohol prohibition ended.

In a book called *The Black Candle*, serialized in *Maclean's* magazine in 1921, she fulminated about a non-existent cannabis problem. Quoting the L.A chief of police as her source, she wrote:

> The addict loses all sense of moral responsibility. Addicts to this drug while under its influence are immune to pain and could be severely injured without having any realization of their condition. While in this condition they become raving maniacs and are liable to kill or indulge in any form of violence to other persons using the most savage methods of cruelty without, as said before, any sense of moral responsibility.

She closed the chapter "Marihuana: A New Menace" with the following:

> It has been pointed out that there are three ways out from the regency of this addiction. First, insanity. Second, death. Third, abandonment. This is assuredly a direful trinity and one with which the public should be cognizant in order that they may be warned of the sharp danger that lies in even curiously tasting poisons which have been inhibited or which are habit-forming.

Whatever her intentions, Murphy was under the influence of U.S. propaganda against marijuana in the southern states, which was a not-so-subtle racist slur against immigrant Mexicans. The political upheaval triggered by the Mexican Revolution had sent thousands of poor northward, and they took their pot-smoking habit with them.

By 1931, more than half the U.S. states had prohibited marijuana. Over the next five years, the U.S. federal government ramped up a scare campaign that culminated in the Marijuana Tax Act and a countrywide ban.

Harry Anslinger, the former director of the anti-prohibition branch of the FBI, became head of the new Federal Bureau of Narcotics, the precursor of the Drug Enforcement Administration established under President Richard Nixon. Anslinger topped even Murphy's lurid and pandering tales of the demon weed. He was responsible for the *Reefer Madness* culture that gripped North America in the thirties and said judges should throw the book at pot addicts, "then throw away the key."[*]

By the 1950s, it was jazz musicians and Beat poets Anslinger blamed. At one time, he even planned a mass arrest of musicians such as Louis Armstrong, Count Basie, Duke Ellington and Cab Calloway.

From 1930 until the 1950s, in Canada, there was little public debate about drugs. Why would there be? The numbers didn't warrant it. Especially for marijuana.

Up until 1938, legal historians believe, there had been only thirty convictions for pot across the country. By 1955, a special Senate committee on the traffic of narcotic drugs concluded: "Marihuana is not a drug commonly used for addiction in Canada. No problem exists in Canada at present in regard to this particular drug. A few isolated seizures have been made, but these have been from visitors to this country."

In 1961, the United Nations adopted a new international convention aimed at curbing illicit drug trafficking. As a

---

[*] Anslinger was also a key player in the illegal and notorious CIA experiments with LSD and admitted to supplying at least one prominent but addicted congressman with morphine. Apparently, that was Joseph McCarthy.

result, Canada adopted a new law, the Narcotic Control Act, that upped the penalty to life imprisonment for distribution offences. I'm not quite sure why—the worst hadn't even happened yet.

Certainly in the United States there was evidence of marijuana use among musicians, poets, painters, folkies, actors, artists, outlaw bikers, the avant-garde and other counterculture types—real threats to society. Still, there was a reason this demographic was known as "the fringe"—in terms of absolute numbers there were damn few of them. It was the same in Canada, as the sporadic court cases made evident. There were few tokers in North America, or most of Europe for that matter, before the sixties, though the numbers then exploded.

In 1967, there were roughly 1,000 marijuana possession convictions in Canada; by 1975 there were 40,000. The numbers doubled one year, tripled the next and quadrupled the year after that. The judiciary initially enforced the egregious iron-fisted penalties on the books—more than half of the people who came to court in 1967 charged with possession were imprisoned. But that changed as the numbers skyrocketed.

Even Margaret Trudeau, wife of the Liberal prime minister Pierre Trudeau, was smoking dope behind her RCMP security cordon. It was evident the law should be changed.

After the release of the LeDain Commission Report on the use of illicit drugs in 1972, the government amended the law to allow judges the option of granting an absolute or conditional discharge, a response to the growing concern about foolish young people being stigmatized with a criminal record for an adolescent folly. It was legal legerdemain—they still asked you at the border if you'd been convicted and *bango*, no Florida vacation. Same if you were a teacher—oh, the court might let you go, but your career was over for being involved with "illegal drugs."

As Cabinet dithered, the judiciary changed their approach to sentencing. In 1967, more than half of those convicted of possession went to jail; by 1975 only one of five did time.

On any given day in 1975 there were twenty thousand Canadians imprisoned. If we as a society had wanted to continue to incarcerate half of all people convicted of marijuana possession we would have had to double the jail capacity. Yet six years later, the federal solicitor general would lament that discharge provisions were too often invoked and complain they were too lenient. The pendulum had swung to the other side. President Ronald Reagan was declaring war on drugs and his bride was telling the world, "Just Say No."

The government has hemmed-and-hawed over the law ever since.

Throughout, and no matter how severe, the penalties had little impact on whether people smoked dope: In Canada and the United States (regardless of whether the state decriminalized), you saw an increase in use from 1968 to 1979, a falling-off during the 1980s and an increase during the 1990s. You see exactly the same pattern in the Netherlands, which has had liberal drug laws since 1976. There was no correlation between the rates of cannabis usage and criminal strictures.

The seventies-era Trudeau Liberal government promised to decriminalize marijuana. But Cabinet always was too divided and there were more important priorities, such as repatriating the constitution. No one since has had the gumption. Today more than 600,000 Canadians have criminal records for marijuana possession.

Conroy has never lacked clients.

In the 1990s, defence lawyers like Conroy began challenging the constitutionality of the Criminal Code law. This litigation strategy, in which David Malmo-Levine was a key participant, culminated in a May 2003 hearing before the Supreme Court of Canada.

Tobacco kills 45,000 people a year in Canada, Conroy said, and the second-biggest problem is alcohol, which kills 12,000 a year, way ahead of all illegal drugs, which kill about 800 people a year. The next biggest problem is prescription drugs. Then there are over-the-counter drugs. One year in Canada there were 10,000 hospital admissions because people took too much Aspirin, he complained. Marijuana has never killed anyone.

Like many of those in the movement, Conroy is a libertarian when it comes to drugs and would legalize them all. Restrict them, sure, but get rid of the criminal law as the regulatory mechanism.

If you read the court decisions and think about the underlying logic, Conroy said, the basis of the marijuana law is suspect. It threatens people's liberty in order to deter them from using a substance that over a prolonged period of use might at worst give them chronic bronchitis—which speculatively might make them a burden on the health-care system, and, aha!, a burden on society or others, ergo, QED, the need to use the weight of the criminal law. Conroy wrinkled his face—huh?

There were identifiable groups, he said, such as pregnant women, the mentally ill, particularly paranoid schizophrenics, and immature youth that probably should not under any circumstances smoke pot. But there are all kinds of people who die if exposed to nuts and we haven't yet criminalized the possession and consumption of crunchy or smooth peanut butter.

The criminal prohibition, nevertheless, was upheld on December 23, 2003, by the Supreme Court of Canada. It backed the government, saying it was okay to jail someone for small amounts of pot and any changes to the law must be made by Parliament.

"We conclude that it is within Parliament's legislative

jurisdiction to criminalize the possession of marijuana, should it choose to do so," said the judgment co-written by justices Charles Gonthier and Ian Binnie. "Equally, it is open to Parliament to decriminalize or otherwise modify any aspect of the marijuana laws that it no longer considers to be good public policy."

Conroy disliked the decision and interpreted it to mean it was time to start lobbying for political change because the legal avenues had been shut down. Young agreed. Both believed the biggest problem with the discussion around marijuana policy and the law was ignorance. Most people just didn't know what's been tried or what might happen if you decriminalized or legalized pot.

The state of South Australia decriminalized in 1987, and although there was some subsequent rise in use, it was no greater than that in two neighbouring states that didn't change their laws. The same thing happened in the American states that have decriminalized marijuana since the 1970s. Jurisdictions with the most severe anti-marijuana laws experienced the sharpest rises in use, Conroy said.

Holland made marijuana possession (also the possession of small amounts of other drugs, including heroin and cocaine) de facto legal in 1976 and coffee shops were later brought under municipal licensing. There was no increase in use. The increases in use noted after 1984 were equal to or less than increases that occurred in the United States, Britain and many other countries that stuck with criminal prohibition. The Dutch rate of marijuana use continues to be one of the lowest in the western world.

Some states and cities in Germany chose this policy in the early 1990s. Italy and Spain adopted this approach for a while. Portugal voted to follow suit. Critics in each case insisted drug use would soar, and in each case it didn't happen.

Like many of those who have been involved in the marijuana debate for any length of time, Conroy thinks pot is a symbol, and that makes it harder for people to deal with the subject dispassionately. For a certain generation and a certain ideology, it represents anarchy, lazy callow youth, decaying morality, property crime and public disorder. Conroy feels we need a period of desensitization so that people can become more disinterested in what happens with the herb. But it has to happen, he added, because the criminal law is not working.

The commercial cultivation of marijuana, once largely confined to British Columbia, has spread nationwide, Conroy said. In Ontario, the harvest has grown by an estimated 250 per cent in the past two years. The Electricity Distributors Association estimates that Ontario utilities are losing as much as $200 million a year from illegal taps of power lines by grow-ops.

Police recently raided massive grow-ops in Moncton, New Brunswick. In Edmonton, real estate agents are exploring their legal liability for selling a house that turns out to have been a nursery. In an effort to control the spread of grow-ops, civic administrations are flirting with unconstitutional laws. It is a bad situation.

"There is so much around, it's unenforceable," Conroy said.

He had outlined the negative consequences of the prohibition in court time and time again—the least desirable elements of society are enriched, empowered and encouraged. At the same time, civil rights, due process and personal freedoms are fettered and trampled as law enforcement agencies struggle with unenforceable laws. The social fabric becomes threadbare. Compared with the tactics used against alcohol consumption, the anti-drug laws have a perverse draconian aspect to them. Even during Prohibition, possession of alcohol was not criminalized.

Conroy believes the government has a range of options for dismantling the prohibition. Regulatory questions are not an issue — there are models for tobacco, alcohol or methadone to choose from. The first step is to acknowledge that one general criminal law is not a good approach for dealing with all drugs. Each substance presents a different risk and a different challenge. Opium requires one approach, marijuana another.

Conroy wants the federal government to get out of the drug-control business altogether. He wants legalization with provincial regulation.

"They should just treat it like booze. Legalization brings it into control, prohibition puts it out of control."

He paused.

"And decriminalization would be good for my business," Conroy said. "You will have more growers and dealers coming to see me to stay out of jail. Lawyers will keep getting rich."

———

Louis Armstrong's gravelly voice echoed through the refurbished basement of the Rogers Building. Once the base for rum-runners, it was now primarily occupied by Pot TV production facilities and Marc Emery's party space.

Chris Bennett was working on a computer monitor. Upstairs they were readying for Emery's homecoming. Downstairs, caterers were laying out buffet tables with poached salmon, ginger scallops, coconut shrimp. There was pop, spring water, juices, organic Salt Spring Island coffee.

"Hi," Bennett said, "have you seen the Bush statement on Iraq? I'm just downloading it."

I walked over to watch.

"I think history plays a big role in forming American opinion, because Bush and all the guys with him, Ashcroft, Walters, they're all fundamentalist Christians," he said. "It's the ideological difference between them and the rest of us. They believe the rapture is going to happen in their life-time—and it better happen soon since they're all in their seventies."

Bennett had a blue tattoo on his forearm: an interpretation of the Seal of Solomon by Eliphas Lévi, a 19th-century hash-head and magician.

"You know I've always said it's because marijuana breeds insolence," he quipped. "Maybe the drug experience in general has a tendency to take you out of your tunnel-vision reality and throw you into this new space. Suddenly you are looking at everything from the other end of the room and you are seeing things in a slightly different manner. That's the threat. People start looking at politicians, people in power and questioning what they are doing, watching the news after smoking a joint and going, 'Oh jeez, this sounds like a pile of crap.'

"It's like it's got the nature of ridicule and whatnot in it. You know what I mean?"

"Yes, I think there's an element of that," I said. His dark red hair was receding and his beard was reaching bushman bulk again.

"It has always been a threat to kings and hierarchies and all that type of layout, that type of structural layout, because people smoke and go, What makes you better than me?" he continued.

I nodded. "It's a little spiritual for me, but maybe."

Bennett was born in Vancouver and grew up in Deep Cove on the banks of Indian Arm. He started smoking weed at twelve after finding some in his brother's dresser drawer, he says, and can remember the first homegrown harvests from Lasqueti Island in the early 1970s.

"I think we could have a mini Dark Ages here," he muttered. "What's taking place in the U.S., with the loss of freedoms and the mass incarcerations, could come here. That's
a very real threat."

Bennett said he wasn't an intellectual fellow in spite of
the books he authored. He dropped out of high school and
ended up on the west coast of Vancouver Island, in Ucluelet,
twenty years ago. He worked as a night watchman at the fish
plant three times a week, grew weed and surfed.

"I had it good," he said. "I went surfing all the time, had
my own house, didn't have to work too much—I was living
the good life, alright."

The Gulf War had just begun in 1990; he was smoking a
joint and reading the newspaper. He noticed an advertisement for an evangelical rally in which a reference from
Revelations about the fall of Babylon was superimposed on
an image of tanks and jets invading Iraq.

"I thought, holy shit, that's weird. I had heard on the
news how Saddam was trying to rebuild the Babylonian gardens. I was like, oh, man, I'm going to read the Book of Revelations and see what's going on. I smoked another joint.
I read the first little bit about the guy taking a bit of the
scroll and eating it. It's sweet in his mouth but turns bitter
in his stomach and he begins to prophesy. I was like, oh,
sounds like he ate something there. I get to the very end
and the last paragraph of the Bible says, on either side of the
river of life stood the tree of life bearing twelve manners
of fruit."

Bennett's eyed welled up and he sighed. Anyone could
see the tree of life was marijuana.

"I always get emotional, because it was really emotional
when it happened," he said ingenuously. "And the leaves of
the tree are for the healing of the nations, and I was like,
fuck, I just knew it was just this whole cannabis thing. The

paper, the fuel, the medicine, and I just started tripping, I felt like light just poured into me."

The next day Bennett started collecting information, any information, about cannabis and religion. He formed Patriotic Canadians for Hemp and became his own one-man band for marijuana in a town where asking for brown toast was eccentric.

"My wife at the time, her whole family was loggers," he recalled. "I had big long dreadlocks. I had my own home-made hemp clothes. I was the modern counterpart of Ezekiel walking amongst the infidels. I had the full attention of the town. I had lived there for a long time too, so everyone knew me. It was local boy gone bad, you know."

He left in 1995, taking his file folders of clippings and photocopies and turning them into one book, *Green Gold the Tree of Life: Marijuana in Magic & Religion*, then another, *Sex, Drugs, Violence and the Bible*. The volumes were fascinating. He followed the plant into the past, traced its connections to the Sufis, the Zoroastrians, the Babylonians, the Brahmans, the Assyrians . . . back into the mists of time.

His investigation of Hebrew etymology and the references to cannabis in the Bible were groundbreaking. He was particularly interested in the anointing oil that Moses was commanded to make in the book of Exodus. This mixture included about six quarts of olive oil, myrrh, cinnamon, other spices and probably hashish or pot, because the recipe included the Hebrew word for *cannabis*. Apparently, the holy hash oil was used every time Moses spoke with God. He entered a tent, covered himself in the mixture, put some on the altar, burned it and, voila, talked to the Lord in the pillar of smoke. What happens if you shift the focus from the relationship between God and Moses, to Moses and the oil and smoke?

"What happens in this scenario, this alternative," Bennett said, "is that Moses becomes like a shaman and on behalf of the tribe he leads, he goes in, takes the sacred plant and ponders what he should do, and then goes out and says, this is what the Lord your God has said you should do."

Bennett stared at me.

What an interesting take. The herb of a thousand faces.

"Now the oil was originally just limited to the high priests," he continued gleefully, "but at the time of the Age of Kings this was extended to include the kings. So we have the biblical account of Samuel anointing Saul, right? And he tells Saul that when you have this oil come upon you, you will feel the Lord's spirit come upon you and great power. Saul is so overcome by the experience he rips off his clothes, and they find him the next day hiding in the baggage. And it's like a classic shamanic experience. You are going to feel God's power and *ahh*."

That's about the time, Bennett said, that Jewish religious authorities appear to have prohibited the old oil routine and associated it with the worshipping of false idols. By the time of Jeremiah, Bennett said, "God is saying, What do I care for this incense of Sheba, this Cannabis from a distant land does not please me."

I was fascinated. Bennett's work suggested the anointing oil was suppressed until the early Christian period, when it resurfaced as a symbol of Jewish independence and authentic tradition: Messiah, the "anointed" one, Christ in Greek.

"In the early Christian movement, the anointing oil plays a major, major role for the first few centuries," he said. "One of the main points of contention with the Gnostics and the group that became the Roman Catholic Church was water baptism versus anointing with this holy oil. The Gnostics say there's only water in the baptism but fire in the anointing oil. Through the anointing oil we are initiated into unfading bliss. They describe Jesus performing an initiating ceremony with an incense that contained a wonder."

He has concluded there is no question that there were psychoactive sacraments in use.

The plant's connection to the world's other major religions is equally rich, he assured me.

He wished he could spend more time on his anthropology. But on top of his TV production efforts, he was working hard to keep his wife, Renee Boje, in the country. She and their two-year-old son, Shiva, were out back in the Zen garden waiting for the band to play and the party for Emery to begin.

Boje was one of the growing number of American refugee claimants in Canada fleeing a hefty jail sentence for a pot-related offence. Ken Hayes, who ran the Spirit Within on Commercial Drive, was another. He had vanished in recent days, after police said they had made an undercover marijuana buy at his store and wanted to talk to him. Steve Tuck, Steve Kubby and Kubby's wife, Michele, on the Sunshine Coast were others—and they were spearheading their own legal challenges of the law to secure medical access to pot. Dozens were arriving every year.

Shortly after California passed Proposition 215, Renee Boje began working for cancer patient Todd McCormick, one of the leading U.S. medical marijuana activists. She was to be an artist for a book he was writing on the production of medical-quality marijuana. McCormick and his pal and co-writer, best-selling author Peter McWilliams, who had cancer and AIDS, had taken their $100,000 book advance, rented an L.A. mansion dubbed "the Cannabis Castle," and were growing medical-quality marijuana for research and distribution to other patients. In the first federal raid on a state-approved medical marijuana site, McCormick, McWilliams, Boje and others were arrested by the DEA who also seized 4,000 plants.

While in jail, McWilliams was thrown into solitary confinement because he was supposedly using cannabis while in prison. He said they were detecting traces from his previous use, since THC stays in the body for months. He smoked marijuana to control the nausea from cancer and AIDS treatments. He died choking on his own vomit under house arrest in June 2000.

The federal government claims to have witnesses who saw Boje watering plants in the grow-op. On the basis of this testimony and Boje's refusal to testify against the others, she faced a mandatory minimum sentence of ten years to life. She chose to flee to Canada.

After telling me his wife's story, Bennett just shook his head and returned to his work. I wandered upstairs to see if Emery had arrived from Saskatchewan. He was at the airport, CEO Michelle Rainey said. I joined her on the couch to wait. The thirty-three-year-old was on tenterhooks awaiting Emery's return after more than two months.

"Has it been easier or harder with him in jail?" I asked.

She guffawed. "My nickname for him is Captain Chaos, and even when he was in jail he was causing as much chaos as you can possibly imagine," she admitted. "If they would not have let the man have access to a phone or a computer, life would have been great. I could just zipper his mouth."

Once he was out of the way, she had closed Iboga Therapy House. As dear as it was to Emery's heart, the experimental free drug treatment was costing $120,000 a year and Rainey said they no longer could afford it. She wanted to see a doctor, clinic or philanthropist take over the research and expand it. She also had managed to bring the earlier cash-flow crisis under control—for the time being. The business was always precarious.

"That man can still spend money," she said.

The cheer from the front of the store told us he was back.

After serving sixty-four days as the most public prisoner in Canada, Emery walked back into his headquarters noticeably thinner and less ebullient. He smiled and embraced each of his staff. The women wept.

While imprisoned, he appeared on open-line radio shows, he published a well-read blog—his own *Ballad of Reading Gaol*—he worked in the prison cleaning toilets, he organized inmate activities, and he exposed the utter moral emptiness of the prohibition and those who blindly support it.

Emery's eyes misted up at the sight of a huge bouquet of flowers—dahlias, birds of paradise, great huge blooms of vibrant orange and pink and scarlet. He unwrapped a gift— an elaborate glass bong. More cheering.

He handed the bong to Kaara to fill. She passed it back and Emery took a huge toke.

"Let my incarceration galvanize you to action," he said. "We need to ensure that the new law allows people to possess. To grow for themselves. And to share with others. Otherwise, it will be flawed."

He took aim at Saskatchewan. "No job will be harder than to liberate Saskatchewan from the dark grip of back-wardness, bigotry and the perverse urge to punish," he intoned. "But we will liberate this province, and we will bring the whole country to the glory of a free nation once and for all, one nation under cannabis."

He spoke with the seriousness of a modern-day Paine, declaring that *these* are the days that try men's souls. It was ever so. Another huge cheer went up and the crowd poured downstairs to party.

Most of the pot world was present—diva Watermelon, Compassion Club foundress Hilary Black and her successor Rielle Capler, lawyer John Conroy, David Malmo-Levine . . . Even Charles Scott had flown in, with Mason jars of his finest bud, samples of the pot he was submitting at this year's Cannabis Cup.

I was surprised, given his plans to go retail and compete head-to-head with Emery. But the first full-page *High Times* advertisement for his Reeferman Seeds had yet to run. Emery would still be oblivious about Scott's intentions. For the night at least, tensions between the two were in the future.

I asked Emery how he was doing.

"I hated the food," he said. "You could get any amount of sugar or junk food you want but forget about fresh fruit or vegetables. They said that would be too easy to turn into moonshine. Yuck!" He laughed.

"It made me realize that once we free the weed, we've got to get involved in prison reform. What we are doing to people is wrong."

MEDICINAL MARIJUANA

the pot of gold

IN UPHOLDING THE VALIDITY of the criminal prohibition of cannabis, the Supreme Court of Canada appended to its reasons for judgment the California Compassionate Use Act of 1996, as well as legislation from Hawaii. The Californian law promises the "seriously ill" access to marijuana where recommended by their doctor if it "provides relief," whereas the Hawaiian law requires a diagnosis of a "debilitating medical condition" that produces one or more of "cachexia or wasting syndrome; severe pain; severe nausea, seizures, including those characteristic of epilepsy; or severe and persistent muscle spasms, including those characteristic of multiple sclerosis or Crohn's disease."

The U.S. government, however, has insisted since 1937 that there is no such thing as medical marijuana. In 1971, it passed the Controlled Substances Act, declaring cannabis to have no medical value. Yet the strongest current assault on the legal prohibition of pot comes from patients and doctors fighting to overcome that blatant ideological lie. Many of them believe marijuana will one day be recognized as a miracle drug; most just know it works and don't want to go to the black market to buy medicine.

Washington has maintained its stance and as recently as 2002 issued a directive to federal prosecutors spelling out the Bush administration's view: "Marijuana and violence are linked . . . Marijuana is a gateway drug . . . marijuana legalization would be a nightmare . . . marijuana is not a medicine . . . no drug matches the threat posed by marijuana."

Not one of those scare-mongering statements can be supported with evidence. Many states certainly have come to that conclusion. Alaska, Arizona, California, Colorado, Hawaii, Maine, Nevada, Oregon and Washington went ahead and passed, or have voter approval for, medical marijuana laws. As has the District of Columbia! California voters in 1996 voted to allow the possession and use of marijuana for medical purposes with a doctor's recommendation. Yet the U.S. Supreme Court said as recently as June 2005 that Washington could still prosecute medical patients, saying state laws didn't shield them from federal prosecution.

The only remaining reason for governmental resistance to implementing a broad, workable medical program in the United States and Canada is that it will make enforcement against recreational users impossible. Police and prohibitionist policy-makers are sure of that. They view medical pot as the Trojan Horse of the legalization movement. But the numbers, the demand and the potential profits that medical marijuana represents are overwhelming even the law-enforcement lobby. With the prodding of the courts in Canada, the federal government has finally established a medical marijuana program.

Ottawa has been dragging its feet, but it is slowly moving down the road and is being forced to open up the medical cannabis market, which many think will prove to be exponentially larger than the recreational market—perhaps $20 billion domestically.

Brian Taylor, the fifty-eight-year-old former mayor of Grand Forks, has been waiting for that payoff for more than a decade. I originally met him in the mid-1990s, when he was just getting on the medical marijuana bandwagon. For Taylor, the pot of gold better arrive soon because he was now paying his bills by bouncing in the local bar and dishwashing when they don't need a heavy.

"Aren't you a little old for that?"

He nodded wearily. "I use the line 'I've fucked bigger guys than you when I was in jail so get out of my way.'"

Taylor sported a long grey ponytail when I met up with him in the summer of 2004 at his home in southeastern B.C. He'd grown up in nearby Keremeos and thought of himself as Native when he was younger because he spent most of his time with friends from the local Indian bands. He had a stylized Haida raven tattooed on his right biceps. He stood in the kitchen area of his double-wide trailer and wistfully stared across the valley at the rays of morning sun lancing through the clouds over the mountains. In an hour or so, he would sell his horse, Rocking Comet, a dark-coloured Morgan.

"I left the water on last week and flooded the grow-room," he sighed. "If I had been in an apartment . . ."

He was running three lights, which cost him roughly $150 to $200 a month inclusive. A house with electric heat would use more power than that, he said, so he was below the radar in terms of getting caught because of hydro consumption. He plugged in the coffeemaker and began to fill the Volcano—inhalation device of choice among the cognoscenti.

"Gets the heart going," he quipped. "It's a very civilized approach."

Taylor unhooked the ballooned cellophane bag. He took a toke like a diver sucking oxygen. A radio was tuned to CBC.

"I wish I had got into the marijuana business in the eighties," he said. "I would be rich right now and driving around
in a fancy car. I didn't figure it out until the end of the eighties when biker gangs were beginning to come into the
Okanagan and offer set-ups for people, fifty-fifty splits."

He took a big toke, held it, exhaled and continued.

"They'd bring everything in, set up your room and you'd
run it and get 50 per cent of it. There was a sliding scale—
you got 50 per cent the first time, a little more the next time
and by the end of the third or fourth cycle, you owned it all.
It was quite a scheme."

Taylor had about 3 hectares on the western lip of the valley. He planted his first hemp crop here in 1995, but the
field today lay fallow. Nearby pot farmers were convinced
pollen from the hemp would ruin their crops, so he grew a
big field at another location. Highly, highly unlikely, but
with a really big wind, maybe, like the apocryphal sirocco
blamed for carrying Moroccan pollen to Spain.

"I had death threats," Taylor recalled. "I had people in
bars coming up to me telling me to get the fuck out of town
or we're going to kick your ass. That sort of stuff. Writing on
my door once—GET THE FUCK OUT!" He shrugged. "Not
very literate, but how much can you get on a door with a big
pencil? It wasn't even a crayon."

His double-wide gazed east at a spectacular vista of
undulating lea, the town of some five thousand folk and the
surrounding mountains, the most distant of them purple in
the morning light. Behind his trailer was a barn that had seen
several incarnations—party central for his band, home of the
Grand Forks Yacht Club and magazine production centre. At
one time, two carpenters were busily producing individual
grow-boxes that resembled wardrobes. It was Taylor's last get-
rich scheme.

Each of the units, of Baltic birch, was equipped with a

single lightbulb, a small bathroom fan and two tiny pumps—
one for the air and the other for the hydroponic system that
fed the plants. The unit allowed anyone to produce an ounce
of high-quality pot weekly with a minimum of fuss and attention. They were even designed to be wheelchair accessible,
because the controls on a standard grow unit are too high.
They were now built elsewhere.

These days, the barn served as a store, activist meeting
centre and home to the monthly *Cannabis Health Journal*.
The staff were currently working without pay until the
finances were more secure.

Taylor has gone through several transformations himself.
He was an aggressive born-again hemp supporter at first, then
leader of Emery's Marijuana Party and now he was a key
player in the medical marijuana movement. His start-up
funding came from Advanced Nutrients, which remained the
magazine's sustaining advertiser for months afterward.

"I've been in the marijuana industry about thirteen years,"
Taylor said as he poured the coffee. "I started in Kelowna. I
was working on the child development centre—I was an
important bigwig in the city. Tommy Capozzi and I ran all
the bingo halls and we made a lot of money. I had quite the
mansion. I was picked to go with the John Howard Society to
tour prisons."

In the Kent maximum-security institution, he met two
twenty-something inmates from Prince Edward Island. They
had gone to Mexico, bought a boat, loaded it with marijuana
and sailed north. The U.S. Coast Guard spotted them off the
coast of Washington State and, with a helicopter overhead,
the would-be smugglers jettisoned bales of pot. By the time
they docked, an escort of Coast Guard and police boats, even
a submarine, were alongside.

"They weren't a danger to society but they got nine-and-
a-half years for that little misadventure," Taylor said. "Nine-

and-a-half years. They were in with murderers. The group I was with, all leading community people, went back to the motel. Everybody was just so upset at what happened to these guys. Finally it got around to, well, did anyone bring any marijuana?" He chuckled.

"What a bunch of hypocrites! Here we were sitting around with these guys in jail for nine-and-a-half years while in our group I think only one person didn't bring pot. Out of the whole group. It was a big eye-opener for me. I made a commitment not to be part of that hypocrisy."

Taylor took up the cause of cannabis the way Oral Roberts took up religion.

With his political career awaiting resuscitation, Taylor directed his energies toward medical marijuana. He formed the Cannabis Health Foundation in the spring of 2002 as a non-profit organization dedicated to promoting safe medicinal practices. Taylor pulled out the current issue of his magazine and pointed proudly to an archival picture on the cover of an elderly couple from Georgia, in the former Soviet Union, sitting in front of a lush behemoth of a *sativa* plant.

"Barry Verigin brought it back," he said.

Verigin's sprawling home was about a quarter-mile away. He was the son of J.J. Verigen Sr., the current leader of the Doukhobors, Russian pacifists who fled to Canada and settled throughout this area, making it famous for borscht and dark rye bread.

The Doukhobors traditionally used the plant medicinally, and hemp oil in their cooking. Cannabis has a long history across the Soviet Union: the steppes are one of its suspected birthplaces, and the record of domestic and religious cannabis use stretches back centuries. It could be found among the archeological ruins, was everywhere in the ancient texts. Greek historian Herodotus described Scythian tribes from modern-day Ukraine throwing flower tops onto the hot stones in their sauna tents. Still, the few local Doukhobors who grew cannabis for the traditional herbal remedies were surprised when draft-dodging hippies arrived in the valley and began smoking their grass. It was a good story and brought Taylor a lot of kudos, though the magazine was a struggle overall. Circulation and advertising were both a problem.

"We distribute through the network," Taylor said.

The network was essentially the growing Canadian Cannabis Coalition, which had its roots in an e-mail list assembled back in 1999 by activists interested in setting standards and exchanging information. About twenty entrepreneurs, volunteers and professionals—including BC Compassion Club Society pioneer Hilary Black and Dr. Paul Hornby—attended the group's inaugural meeting in Grand Forks, hosted by Taylor. The group grew from there into a strong lobby voice.

"We have one hundred advertisers that are holding us together but we have to morph," Taylor added. "We have to get bigger or find another revenue stream. One thing that might work is to distribute with a donation expectation. That way we can up our circulation and keep growing in terms of numbers, which helps us on the advertising side."

Other publications view pot through the prism of popular culture and pitch themselves at the young, predominantly male marijuana grower and consumer. They have a broader spectrum of advertisers to draw from because of their focus, and, in the case of *Cannabis Culture*, heavily subsidized advertising from Emery's seed company.

"They're after a different market than we are," Taylor said of the other publications. "We're after the shirt-and-tie market. We don't say 'fuck.' We say 'penis,' if we have to. We don't do other drugs. We don't do pee testing. We don't advertise pit bulls. These are all things that we think would put us into another category and keep us out of schools and libraries and doctors' offices."

He was after a serious audience, people who had got beyond the snicker factor and were trying to find solutions to the thicket of concerns keeping marijuana from people who needed it for pain relief. Dr. Lester Grinspoon and Laurence McKinney especially inspired him.

Grinspoon, a faculty emeritus of the Harvard Medical School in the Department of Psychiatry, is the dean of cannabis researchers. He started studying it in 1967 and published two groundbreaking works—*Marijuana Reconsidered* in 1971 and *Marijuana, the Forbidden Medicine* in 1993. He has been at the forefront of the fight to rehabilitate the plant's pharmaceutical reputation.

"What is the government's problem with medical marijuana?" Grinspoon asked. "The problem, as seen through the eyes of the government, is the belief that as growing numbers of people observe relatives and friends using marijuana as a medicine, they will come to understand that this is a drug which does not conform to the description the government has been pushing for years. They will first come to appreciate what a remarkable medicine it really is; it is less toxic than almost any other medicine in the pharmacopoeia; it is, like Aspirin, remarkably versatile; and it is less expensive than the conventional medicines it displaces."

McKinney is a Harvard MBA who twigged to marijuana's medical potential back in the early 1970s. He supplied the seeds that were the genesis of the U.S. government's marijuana farm in Mississippi, he connected medical marijuana pioneer Robert Randall to the UCLA doctors who created the first American "medical cannabis" program, and in 1975 he figured he could get a patent to extract THC from cannabis in India and ship it back to the United States.

The Purdue Pharma drug company was willing to back him and he founded the Cannabis Corporation of America—years before the creation of today's main firms, GW Pharmaceuticals in Britain, HortaPharm in Holland, Prairie Plant Systems and Cannasat in Canada. McKinney said he could raise $100 million in a week if the United States abandoned the prohibition. In 1980, he was awarded the first cannabis improvement patent—a $29.95 device called "the Maximizer" and guaranteed to improve your smoke. U.S. paraphernalia laws killed the product. McKinney changed the name of his company to Cambridge Pharmaceutical Laboratories and began selling natural skin products unconnected to cannabis.

Taylor said his main concern about medical marijuana activism was the vicissitudes of the law. Remember old John Sinclair, the pot dealer immortalized by John Lennon back in the days of Nixon? The wrong judge, the wrong part of the country, the wrong day of the week, and you could lose years of your life. Look what was happening to Don Briere. Look what happened to Emery.

Taylor and his girlfriend were splitting, in part because they disagreed about how in-your-face they should be about pot. She favoured a more low-key, work-with-people strategy; Taylor wanted to kick the stall down.

A woman arrived just as he was discussing the difference of opinion.

"Hey, Barb," he said.

Barb Cornelius was his ex, but still his accountant. She has lupus, uses marijuana for its symptoms and bakes cookies. She also gives seminars on how the marijuana industry can benefit municipal economies.

She put her jacket on a hook. "I'm still trying to figure out how to do the edibles thing," Cornelius said to me. "I'm supplying doctors already. Cancer clinics."

But she was perplexed as to how to determine the potency of baked goods for those who didn't want to smoke. "It would be nice to get some testing done so we know the strength," she said. "That's always the issue—is it too strong or too weak? That's the real challenge. How do you gauge what a cancer patient needs in a single dose? Brian will eat three cookies, compared to the half most patients are taking. I haven't been able to figure out how to test or who can test. The government supports edibles but they won't help us to develop this. And they won't let you make concentrates, so pot butter is illegal."

Taylor nodded vigorously. "They're trapped in a position where they can't allow things that are not controllable," he said. "They are not against hash and concentrates being used. They just don't know how they are going to license people to make them without losing control over the whole system."

He thought the government was fast approaching a crossroads. Health Canada would have to look at a decentralized supply system or the individual licensing of patients.

Taylor wanted to see small farms spread around the country, a competitive, free-enterprise diversified approach. He thought many people would still grow under lights, and nutrient, growing equipment and light manufacturers would keep doing well.

"I've been trying to get science and technology money applied to this area," Taylor said. "I have a guy who has developed a unit that runs on centrifugal force. He spins his pot at thirty revolutions a minute inside this thing we call Willy Wonka's Chamber. We have become a conduit for products coming out of the underground onto the open market. Vaporizers are another good example, where we have the convergence of technology into this new open market. The Americans, by enforcing their paraphernalia laws, have made it really lucrative for us. We sell tons of stuff across the line. That is our biggest customer. We just ship it labelled 'Medical Equipment.'"

From his veranda, he pointed to the U.S. border, a slash on the mountains at the end of the valley. "You know, the town of Molson's just down the road," Taylor said, and grinned.

It was one of the many communities along the border that benefited during Prohibition by producing alcohol in Canada and then smuggling it into the dry United States at a premium. Like the pot growers of today, the rum-runners set up in rural locations in the B.C. Interior or on the Prairies where the border was little monitored and smuggling a breeze.

"It's sort of fitting, don't you think, that here we are at the end of another era of prohibition. Just consider the size of the legitimate medical market if, as expected, even a small percentage of those who suffer from AIDS, cancer, chronic pain, arthritis, premenstrual syndrome or degenerative diseases like multiple sclerosis seek relief from marijuana." Arthritis alone affects one in seven Canadians.

"My sister has leukemia and she's a user," Taylor added. His dad used it too, and maintained a personal grow unit in his seniors' apartment up until he died.

"The bankers say it's one in two—50 per cent of the population is directly affected by the marijuana industry."

He looked at his watch. "I got to go. Time to sell Comet." He would soon relinquish the editorship of the magazine, as well. He sloughed off the melancholy with a toke and headed out the door.

The Vancouver Island Compassion Society (VICS) occupies the ground floor of an old mid-century home in downtown Victoria. There are lots of plants, a sofa, a bookshelf and Chinese scrolls bearing images of cranes and landscapes. As well as being the capital region's central compassion club, it was previously the city's first school of Chinese medicine.

"I wanted to make it comfortable for a fifty-five-year-old woman who's just been diagnosed with breast cancer," founder Philippe Lucas said, leading me through to a large presentation room in the back. "This is an office designed with Martha Stewart in mind. There is no smoking here or in the environs."

Although, here in the back on his desk, there's another Volcano machine. "This is fantastic," enthused the slight, fair-haired, thirty-four-year-old former teacher. "Nothing else comes close to it on the market, but it's $700 with our discount and that's too much for people to afford." As in Vancouver, most of his membership is on some kind of disability pension because of a medical condition.

Lucas is one of the most visible faces and one of the most articulate voices in the national medical marijuana debate. He sat on the City of Victoria downtown advisory committee, ran for council and actively participated in civic issues. On top of that, he works hard to integrate his services with local social-welfare organizations. He has taught at the University of Victoria, which placed nursing students in the VICS. He regularly addresses AIDS Vancouver Island, the Hepatitis C Society of Canada, Persons with AIDS . . .

"I had twenty-three chiefs of police from China come in and I did a presentation to them," Lucas continued. "They were here to look at our legal system, and one of their hosts was our landlord, and I told them what we do at the VICS for an hour and a half, with him acting as a translator."

While the Chinese have an issue with "illegal drugs," herbal medicine is something they completely understand, he said. Cannabis has been part of the country's pharmacopoeia since before Europeans were bathing properly.

Lucas also is conducting research, in conjunction with the University of California and the University of British

Columbia, on marijuana's effects on hepatitis C, pregnancy-related nausea and pain. The results so far in the pregnancy study indicate that marijuana was found to be very effective or effective for more than 90 per cent of women who suffered severe morning sickness, both for nausea relief and appetite stimulation.

"Back here is where we make our hash as well," Lucas said, pointing to a set of fine-mesh screens sitting on a nearby counter. "My co-worker Chad is the expert and he builds these screens."

Hash isn't recognized by Health Canada and remains illegal, but compassion clubs are clamouring for Ottawa to change the law and do some research. Hash and kif are by-products created by isolating and concentrating marijuana resin glands. Cannabis resin contains the most cannabinoids, such as THC, which give pot its kick, and terpenoids, the essential oils that give it aroma and flavour. The resin is held in a gland on the end of a trichome stalk, an extension of the plant. Hash, kif, oil and other concentrates are more potent, and patients don't have to smoke so much to get the desired effect.

You can isolate the trichomes by rubbing the flowering plant with your hands and then scraping off the resin and pressing it into a ball—which people do in places such as Nepal. A more common method, particularly in the Middle East, is to shake, beat or press the dried flowers and leaves on a fine mesh, set of screens or even muslin. The powder that falls through is smoked as kif. You can compress it into hash. More recently, ice water has been used to mash the cannabis and extract the trichomes via the principle of density.

"That water-extraction hash is way overrated," Lucas said. "I think what it's done is democratized the entire hash-making process nicely, but you lose the feel for it. We've done an actual comparison. I did a by-product seminar for Marc Emery. Chad and I took the same amount of pot—I made an Ice-o-lator bag of hash and he hand-screened his shake. With the same amount, he ended up with twice the amount of hash and was done in half the time. And his product was better. It tasted better."

There are good scientific reasons for that. Outside of the cannabinoids and psychoactive chemicals in pot, the flavonols and terpenes are water-soluble. They're washed away and you lose flavour by making water-extraction hash. "I also think you lose some of the therapeutic effect," Lucas said.

But today, hash and other by-products are not on his mind. Lucas is concerned about the recent raid of his club's grow-op—the so-called Vancouver Island Therapeutic Cannabis Research Institute. Computers, hydroponic equipment and nine hundred plants were seized. The pot was for the nearly four hundred patients at VICS and Canadians for Safe Access (a mail-order service for those outside of the city).

The club couldn't afford to lose $40,000 in equipment and Lucas was on the lease. He opened a large three-ring binder filled with pictures of the operation he had designed. They were stunning. Hundreds of luxuriant, verdant plants— thirty-five strains. And then photos of the severed stumps, butchered plants and damaged growing equipment left by police. His eyes welled.

"Now we're back on the black market, [even though] 90 per cent of Canadians support medical marijuana," said Lucas, who's also director of communications for DrugSense. "This is not how Canadians want their law-enforcement resources spent."

Lucas began using pot as a medication after a 1995 employment medical examination revealed he had hepatitis C. He began looking into cannabis and credits it with liberating him from two vices: "For me, marijuana was an exit drug from alcohol and tobacco, not a gateway drug."

Pioneers Hilary Black and Dennis Peron inspired him. One of California's best-known medical marijuana activists, Peron was a war vet who had gone to Vietnam and come back to the United States as committed to the counterculture as when he left. He was a key figure in San Francisco's gay political scene and started the Cannabis Buyers' Club back in 1991.

Most people don't realize that nine U.S. state legislatures and the District of Columbia have endorsed medical marijuana and try to protect bona fide patients from prosecution for personal possession and use. There is even a federal medical-marijuana program that was established in 1976. But only a handful of people continue to receive a monthly tin of U.S. government pot, because Washington stopped accepting compassionate-use applications in 1991, in the face of exponentially increasing numbers. They said the program gave "the wrong signal" and "there is not a shred of evidence that smoking marijuana assists a person with AIDS."

That's one of the reasons politically active gays such as Peron demanded state support. Peron was central to the development of Proposition 215. It became California's Compassionate Use Act, which exempts from state criminal prosecution patients obtaining and using marijuana with a doctor's recommendation for "cancer, anorexia, AIDS, chronic fatigue, spasticity, glaucoma, arthritis, migraine, or any other illness for which marijuana provides relief."

In response to the proposition, the U.S. government funded the National Academy of Sciences to scrutinize the efficacy of marijuana as a medicine. The 1999 NAS report acknowledged pot's therapeutic value. As more and more research continues to establish the medical worth of marijuana, governments are finding it increasingly difficult to defend absolute prohibition.

The more Lucas learned about marijuana, the more he read about Peron and Black, the more he decided he wanted to operate a compassion club. Before long, he was growing his own so he wouldn't be subject to the vagaries of the black market.

Lucas officially opened the non-profit VICS in 1999, initially in Oak Bay. A year later it moved downtown, and later it moved again—to within a block of the biggest local police station. Discretion and community relations are its hallmarks. Like the Vancouver club, Lucas's has always been very thorough about its registration process—this was not a Da Kine Café.

Lucas was arrested for cultivation in 2000, but the charges were dismissed by Judge Robert Higinbotham, who said he "enhanced other people's lives at minimal or no risk to society . . . He provided that which the government was unable to provide: a safe and high-quality supply of marijuana to those needing it for medicinal purposes."

The club uses the quote on its literature.

"All our members have doctors' recommendations," Lucas emphasized. "We phone in those registrations to confirm them with the doctor; otherwise we wait for a fax confirmation. And all of our members have to sign a contract stating they won't reuse or redistribute the product. And that they won't use the product in the general area of the organization. It's frustrating to have to tell people where and when they can use their medicine. But we feel it's a necessity right now, with the law the way it is. In order to protect the other 429 members, we can't have one member smoking pot outside our organization, drawing unnecessary problems, heat or complaints."

The man who gave cannabis-using Canadians the greatest hope that the end of prohibition is in sight was former health minister Allan Rock. He opened the door to legal cultivation and introduced a regime that plays havoc with police grow-busting strategies.

In July 2000, the Ontario Court of Appeal struck down the pot possession section of the federal anti-drug law, saying it violated the Canadian Charter of Rights and Freedoms because no provision was made for medical users. One year later, Canada became the second country (after the United States) to adopt a system regulating the medicinal use of marijuana. Holland followed suit.

Canada's response to the judiciary's concern was to implement the Marihuana Medical Access Regulations. They outlined three categories of people who can possess cannabis: those with terminal illnesses with a prognosis of death within one year, those with symptoms associated with serious medical conditions, and those suffering from symptoms with other medical conditions. Severe arthritis, cancer, AIDS, HIV infection, MS and several other ailments are specified.

For those allowed to grow, the rules set maximums for the number of indoor and outdoor plants, authorize a grower to receive and possess seeds, and allow for site inspections and criminal-record checks. Ottawa also awarded Prairie Plant Systems of Saskatoon a contract to grow marijuana for research and qualified patients.

Lucas thinks the program has been a disaster—patients have had enormous difficulty obtaining an official exemption from Health Canada to avoid police harassment, and at first, many thought the government's pot wasn't up to snuff. In Lucas's opinion, the country was having difficulty because doctors were dragging their heels.

The mainstream Canadian medical community seemed as confused as ordinary people about what should be done. The Canadian Medical Protective Association and the Canadian Medical Association told doctors not to participate because of potential legal liability. They argued doctors should not be the gatekeepers to the use of marijuana because there had been none of the usual testing for dosage and quality that drugs usually undergo before public release. They also maintained there was no solid evidence, only anecdotal support, for marijuana's effectiveness and scant data as to its medicinal qualities. They feared future lawsuits from patients if pot proved to have unexpectedly pernicious side effects, such as occurred with tobacco.

The lack of research on cannabis is also one of Lucas's prime concerns. Ottawa announced a five-year, $7.5 million Medical Marijuana Research Plan as part of its response to the judicial slap. But only two studies were approved and only one was proceeding in the final year of funding. The study on AIDS wasting and appetite was cancelled after $800,000 was spent. The single study was at McGill. After nearly four years and $270,000, they were still recruiting.

"To us, this is unacceptable," Lucas said. "This can be done much more easily. It's frustrating. They still haven't seen fit to initiate direct contact and research with us, or offer us some kind of licensing regime that would make legal what we are doing now."

Lucas is among the most strident critics of Health Canada and the medical marijuana program. Through a Freedom of Information Act request, he learned that 30 per cent of patients originally returned the government-supplied pot. He conducted tests that indicated the initial batch of cannabis contained less than 6 per cent THC.

"I have to tell you that if we were talking about MS patients returning their antispasmodics, or AIDS patients returning their anti-nausea drugs, we would have a significant health scandal on our hands," he said. "For some reason, and because it's medical marijuana, it doesn't strike the same chord, although we are still dealing with AIDS and cancer patients and critically and chronically ill folks."

He pulled a small foil pouch from a drawer and emptied some of the contents onto the desk. It looked like a handful of pot from the days of Mexican mini-bricks, the ground-up whole plant—stem, sticks, seeds and all.

"There's no way I could sell a gram of this to any of our members without them throwing it back in my face," he maintained. "We only sell triple-A, high-grade product—we create what I like to call 'pot snobs.'"

That's why he was so upset about the latest police raid. They destroyed the medicine of 430 VICS members, but also a kilo put away for a $500,000 "smoked cannabis and chronic pain double-blind clinical study" funded by the Marijuana Policy Project (MPP) in the United States. They destroyed genetics that were unique to the VICS and set back research at least a year. Lucas found it particularly annoying that health bureaucrats pushed pilot programs for safe-injection sites and free heroin trials but stymied attempts to open access to medical marijuana.

"I, of course, completely support all of these harm-reduction initiatives, but to place more importance on the health and welfare of heroin addicts while completely dismissing that of an AIDS patient or a hep C patient who might need medical marijuana—" he threw up his hands. "To me, it just doesn't sit well. They've been resistant since day one on this program. This was a program that was initiated as a result of a court finding that they needed to do something. I really think we are just not moving forward."

In five years of operation, fewer then eight hundred patients had been registered for a marijuana exemption at a cost of $12 million. It's the illusion of access. Lucas saw the future darkly.

In California, there are seventy thousand reportedly registered medical marijuana users and most of those are getting their pot through compassion clubs. Lucas said he even knew of a doctor who spent the day driving his Jaguar between three clubs doing nothing but picking up bags of cash. In

Oakland, the medical cannabis clubs were said to be generating $70 million a year in gross revenue. Lucas said that at the least, he wanted to see a legal distinction drawn between medicinal and recreational cannabis.

"The police don't differentiate, which is why our production facility was busted without giving due consideration to the research and the medicine that was being grown. We have people who are suffering all over Canada right now who could benefit from access to medicinal cannabis, and our current federal program is denying that access. I have to point out that not only are we—the compassion clubs— supplying more people than Health Canada, we are doing more research than Health Canada and we're doing all this at no cost to the taxpayer."

For cannabis, Lucas believes the only thing that makes sense is legalization with a tax and a regulated regime, the same kind of regime used for alcohol. You can have an age restriction and regulations to govern quality control and commercial sales. Home growing would be allowed and there would be community-based research, production and distribution facilities.

"I see a centralized role for Health Canada without a doubt, because it's not every city that's going to have a compassion society. I think it's important that there be a centralized supply available through pharmacies. But I think that for those cities and those areas that do benefit from having a compassion club or society around, we could take away a lot of the fears and the potential harms of the black market, in terms of cultivation and distribution of this product. Our production facility was a lab setting. Everything was tested for purity and consistency. That's the kind of thing we can offer medical marijuana users, and I think that's the direction we should move."

The other point, he said, was that the government was forcing people to smoke. There were no alternatives under the federal program. The VICS and other compassion clubs offered alternatives—edibles, oral mucosal sprays, tinctures and oil-based products.

"We are doing the harm reduction that the government really should be," Lucas lamented, shaking his head.

Research around the world suggests without question that marijuana helps treat chronic pain, MS, epilepsy, glaucoma and post-traumatic stress disorder. In Israel, they were doing direct applications of synthetic THC to brain-trauma patients and a company named Pharmos was seeking FDA approval for a synthetic cannabinoid that would be ingested and used by paramedics to forestall brain damage.

In Holland, by comparison, they created a medical marijuana program two years ago by hiring two different growers to produce different strains for different conditions. Healthcare coverage paid for the cannabis the same as for any other medication. If you bought pot through a pharmacy, it was covered by your health-care plan. Already one thousand people were signed up for the program versus the eight hundred Canada had approved. Doctors in Holland were onside. They said a medical marijuana program was required, otherwise people were driven to the black market where there was no quality control as well as myriad other dangers.

Sitting in his back office fingering the government marijuana, Lucas said that is the biggest problem—the risks the government is imposing on sick people.

"I think cannabis is much better regulated under natural health products legislation," Lucas said. "I think it is much more in keeping with traditional Chinese medicine, with herbal medicine, than it is with standard pharmaceutical medicine. The side effects are so few and far between. I'm not saying all cannabis use is safe. I'm not saying all cannabis use is healthy. But I do not think it should be given a restrictive regime above and beyond that which we use for very dangerous, therapeutic drugs. All that we're asking for is a medicinal cannabis policy that is based on science, reason and compassion. Right now what we're seeing is a policy based on fear, misinformation and, really, hysteria and a tremendous lack of compassion."

Health Canada should be doing better, he said. Tens of thousands of Canadians, he believes, want access to medical marijuana but are being stymied by the bureaucrats.

About an hour up the Island Highway, at Duncan, Eric Nash and his partner Wendy Little were growing marijuana legally. The couple, two of the several hundred people allowed to cultivate for medical use, had just published *Sell Marijuana Legally*, a step-by-step guide to making money by becoming federally licensed to sell pot. Theirs was exactly the kind of model Lucas favoured.

Little, 44, was a teacher in the health-care system who worked for non-profit groups and private firms. Nash, 47, worked for the provincial government and the City of Victoria as a communications consultant. The couple entered the Health Canada program as designated growers in 2002, and now supply marijuana to five chronically ill patients from ninety plants grown at their Island Harvest facility.

"People were always asking, 'How do we get started?' and it just made sense to put it all together in a book," said Nash.

When we met, they were trying to win authorization to grow for thirty more customers and for another 450 plants. It was never the government's intention to allow the kind of commercial supply network Nash and Little would establish and that Lucas had growing. The government feared such a situation would require a significant administrative infrastructure for regulatory surveillance, exacerbate cross-border tensions with the United States, create problems of diversion and aggravate existing drug abuse by making policing impossible.

Lucas, Nash and Little, and just about everyone else who actually worked in the medical side of the industry, disagreed.

Nash and Little began researching marijuana half a decade ago after a relative with Parkinson's disease asked for help buying some pot. Today, they are a hub in the cross-country medical marijuana movement and maintain an important Internet resource—medicalmarihuana.ca. They also founded Medusers, an on-line legal patients' and growers' group representing about one in ten of those registered under the federal program. And they teach a university course about the system.

They have honed their public presentation and are always prepared for the journalists who arrive or call regularly. They are perfect interviews, speaking in sentences and repeating answers to the same questions over and over again without ever sounding tired of explaining why what they do is no different than any other small business.

"Our book is about our intent to comply with the government program and how to do this in a legal framework as opposed to the black market," Nash told me. "It's been incredibly satisfying. I've never done anything in my life this satisfying. We are supplying a product that helps people in their day-to-day existence deal with their pain issues."

Nash and Little grow two different strains, a *sativa* and an *indica*, which they sell for $100 an ounce. Aside from providing for their local customers, they are shipping to patients in Alberta, B.C. and Ontario, who sign for the product on delivery.

Their powerpoint presentation always ended with the message: "As legally authorized producers of cannabis in our community, we have experienced encouragement and support from the public tradespeople — electricians, plumbers and fire department officials, pharmacists, family, friends, business owners, nurseries, horticultural centres and the agricultural sector."

Nash and Little said they have never experienced any problem associated with security or violence growing pot and that common-sense security measures were all they needed.

"Beyond prohibition," Nash added, "security will not be such an issue, because the regulated cannabis infrastructure will provide an open and adequate public market. Thus, market value of cannabis will be reflected by a legal supply and demand, and cannabis prices will drop."

He emphasized that there were no extraordinary or inherent risks associated with the crop production, maintenance, drying, packaging or shipping. From their experience as legal growers and parents, both think there was no risk to children from these farm-related activities. Their story is at odds with all the myths police perpetrate about grow-ops. Nash and Little regularly make presentations to groups across the country and a big part of their shtick is satirizing police propaganda. Growing pot really is no different from growing any crop.

"In the past two years of our private-sector cannabis production, distribution and sales at Island Harvest, we have never experienced a single problem with our facility, security or cultivation," Nash said. "We conclude from our first-hand practical experience and knowledge that a legal, safe cannabis regulatory system can function within Canadian society."

Nash's persistence and his low-key approach paid off. In the summer of 2005, Health Canada approved his expansion plans. Under the corporate name of PhytoCan Pharmaceuticals, Nash hopes to grow a standardized crop and produce a spray, liquid or solid organic-cannabis product that can be dispensed in pharmacies. It would be a homegrown medicine similar to Sativex. In the face of the unrelenting criticism of its program, Ottawa appears to be gradually responding.

————

But across the Strait of Georgia, Dr. Paul Hornby, the guru of Advanced Nutrient's research and development team, admits he's paranoid. "I dream of the day when I can do this work without fear of the door being kicked in," he confided. "Marijuana is a herb—a very, very useful herb. But the freedom to do research with no risk is just a dream."

Hornby pleaded guilty in March 2003 to growing marijuana for the BC Compassion Club Society. He received a one-year conditional sentence that was upheld on appeal. Police seized nine boxes of marijuana weighing 18 kilograms, seven plastic bags of buds weighing 980 grams, forty-three dried plants, 367 living plants and 1,892 clones. The estimated street value of the pot, police said, was more than $500,000—but all of it was being sold at cost to medical patients, who saw the prosecution of their main grower as police persecution.

Hornby's work for Advanced Nutrients, he emphasized, does not require him to break any laws. "Any activities that directly involve cannabis plants are carried out by other people," he said. "All I do is analyze data and assist in product development."

If there is one reason the Fraser Valley plant-food and fertilizer firm has become an international force in the marijuana industry, it is the work of Hornby and his colleagues. Not only have they designed products for growing marijuana, they also have conducted some of the most extensive private research into the plant. They have produced sophisticated knowledge about how to manipulate the chemical components of the pot plant and produce a multitude of different strains.

Hornby says it was Hilary Black who initially turned him on to the plant's medicinal properties, even though he has toked since he was a fifteen-year-old. She blew his mind, he said, with her knowledge of what specific strains of the plant would do. One strain, for example, would relieve symptoms of multiple sclerosis but do nothing for glaucoma. Another strain of the plant seemed to help with glaucoma but do nothing for nausea.

"The strain-specificity blew me away and I've been on that track since that time. I wanted to know why," Hornby said. "This is my challenge now—to figure out what cannabinoid ratio will effect MS, which will effect glaucoma, which will effect epilepsy."

Hornby runs a company that tests and develops plant and human nutrition supplements, vitamins and other substances. At the moment, he said, he was investigating oral preparations of marijuana. He had developed a method for pre-treating organically grown cannabis to move the level of THC up or down and to produce an activated oral dose of the medicine (in a capsule).

"We have the first standardized medicine ever," he said. "We developed it. We have it on the shelf. We do it the same way every time, so we measure how much is there and get a standardized product—50-milligram caps. Whatever you like. And we're doing case studies right now with six or seven people with these capsules to see the effects."

Advanced Nutrients is only one of several companies that hope to cash in on the nascent but potentially massive medical marijuana market based on these agents. The first attempt at creating a pot pharmaceutical product was in 1985, when the U.S. Food and Drug Administration approved dronabinol (Marinol), which was developed with much funding from Washington. But it is expensive and takes an hour to work. Most patients prefer smoking the herb, which is a cheaper alternative. Inhaled marijuana also produces a near-instantaneous effect, so patients can gauge their dosage more effectively by controlling titration.

GW Pharmaceuticals in England has created an electronically controlled dispenser to spray cannabis extract into your mouth. It is nearly as quickly acting as smoked cannabis. Nasal sprays, vaporizers, nebulizers, skin patches, pills and suppositories are also in the works.

Some researchers are working on isolating and separating the cannabinoids in the same manner THC has been synthesized; others see the whole plant, with its combination of chemicals and the manner in which they interact, as holding the most promise. Cannabidiol, for instance, is being hailed as an anti-anxiety medication and an anti-convulsant when not bound with THC.

Interest in the plant's medicinal properties has been fuelled in the past decade by the discovery of an endo-cannabinoid system within the body that chemicals in marijuana stimulate. The respected journal *Nature Medicine* said this family of substances "has an important role in nearly every paradigm of pain, in memory, in neurodegeneration and in inflammation."

I have a sheaf of testimonials from patients who believe the quality of their lives, if not their continued survival, is the result of marijuana.

Patient groups say as many as one million Canadians want access to medical marijuana but are being frustrated by the politics and the stigma surrounding the drug. Indeed, medical marijuana patients are among the loudest critics of government policy—and of the media, for treating the debate about their needs as some kind of stoner joke. Palliative-care patients can get all the morphine they need for pain management, but if they want a decent toke to lighten their mood, well . . . the government says they should apply for a permit and go see the pusher on the corner.

In the already-begun jockeying among companies, people such as Hornby who have long research-based involvement with the plant are being courted and hired. He joined Advanced because of its commitment to medical marijuana and activism to reform marijuana laws. So did Ed Rosenthal, who was busted and convicted in California under similar circumstances—growing for sick people.

"I was arrested in connection with providing medicine," Hornby said. "The arrest, trial, conviction and media coverage were travesties of justice. I was a non-profit provider and researcher of medicinal herbs. It was totally wrong for law enforcement to have spent its resources to attack me."

BC Compassion Club Society founder Black (who was distributing Hornby's pot at the time of his bust), dean of cannabis researchers Lester Grinspoon, HortaPharm researcher Dr. David Pate and Ontario lawyer Alan Young have joined Cannasat Therapeutics Inc. The Toronto-based firm was created by former media mogul Moses Znaimer, clothing retailer Joseph Mimran and the Hill & Gertner Capital Corp.

Established in January 2004, Cannasat intends to produce therapeutic cannabis products, just like a traditional drug company, according to vice-president Andrew Williams. Cannasat wants to conduct large-scale clinical trials with the intent of seeking approval from Health Canada for new marijuana-based medications. To facilitate that goal, the company has bought a minority interest in Saskatoon-based Prairie Plant Systems, the fifteen-year-old private biotech firm with the exclusive multi-million-dollar contract with Health Canada to grow marijuana.

Prairie Plant Systems is the only commercial-sized licensed grower and distributor of cannabis in the country.

Theirs is the only commercial-sized pot production facility that meets the Good Manufacturing Practices biosecurity standard required by the government. But around the globe—in the United States, Israel, France, the United Kingdom and the Netherlands—other private and public companies are researching and developing similar cannabinoid-based medicines. But most are examining specific, synthesized components of the plant rather than following the organic, whole-plant, herbal medicine tack favoured by Hornby and Advanced Nutrients.

GW Pharmaceuticals is considered a leader in the field, in part because of its partnership with one of the most experienced pot growers, HortaPharm. (Its chief grower, Dave Watson, is said to have created one of the most renowned strains of marijuana, Skunk No. 1.) GW expects that the strain-specific research HortaPharm has done over the years (which is very similar if not identical to what Advanced Nutrients and guerrilla growers are doing) will help it develop non-smoking-based products. The firm's success and a $100-million investment by pharmaceutical giant Bayer were among the developments that excited the number crunchers at Toronto's Hill & Gertner.

"We found out they were publicly traded and had raised $150 million, had a market cap of between $300 and $600 million without even having a product on the market," Williams said. "So, as investment bankers, we looked at that and went, 'Hey, this is interesting!'"

Medical marijuana, he said, wasn't something the Bay Street suits had heard about, but the more they dug into the issue, the more they liked what they saw. "This plant is incredibly versatile—which is probably why so many people use it," Williams enthused. "Medically, there seem to be some real medical applications."

So Cannasat hired HortaPharm's Pate and Grinspoon as

its scientific advisers. It prominently featured Grinspoon's view of pot on their promotional material:

> "There is very little to support the proposition that smoking marijuana represents a great risk to the pulmonary system. Although cannabis has been smoked widely in this country for four decades now, there are no reported cases of cancer or emphysema which can be attributed to marijuana. I suspect that breathing a day's worth of the air in Houston or any other city with poor air quality poses more of a threat than inhaling a day's dose of smoked marijuana. Furthermore, those who are, in today's anti-smoking climate, concerned about any toxic effects on the pulmonary system can now use a vaporizer, a device which frees the cannabinoid molecules from the plant material without the necessity of burning it and thereby producing smoke.
>
> As for the psychoactive effects, I am not convinced that the therapeutic benefits of cannabis can be separated from the psychoactive effects, nor am I persuaded that that is always a desirable goal. For example, many patients with multiple sclerosis who use marijuana speak of mood elevation as well as the relief of muscle spasm and other symptoms. If cannabis contributes to this feeling better, should patients be deprived of this effect?

But the strident anti-pot policies of successive U.S. administrations have fettered research. In the United States, the medical program is based at the University of Mississippi and it is next to impossible for researchers anywhere else to get needed approvals. In Canada and Europe, the climate is less oppressive but still fettered.

"I think a whole new class of drugs will be derived from the plant," Williams said. He pointed out that the opium poppy is used to produce more than twenty drugs on the market today, but there were only two synthetic medications based on marijuana available—both used primarily in cancer treatment—until GW's Sativex arrived.

"We think there is lots of room for lots of different drugs to be developed."

So did Young. He joined Cannasat because he thinks there is little to be won through litigation since the Supreme Court of Canada upheld the constitutionality of the pot prohibition. He believes that because the courts have endorsed the need for a viable medical program, Ottawa will be forced to open the marketplace.

"I was originally recruited in 2003 by venture capital people to see what kind of market was available for cannabis, because there was a lot of feeling in 2003 that we were moving towards legalization," Young said. "People actually thought we might be into that large, booze-like market. I advised the venture capitalists that the only market available right now is to develop the medical market."

Young said Cannasat is in the initial stages of raising capital, submitting protocols to Health Canada and developing a working relationship with Ottawa. He was peeved the federal government gave GW an early entry into the market, even though its home country remains leery.

"Geoffrey Guy, founder of GW—his mantra is, We will develop marijuana that does not get you high," Young said. "One of the reasons I'm not supporting GW and their product is I don't believe that's a possibility. I also think it demonizes the plant unnecessarily and it raises the spectre of genetic modification."

In spite of Young's criticism, there is no question that the market will offer different methods of administration for marijuana-based medication and both synthetic and organic products. If you need a quick-action response, you will probably want to inhale the drug. If you have nausea, for instance, you can't wait for an oral preparation to be metabolized through the liver. But if you have chronic pain, you may want a patch that delivers a steady, controlled dose. Regardless, everyone believes a whole class of people will choose to continue smoking, whether they roll it or use some sort of vaporizer.

"What makes it interesting for us too," Williams said, "is that it's really tricky to describe what you are doing because so many people have such strong feelings about this plant. There's a lot of misinformation, a lot of myths. Our mission is really to understand the science. We want to do strain-specific research similar to what HortaPharm did. That's our goal."

But before the company can do anything, the long arduous road of regulatory approval lies ahead. To do clinical trials, it must raise tens of millions of dollars—which will probably require a public offering.

"We're excited," Williams said. "We look at this as a long-term R & D play. There will be lots of competition and lots of companies interested in this plant. It is a pretty remarkable plant when you get into it. Cannabis is so safe—you can't overdose on it, you can't smoke yourself to death and if you look at the side-effect profile of other drugs that have got approved . . . well, the prohibition exists only because of the American war on drugs and the incessant media barrage against cannabis."

———

Rain lashed the car. "Here comes Rielle," David Malmo-Levine said, pointing to a slight, curly haired woman gingerly running down the rain-slicked cobblestones. "She's on the cutting edge of medicine."

He opened the back door of the car for her. "I'd like to go back to the Drive if you wouldn't mind giving me a ride," Malmo-Levine said in a southern drawl. "I'm afraid I must rely on the kindness of strangers."

Rielle Capler, his girlfriend, climbed into the back seat shaking the rain from her hair.

"Hi," she said.

"Can you drop Rielle at the compassion club?"

It was only a few blocks up the street from Da Kine. As we drove east to the Drive, Capler introduced herself.

Half a decade ago, in June 1999, she was visiting a friend in Nelson, in the Kootenays. They decided on the spur of the moment to attend what turned into the first meeting of the country's key medical-marijuana advocates, hosted by Brian Taylor.

Initially, people at the meeting were trying to find common ground and failing badly. Capler had experience facilitating and told Taylor she could help. By the end of the day, she had midwifed the birth of the Canadian Cannabis Coalition. Bill Small, a director of the BC Compassion Club Society in Vancouver, approached her afterward and offered her a job.

"I was interested in natural medicine and had been studying psychology but realized that psychology wasn't covered under our health-care plan in Canada," she explained. "None of the kind of counselling or natural health care was, and that bothered me. I didn't want to become a psychologist and cater to people who could afford it. I was also interested in all the pharmaceutical drugs that were being used and were covered. That's all that was covered under our health-care plan. So I went and studied the health-care system. I did a master's in health care administration and learnt a lot about the system."

She was also a veteran activist—one of the central organizers in the protests at the Asia-Pacific Economic Cooperation

Conference at UBC, the recent high-water mark in Canadian nay-saying. The club was a perfect fit and as an organization, needed her skills.

"I think [those operating the Compassion Club then] had come up with a mission statement and had decided to run non-hierarchically and use consensus as the decision-making model, which is the background I came from too," Capler remembered. "So those two things were really interesting for me. They wanted to utilize, basically, my education, my strategic planning and policy and all that kind of stuff. So I came along and added that to the mix."

Today it has a staff of more than forty and offers some three thousand members a daily menu of eight to ten types of cannabis, hashish, tinctures and baked goods. There are multiple phone lines and a smoking lounge. More and more patients frequented the Wellness Centre (part of the club) as the health-care system trimmed what it would pay for. It has two herbalists, two clinical counsellors, doctors of traditional Chinese medicine, a reiki practitioner, an acupressure message therapist, an herbal apothecary and a yoga instructor. A sliding fee schedule is offered.

Most of its members are on social assistance. They're sick and can't work. The office is mobbed on welfare Wednesday, the traditional day at the end of the month when government cheques are issued. On a slow day, probably about one hundred people pass through.

"It's been slower lately, a lot slower in the last few months," Capler said. "For a while it was just packed every day. A couple of things have happened and we have kind of accommodated our infrastructure to deal with that. We have two computers and two tills so there are two lineups. But also competition, different places down the street, so consumers have a choice. They can go wherever they want. And the prices are dropping considerably, that's another thing."

The club gave away a lot. Every member was eligible for 2 grams per week at no cost. Not everyone took advantage, but the club distributed a lot of free weed.

Capler thought the current legal situation was a hyper-hypocrisy. Health Canada was stonewalling rather than creating a medical marijuana program that worked. She considered the provincial government "ignorant and uncaring" with its 1960s rhetoric of "marijuana is evil." She was especially outraged that Ottawa hired a U.S. pharmaceutical scientist and former director of the National Institute on Drug Abuse to counter complaints by Canadians about the Marihuana Medical Access Regulations. He also worked for Solvay Pharmaceuticals, which manufactured Marinol, the synthetic alternative to marijuana.

Malmo-Levine groaned dramatically when she mentioned this. Capler laughed.

"I started smoking when I was fourteen and I was supercurious about it. It was fun, it was something, like it was a whole magical experience to try something new I had heard about. A friend who was a year older took me out into the middle of this park on a snowy day in Toronto. We had snow up to our thighs, smoked a joint and didn't feel anything."

Later, she tried it again and really liked it.

"For me it opened up whole new thought patterns, it really opened my mind. I would think in different ways. Make different connections. I really enjoyed it. It felt good— I smoked tons in high school and was a straight-A student. I laugh at people who say, 'Oh, it makes people unmotivated and it's really bad for kids.' I was a straight-A student."

Malmo-Levine sparked a big spliff and passed it to her.

She believed, and polls supported her, that there was complete acceptance and tolerance of cannabis as a medicine in Canada. Even people who were pretty conservative and older, like her dad and his generation, believed that if it helps people, people should have it. If it helps, why not let the sick and dying have a reefer without the stigma of committing a crime?

"The program that Health Canada is running is a sham, but people believe—most people believe it's legal," Capler complained. "Compassion clubs have been serving people in medical need for a long time and risking arrest and being very vulnerable—the club in Toronto was raided by police at gunpoint, the club in Victoria has been raided twice. There is this climate, yet it's, you know—people think it's all legal and fine. It's not."

People who are sick are caught in the middle.

"I talk to people every day who are stress cases because of trying to get their doctors and specialists to fill in the form," she said. "They still have to break the law to get their medicine."

She, Black and Lucas have co-authored "A Roadmap to Compassion: The Implementation of a Working Medicinal Cannabis Program in Canada." The report is an indictment of the Marihuana Medical Access Division.

The government's own polls indicated that more than 400,000 Canadians claimed to be already using cannabis for medicinal purposes—roughly eight hundred with the proper permit. Patients could not get the prerequisite doctors' letters. Worse, bureaucratic obstacles such as yearly renewals and the required support of a medical specialist meant patients threw up their hands and instead went to the local compassion club or the corner. The "Roadmap" laid out a distilled vision of what the country's compassion clubs wanted Ottawa to provide:

- community-based, non-profit cultivation and distribution of cannabis

- guidelines for site inspections and testing of cannabis for strength and purity
- financial support to allow patients to access cannabis
- education programs to ensure safe and successful use of cannabis products
- research to produce high-quality cannabis and an understanding of which strains do what

They believed physicians should be able to prescribe cannabis in the same manner they prescribed other far more dangerous controlled substances. There was no reason to place cannabis in a stricter regulatory regime.

Under the national compassion club policy, health-care practitioners confirm the patient's diagnosis and symptoms, and "recommend," rather than prescribe, cannabis. In the authors' view, cannabis is an herb, therefore it isn't the sole bailiwick of allopathic physicians. Naturopathic practitioners, Chinese herbalists and others were recognized by the compassion clubs as competent to issue recommendations.

Capler sees Canada eventually legalizing marijuana, and people being able to access the medicine from their own sources, whether from a café, from a compassion club or from pharmacies and other health-care services. Someday medical users would have an assurance of quality and the cost would be covered under their health-care plans.

"It could happen as soon as the will is there," Capler said. "It could happen really quickly. It needs to happen. People are sick, they need relief and they don't want to be criminals in order to get that relief, and they don't want to become poverty-stricken in order to get that relief. We live in Canada— there is an expectation that the health-care system will cover our costs . . . universally."

A TALE OF THREE CITIES

RICHARD COWAN FLAGGED A TAXI at the Amsterdam airport and I joined him for the ride into the city in late November 2004. Yale-educated, scion of Republican oil money, buddies with William F. Buckley Jr. and similar icons of the U.S. conservative right, Cowan was a founder of the Young Americans for Freedom and went to work for the Committee to Re-elect the President—Richard M. Nixon. A former president of the Yale Young Republicans, he became a convert to marijuana legalization when he discovered the number of young Americans who were being imprisoned under the punishment policies of the early 1970s.

Cowan was an early supporter of the National Organization for the Reform of Marijuana Laws (NORML), and twenty years of struggle later, served a three-year stint as its executive director. Afterward, he decompressed from the Washington, D.C., hustle by living in Amsterdam among the expatriate American community. Several U.S. growers busted in the seventies moved to Amsterdam to avoid jail time, and helped accelerate the Dutch seed boom. The aging Texan felt completely at home.

Advanced Nutrients had bid to purchase his popular and informative website, marijuananews.com. He was in the final stages of handing over the operation when the deal went south.

"They, like a lot of people, have a stake in ending prohibition," Cowan said as we sped into the city. "They recognize that their business will be many times bigger if it is legalized, so they are strongly supportive of legalization. Which is all that ultimately matters to me."

The Da Kine fiasco, as he called it, riled him. For thirty years the pot community had been unable to get its act together. It was as if the marijuana movement were intent on being one long, shaggy stoner joke.

"Da Kine was not doing anything the Compassion Society is not doing," Cowan said. "Legally, of the Vancouver Compassion Society's two thousand members, only a few have official exemptions from Health Canada. So if you don't have an exemption there's no difference."

He blamed the media for muddling the pot debate. "Must every article that has anything to do with cannabis contain the phrases 'up in smoke' or 'gone to pot'? It's endless. I called it the giggle factor. When I first got to NORML, that's what struck me—the impossibility of getting serious attention. I once said to reporters, 'What does marijuana have in common with masturbation?' They'd smile and titter. I'd say: 'That's it! People can't talk about it without laughing. You can't have a serious conversation about it.' The headlines condition you to think whatever follows is a joke. So, when you read that there is no fatal dose of pot, that marijuana is a medicine, that it is more benign than Aspirin, it's a joke, you don't take it seriously."

Cowan was close friends with Todd McCormick, and the late Peter McWilliams, best-selling author of *Life 101* who was diagnosed with cancer and AIDS in 1996. His book *Ain't Nobody's Business If You Do* is one of the bibles of the American civil liberties movement. McCormick and Cowan lived together in Amsterdam in the mid-1990s and moved back to California in 1997 at McWilliams's urging. A severe manic depressive, in addition to a lot of other things that caused him problems, McWilliams wanted to get the medical marijuana business off the ground in California, and really threw himself into the cause after Proposition 215 passed in November 1996.

Cowan set up a website for McWilliams, using the URL marijuanamagazine.com. That led to a gig in 2000 on Emery's Pot TV and regular visits to Vancouver. He was peripatetic, moving regularly among the three primary principalities of cannabis cultivation in the industrialized world—California, British Columbia and Holland.

"I think the medical need will force a change in the law—patients don't have five or ten years to wait," Cowan said. "Anyway, I just think the medical issue is the thing that destroys all of the arguments. Theoretically, why not just make it available by prescription and get over it? The system is set up to make a distinction between recreational use of substances and the medical use of substances. There's absolutely no reason not to do this."

Cowan has devoted a lot of energy, thought and most of his adult life to trying to change people's minds about marijuana. He was flummoxed. "Look around," he said, as the cab moved through the narrow, affluent streets and over canal bridges clotted with shoppers. "Do you see pandemonium? Is there ruin and riot? Marijuana has been de facto legal here for thirty years. Life goes on normally." There was no denying that. The cab dropped us at our respective hotels.

Nol van Schaik roused me from my room and pulled me across the darkening Leidseplein in central Amsterdam toward the Bulldog Coffeeshop. We stepped out of the sleet and bitter wind that was scouring the cobbled square. Late November in Amsterdam can be snotty—an ever changing mix of rain, sleet and snow.

"I've been coming here for twenty years," he said. "You'll love it and it will be quiet."

He was a stereotypical Dutchman—blond, good looking and gregarious.

"Nol," a voice from near the bar called out.

Henk de Vries, owner of the Bulldog chain, embraced van Schaik like a long-lost brother. "You got out of jail," he said.

"Yes, yes, the French threw out the charges, but now I hear they are trying to appeal." He shrugged. "How can they do this? I have sold tons of hash. Tons. Now they want to resurrect charges for 200 pounds from another time, another era."

He shrugged.

De Vries grinned and shrugged, too. He was a grey-haired barrel-chested man in a tailored leather coat, a blue-jean shirt and blue jeans.

I extended a hand. Van Schaik, tanned and fit in a yellow chamois jacket and heavy green sweater, introduced us.

"Vancouver," de Vries said, gripping my hand. "You know Nol, I was in this place, Da Kine . . ." He put his hand to his thinning hair and closed his eyes. "I couldn't believe it." He had not even had time to chat with the owner, de Vries said, shaking his head at the memory. It was only happenstance that he decided to leave rather than wait. "Five minutes, Nol," he said, his voice rising, "five minutes later, the police arrive."

Both old dealers guffawed. The old Spidey-sense still tingled.

"My God, I thought. Five minutes more, I would be finished. I'm on the surveillance pictures, I'm sure. They take those pictures for hours before they move in—and I already have trouble getting in and out of Canada because of marijuana."

"They used to call Henk 'the Matchbox,'" van Schaik laughed, "when he was dealing at the pop festivals in Rotterdam."

"The shop they busted," de Vries continued, "it's a big person. It's not a hippie who just opened a coffee shop like this. He was a big guy."

"I know," said van Schaik. "He invited me to come over and said he would finance everything. I said I'd been through that."

De Vries nodded. "Go sit there, I'll join you in a moment."

Van Schaik and I grabbed a coffee and sat down.

De Vries was one of the original coffee-shop owners from the seventies—in business for twenty-seven years. Van Schaik was a second-generation owner.

In 1976, the Dutch parliament passed a law that separated drugs into different classes, the so-called hard and soft drugs. Cannabis was deemed to be a Schedule II drug, as opposed to others such as LSD, cocaine, heroin or methamphetamines. Possession of less than 30 grams of cannabis was permitted, and coffee shops were allowed to sell marijuana and hashish to adults.

Since U.S. President Ronald Reagan launched the war on drugs, the Dutch have been under increasing pressure, particularly from the United States, to reverse that policy. "It's solely because we're the only drug dealers in the global phone book with a telephone number and an address," van Schaik quipped. "They can find us on the Internet."

In 1994, the Netherlands tightened the rules on coffee shops to reduce the acceptable maximum purchase from 30 grams to 5 grams. Coffee shops were restricted on the amount of stock they could have on hand. The Dutch also increased penalties for growers and began targeting commercial cultivation.

The result was a significant reduction in the number of cannabis cafés. Where once there were nearly 1,500, now there are only about 780, of which 270 are in Amsterdam. A ban on alcohol in coffee shops in 2004 was to be followed by a ban on tobacco in 2005 and the end of smoking on the premises in the name of health, not prohibition. For Dutch coffee shops, times are tough.

De Vries set up the first Bulldog in 1975, and his is now the biggest chain of pot shops with its own line of merchandise. Bulldog clothes are designed and tailored in Milan. This particular outlet, already decorated for Christmas with lights and boughs of holly, served alcohol upstairs, cannabis downstairs. In this refurbished century-old police station, you could get high in a now-opulent cell. Like van Schaik, de Vries was a multi-millionaire.

"We must find Reeferman, afterwards," van Schaik said. "Remind me. A bunch of foil packages arrived from Canada. I thought it was smoked salmon." He shook his head. "I thought I was doing the staff a favour and told them to open them up and give it out as treats. It was his pot."

I cringed at visions of Scott arriving at the most anticipated event in the pot grower's year to compete with his idols—without dope. The Cannabis Cup is a seventeen-year-old advertising gimmick dreamed up by an editor of *High Times*. A typical transplanted New York hustle, even the local coffee-shop owners don't particularly get it. But they're happy to take the coin, which is considerable. A judge's pass runs $200 and allows you to visit the city coffee shops and buy your own pot to smoke, then vote for the best. Vendors such as Reeferman and other seed companies drop US$10,000 each for a presence. It is a growers' event—a chance for a lot of otherwise reclusive gardeners to meet, exchange tips, compare product and party.

I told van Shaik that Scott undoubtedly had a fallback plan.

Van Schaik got into the cannabusiness in the late 1980s. Before that, he was a 250-pound weightlifter, gym owner and national coach of the Dutch bodybuilding team who didn't smoke or drink. Then he got involved with a local U.S. football team and travelled to Germany for a game. Some of the other players were smoking pot on the bus, and he was Rebagliatied. The highlight, van Schaik said, was when he got off the bus and obliviously walked into a small pond. The other players howled.

He rolled a large cone-shaped reefer with tobacco, the European style. "After I started smoking and visited a few coffee shops, I decided to open a coffee shop. My father and grandfather were both bar owners, so I knew how this business worked—except it was with hash instead of alcohol."

His was the twenty-second coffee shop in Haarlem, a tourist centre just outside of Amsterdam. "We started on the edge of town in a 300-square-metre [over 3,200-square-foot] old taxi garage," he recalled. "That's where I started Willy Wortel's fourteen years ago." He took a toke. "I started my coffee shop in 1991 and 95 per cent of the goods I sold were not from Holland. They were smuggled in. Five per cent were from [local] gardens. But that is the year homegrown started coming up. It didn't get out of Amsterdam because there wasn't enough quantity. Now 80 per cent of my turnover is Dutch marijuana. Only 20 per cent of my turnover—and I have ten different hashes on the menu from all over the world—only 20 per cent is hash and a percentage of the hash is Ice-o-lator and Pollinator Dutch hash."

As in Canada, the increased emphasis on the interdiction of foreign supplies in the late sixties and seventies in Europe stimulated domestic production in the Netherlands. The American Sacred Seed Company brought genetics and know-how to Amsterdam in the early 1980s. Henk van Dalen, owner of the Dutch Passion Seed Company, developed the first feminized seeds—growers no longer had to weed out the male plants, distinguishable by their testicle-like pollen sacs and lack of psychotropic properties.

The problem with the Dutch system, he said, is that coffee-shop owners have to be crooks at their back door, tax collectors at the front and genial hosts in between. The clamp-down on growers not only would be counterproductive, but also would resuscitate the gangs that had once dominated the pot trade. He said currently he bought from Moroccans who smuggled a kilo or two in the trunk of their car, grandmoth-ers and uncles and invalids and people on social assistance—the smuggler's version of the mom-and-pop grow-op.

"The hydroponic industry got rid of organized crime," van Schaik said. "I deal with one-kilo, one-and-a-half-kilo people, not people who drop me a kilo of hash and say, 'There's 1,500 more kilos of that. Give me a call next week and I'll come back up.'"

Four or five offices existed in central Amsterdam where he could go, sample several kinds of hash, make a choice, pay the price and wait. Moments later someone would ring the doorbell and he would be told it was for him. On his way out, he would be handed a bag containing his purchase—a kilo of Red Lebanese, say. All very civilized.

In 1994, the local officials began scrutinizing the coffee shops three or four times a year looking for underaged teens, health violations, hard drugs and other business licence vio-lations. They have no problems in his city, van Schaik said. "No complaints at all. Zero in three years."

All the talk of the Netherlands reverting to prohibition was bunk, he said, but things were definitely getting tighter and the law against smoking tobacco in coffee shops was going to have repercussions. Europeans love their hash and often their pot rolled with tobacco. There was also talk of banning foreigners, primarily because cannabis customers were pouring across the German border and causing traffic nightmares and other headaches for some Dutch towns.

"The naked facts are, we have a minister who is a reformed Catholic and shouts off a lot of things," van Schaik laughed. "But control of the policy of coffee shops is in the hands of the local councils and the mayors. He can only ask the mayors to follow up on his stupid requests. They say, 'Why are you doing this?'"

The minister sees problems where none exist, van Schaik insisted. Taxes would decide the issue. The coffee shops generated some $3 billion in gross economic activity, van Schaik estimated, nearly $340 million in tax revenue. In his case, he employed twenty-four staff in three coffee shops. The government was always trying to get more, he complained. They even tried to get the coffee-shop owners for back taxes and on their wholesale transactions. But who, buying wholesale on the black market, is going to provide the government with a set of books showing a profit? In de Vries's case, they wanted tens of millions of euros. He balked and eventually beat them in court.

That's because the figures tossed around are so flexible that it's difficult to determine what, if anything, might be owed on transactions that are illegal. As with distilleries during Prohibition, the books produced by coffee-shop owners are suspect because their wholesale purchases are done on the black market and unrecorded. Each maintained two sets of books. Certainly, a huge amount of economic activity was associated with the coffee shops, but quantifying it—as with all underground activity—was another matter. Still, the Dutch were reaping more benefits and had more control in terms of regulating the cannabis industry than those countries enforcing a prohibition.

"The municipalities not only get their cut of the taxes," van Schaik said, "they don't have to spend any money sweeping the streets clean of dealers. Our mayor urges us to put in more rooms—we have four now above our coffee shop. He wants us to put in more rooms because cannabis tourism brings money to town. We are part of society, as much as our minister tries to paint us like crooks that ruin society."

As a result of the pressures, van Schaik moved most of his grow operation to the coast of southern Spain in 2003. There, in a nation of 41 million people, one in three admit to marijuana use and there are more than four hundred grow shops. Van Schaik rented a hilltop mansion surrounded by olive trees near Málaga, where a couple of Amsterdam-like coffee shops had sprouted on the beach thanks to transplanted Dutchmen.

Van Schaik was considering a cannabis destination resort on the shores of the Mediterranean. He had a legal opinion that said Spain's constitutional guarantees to privacy were strong enough to keep police at bay unless they could prove you were growing for commercial distribution. He was doing well—until France insisted Spain arrest him on a fifteen-year-old warrant. He turned fifty in prison. "My whole family was in a huge villa with a pool . . . 105 plants in the garden—and I end up being in prison," he lamented.

Van Schaik and his partners had been caught years before at the French border in a truck loaded with 400 kilos of Moroccan hashish. "The customs officer went to put the handcuffs on me, I head-butted him and ran."

The gendarmes chased him. One grabbed his hip bag and it ripped off. That's how they got his passport, driver's licence and car registration. That's how they knew who he was. But after two seasons as a fullback in a European U.S.-style football league, van Schaik was difficult to snare. He remembered what that Canuck coach had told him—*Keep those legs moving, keep those legs moving*. He did. The cop on his back fell off. Another tripped him, van Schaik got up.

Keep moving, keep moving. He broke free and sprinted. *Crack!* A shot rang out. *Crack!* Another.

He ran through a construction site, bounced into a fence. He glanced back. They were farther behind than he had expected. High on adrenaline, he scaled the fence, landed on the other side and took off. Literally. Like Wile E. Coyote, van Schaik found himself running on air and tumbling into a ravine.

"I was so lucky nothing was broken," he recalled. "I ended up halfway down the hill behind a bush, one big slice of flesh out of my knee, blood everywhere, cuts and bruises."

Spotting a river and a medieval arched bridge, he splashed through the water and hid.

"I waited until dark and crawled back," van Schaik recalled. "They almost got me, I jumped in the water again. I got to a truck stop and in the parking lot walked over to a Scottish truck driver. He said I could hide in the back . . . Thirty-six hours to get to Holland. I didn't get out. I went to Morocco 96 kilos, I came back 78 kilos."

He ordered another coffee and passed me a large beryl-like bud encrusted with vibrant crystals. "That's Sticky Fingers, our home brand."

He was considering writing a book about his exploits. *"Cannabis, Cappuccino and Conflict,"* he planned to call it. "Because I smoke marijuana, I drink a lot of cappuccino to level the yin and the yang of my energy and I always cause conflict."

Van Schaik supplied pot to Colin Davies, the disabled British cannabis crusader, during his 2001 attempt to open a coffee shop in England. Called the Dutch Experience, it was raided on the first day and Davies was busted. The courts made an example of him, just as they had Emery. He was sentenced to three years in prison. Van Schaik said he would be jailed too if he returned to the United Kingdom.

"I tried to open a coffee shop in Belgium," he said. "Too much heat. I was arrested and locked up for two months in Spain, and I did six weeks in France. I'm getting a bit tired of it now."

He began to roll another tobacco coner. The late Pierre Berton would be proud, I thought.

"I don't feel like a radical," van Schaik continued. "That's why I'm outraged. I feel like a normal businessman who pays a lot of tax and gets called all kinds of names."

He was becoming more of an activist as a result of his most recent brush with the law. That was how most were politicized, he said.

"I'm in touch with all kinds of cannabis communities in European countries," he explained. "I am doing this for my future. I have a daughter and a son, twenty-six and twenty-two, and I have two grandchildren, and I want my grandchildren to be third-generation coffee-shop owners. That's why I have to maintain my status and my licence and these policies."

Van Schaik wanted to produce TV programs, raffle off one of his coffee shops (he figured each was worth about one million euros), set up a dealer-for-a-day contest, film a series of *Survivor* in a coffee shop . . . He even had two college students working under him in an internship program. He planned to have an Internet TV channel, just like Pot TV, containing European policy material on medical marijuana, documentaries, music programming . . . start in English, then Dutch, French, Spanish, German, Portuguese and maybe Russian. He was a European Marc Emery.

"I can be the activist I am because I can afford it," he said. "It doesn't make me rich, but I live the way I like it. I am completely convinced I am doing nothing wrong."

Henk de Vries finally came and joined us. "You know, I never talk to the press—who needs it," he said to me. "Let me get you drinks."

He waved over a waiter, ordered wine and lit a cigarette.

"You are from Canada," he said turning his attention back to van Shaik and me.

"I think personally that Canada should learn a lot from the Dutch laws," de Vries said. "They are liberal, but they can see the mistakes Holland made starting a coffee-shop licence. From the moment they say we got a blind-eye policy, all the countries of Europe get all over them. From the first moment, until today."

He thought Canada should legalize, make everything above-board and on the books. Forget about halfway measures—they were causing the problems in Amsterdam. In his view, the battle in Europe was over. There were too many other pressing issues on the political agenda, anti-smoking campaigns were spreading, and there was no unified constituency lobbying for change. At the same time, by taking a low-key, tax-and-regulate approach, the government had made coffee shops less bastions of counterculture and more like other restaurants or bars.

"The government is making it closer and closer [with regulation]"—his hands rose to chest level and mimed strangling—"closer and closer, tighter and tighter. Regulating us to death. Canada should see the difference."

De Vries said everything had changed from the old days. The coffee-shop culture he valued was gone.

"I liked the cannabis culture. I love to go to a bar or a place where I can sit and relax, like Vancouver. That's fantastic, fantastic. I think that Vancouver is going to do it better in the future than Holland. In Holland, the coffee-shop culture is dead. It's over and out. That culture is gone. It is like booze now. We exist because we know how to talk to the police people and the tax department. It's business."

He said the country had proved you could make pot boring and regulate it just like booze by turning it into an identical product. And when you did that, van Schaik thought, it lost some cachet.

"You know how Canada should do it?" he said. "Not like this Da Kine. Not by opening one. I'll tell you how Dutch coffee shops survived. Not by opening one. By opening a dozen. Like Amsterdam's smart shops [which openly sell magic mushrooms, ecstasy and other hallucinogens]. They came after we did and established themselves over two months. They opened a series of shops initially; the police closed them. But these guys had other buildings and they opened them right away; the police closed them. They opened others. It was like seeing mushroom spores spread— and finally the police gave up."

He was probably right. It was easy to close a single café like Da Kine, much more difficult to close a dozen and a dozen more and a dozen more. Briere had established the model of what wouldn't work—at least, not without an army of people ready to do the same thing, open a pot café, and ready to pay the price. To win a campaign of civil disobedience you must have numbers. Gandhi's cotton and salt campaigns succeeded because his supporters could overwhelm the system. For only a handful of people, even several hundred, there's always room at Her Majesty's inn. You need legions willing to clog the courts. That wasn't going to happen: pot always will be a minority's vice. The laws governing the recreational use of marijuana are going to change much more slowly than activists want.

"But there is no doubt about it," de Vries said, sipping his wine, "I start a new business in Vancouver within two to three years—for sure. For sure. I love Vancouver, really. I have been in contact with the guys in Blunt Bros [whose pot-friendly café was gutted by the springtime fire]. They're going to get that new building across from Emery's place. They've financed the restoration. I've been in it, and it's going to be great. Great big potential all around."

Van Schaik and I crossed the Leidseplein again, walking into the teeth of the squall to the Melkweg, where the final countdown for the Cannabis Cup was underway. The trade-fair portion of the festival featured a dozen or so seed companies, pipe manufacturers, paraphernalia dealers and novelty suppliers. There were incredible edibles: THC-laced chocolates in perfect imitation of regular candy bars—Blunty instead of Bounty, Stoners instead of Snickers—and Potella instead of Nutella spread . . .

We found Charles Scott at the Reeferman booth with Ken Hayes, the American refugee who ran the Spirit Within across from Da Kine. He planned to remain a global fugitive until the United States tired of prosecuting pot growers, or forgot about him.

Scott was happy to see van Schaik, and called the loss of the marijuana he sent a few weeks earlier insignificant. He had entered in the Cannabis Cup other pot he sent separately, and only the judging remained.

We headed for the main hall. There, the Tall Brothers from Vancouver were performing a 1938 classic, "If You're a Viper."

The crowd was older, almost entirely male. There were a few Goth chicks, women with tattoos, earth mothers and Rastafarians. This was a celebration of marijuana culture—nearly half a century of counterculture history on display, the remnants of the sixties revolution refusing to surrender.

There was Stephen Gaskin—wasn't he dead? Well, no. Today, Saint Stephen, as the Grateful Dead immortalized him, was offering growing tips. An icon from the Summer of Love—Haight–Ashbury circa 1967—he founded the Farm in Summertown, Tennessee, a successful alternative community. He and his wife, Ina May, were a veritable *American*

Gothic of the marijuana movement. Eddie Lepp, California's cannabis king, was here too, in an outfit bedecked with marijuana leaves and celebrated as Freedom Fighter of the Year. The fifty-two-year-old Vietnam vet was the first person arrested, tried and acquitted in the summer of 1997 as a result of the protection offered by California's Proposition 215 legislation. He again faced charges, as police had raided his 8-hectare farm in northwest Lake County on August 18, seizing twenty thousand marijuana plants—a crop worth more than $80 million, authorities said. The genetic stock had been supplied in part by Reeferman. Lepp made no pretense of hiding the pot farm, touting it as "the world's biggest medi-garden."

In a corner, broadcasting over the Internet and flogging his latest book of poetry, was John "They Gave Him Ten for Two" Sinclair. He looked like an elderly Leon Trotsky. A cast of characters was on hand, most of them part of the global cannabis caravan for decades—Eagle Bill, hawking his version of the Volcano vaporizer; Lawrence Cherniak, an Ontario-based actor, selling his renowned coffee-table books of hashish photographs . . .

Ben Dronkers, founder of Sensi Seeds and the man who inspired Emery, stood nearby. The fifty-three-year-old had all his kids working in the company, and five of the six smoke cannabis. He also operated the Hash Marijuana & Hemp Museum in Amsterdam and overall in 2005 employed about one hundred people. In recent years, he sold about 4 million euros worth of seeds annually. A third of his business was export. I asked him where he thought things were going—was he as pessimistic as his colleagues?

"All the laws for the last six or eight years have been going in a negative way," he said, then took a sip of white wine. "Rather than more regulation and legalization, there is more oppression and more priority being given to marijuana growing, for example. They even designed the medical marijuana program to fail."

Although the Dutch pot program was considered a good model, the price in the pharmacy was roughly twice that in the coffee shops. So the government had a glut of marijuana on its hands and was forced to lay off one of its two growers.

"It's insane," Dronkers said. "They are putting people in prison again for growing marijuana. It's crazy. If you ask them, Would you put anybody who smokes tobacco in jail— Would we put these people in prison because they smoke tobacco? Is that the next step? You know, like we have an anti-smoking campaign, so should we stop young people from smoking by putting them in prison?"

He did not seem to expect an answer.

"The ignorance and the stupidity of people who systematically keep this plant forbidden, I don't know the reasons any more—is it just Pavlovian? Or is there really high interest of big oil companies, pharmaceutical companies, liquor companies who would rather sell beer and whisky to the kids than see them smoke? I don't know."

Dronkers said he wanted the plant legalized. "What is the problem? Let farmers grow it. And it's not the Dutch farmers who will benefit, it will be the south of France, the south of Spain—where they can grow good wine, they can grow good marijuana. Why not? It should be an open market, something like—well, there are so many possibilities."

He gestured to encompass the crowd, the ancillary industries, the music, the good times. "I think in twenty-five years, two generations from now, people will think, What silly people, those who had the drug war."

Later, inside the darkened auditorium, I stood beside Hayes, who was wearing his *Hard Day's Night* T-shirt, awaiting the announcement. Scott was somewhere down front amid the several hundred people crowded into the room. There was a drum roll and we heard a voice announce, *"This year's best sativa—Love Potion #1 from Reeferman Seeds."*

Hayes jumped. A moment later we saw Scott on the stage, grinning and waving both arms.

"Go, Reeferman!" someone shouted.

Camera flashes strobed. There was huge applause. A win like this could mean a $1 million gross in seed sales, Hayes whispered.

"B.C. Bud rules. B.C. Bud rules!" Scott shouted from the stage. "Well, someone said to me, show us the bud. This is the year the B.C. boys have shown Amsterdam the bud."

Shortly afterward, God Bud, from BC Bud Depot, was declared the year's best *indica*. No more evidence of the province's ascendancy was required. A clean sweep for the colonies in both important strains. Scott came to the back of the hall clutching the stylized silver trophy—a crucible held aloft by a cannabis leaf. He borrowed my cellphone to call his wife in Canada.

Minutes later he hung up, beaming. "She told me congratulations—but she said she knew it would win!" He was clearly ecstatic.

For him it was more than a confirmation of his breeding skills; this win was a huge leap forward in terms of recognition. He had been wandering for many years in the wilderness. Finally he felt accepted.

Dave Watson, the U.S.-born grower from HortaPharm, one of few licensed marijuana producers, congratulated him. They fell into a long conversation about particular strains and how to manipulate the cannabinoids. Perhaps they could work together—they'd stay in touch.

After Watson left, Scott grinned. "You know, I've got three better strains at home. And a great big bag of seeds back at the hotel. I guess I better call the airline and postpone our flight home."

Five months after the Cannabis Cup, I emerged from the BART subway station in downtown Oakland squinting into the California sunlight glinting off a red Ferrari ostentatiously parked outside the Cannabis Buyers' Co-op. The licence plate read: GROWHYDROPONICS.COM.

Inside the co-op there was the usual head-shop collection of vaporizers, rolling papers, lighters, paraphernalia and hemp products. The co-op also produced and sold one of the state's most recognized cannabis-patient cards, which allowed the bearer to buy from a menu of cannabis products at more than one hundred outlets, including medical-cannabis dispensaries for patients and pot clubs that sold to recreational users.

Next door, the hydroponic shop offered equipment and advice on growing. Two doors down was the Bulldog Café — christened in homage to Amsterdam. Here, members of the club could order from a menu of cannabis products, and sit and enjoy a cappuccino and a smoke.

Prices were about twice those in Vancouver: an eighth of an ounce of good stinky sold for US$40, less potent weed for US$30—plus state sales tax, of course.

"It's called Goo," Richard Lee, the owner, told me, holding up a bud of marijuana heavy with scents of orange and sandalwood. "As good as any of your B.C. Bud."

From his wheelchair in a small room behind (appropriately enough) a Dutch door, he dispensed the pot in small glassine bags, the edibles packaged in satirically labelled wrappings—Kiefkat, Indo' Joy, Stoners, Reefers . . . There was chocolate milk infused with THC as well as cheesecake laced with pot. You could also order a big bowl of spaghetti and meat sauce with a bun for $5. A sign read: *Must roll your own. Our dispenser cannot do so.*

"We're trying to be low-key responsible neighbours and so far it's working out well," Lee said. "We're celebrating our fifth anniversary."

Throughout this downtown neighbourhood are similar outlets, the oldest dating back to the early 1990s, the co-op to 1995. They call it Oaksterdam. Across California the growing network of medical-marijuana dispensaries and clubs is using the state's constitutional privacy rights to keep police at bay. There were an estimated twenty thousand registered users in the Bay area, and scores of outlets, some offering more than sixty strains.

Lee has been at the forefront of the fight that established this marijuana-friendly enclave in the belly of a country whose federal government is engaged in a war against the drug. While Washington desperately seeks to maintain the worldwide pot prohibition, more and more states are choosing to decriminalize (although cultivation and distribution remain criminal offences), and many are supporting medical marijuana.

In Oakland, cannabusiness is hailed by some as the catalyst for urban renewal in a once blighted neighbourhood. The model led to the passage on November 6 of Measure Z—the Oakland Cannabis Regulation and Revenue Ordinance. Electors voted by 65 per cent to tolerate private adult sales, cultivation and possession of cannabis, with envisioned regulated retail sales and smoking dens.

It's a noble experiment, though to enact such a policy would require changes to state and probably federal law.

"This is just the beginning," said Mikki Norris, who leads

the Cannabis Consumer Campaign, a lobby group advocating a legalized, tax-and-regulate approach. "The debate is
finally moving in the right direction."

Her group believes the state alone could save US$150
million or so in enforcement costs and raise an estimated
$1 billion in tax revenue. Across the United States, she said,
the savings and the revenues would be enormous.

The cost of enforcing state and local pot laws is
pegged at $7.6 billion, about $10,400 per arrest. Annual
U.S. policing costs associated with cannabis are $3.7 bil-
lion. Judicial and legal costs, $853 million. Correctional
costs, $3.1 billion. Total arrests in the United States
increased 165 per cent in the 1990s, from 287,850 in 1991
to 755,000 in 2003—with no discernable effect on use.
Today, it's believed more than one million American teens
are selling marijuana.

The question, though, is whether pot opponents here
will be able to attack the initiative and defeat it the way
Vancouver shut down the Da Kine and dampened optimism
among pot users that liberalization was on the horizon. I
came not only to see Oaksterdam, but to attend the thirty-
fifth annual conference of the National Organization for the
Reform of Marijuana Laws (NORML). Some five hundred,
primarily American members of the oldest pro-pot activist
group gathered to celebrate their advances and mark the
generational change in leadership.

Keith Stroup, long-time president, was relinquishing
the reins. Inspired by Ralph Nader, the sixty-year-old Washington, D.C., public-interest attorney founded the group in
1970 with $5,000 from the Playboy Foundation. He ran
NORML from 1970 to 1979 and returned in 1994 to take the
helm again after the organization was riven by personal
feuds. But times had changed and Stroup felt he had to
move on, especially now that he had recently remarried.

There were 350 lawyers on NORML's national legal committee and its 115 chapters did good work, but over the years it had often become part of the problem, not the solution. Stroup's legacy was problematic. When he left the first time, he was better known for hanging with Jimmy Buffett and assorted rock stars, for having sex in Hugh Hefner's grotto during a fundraiser and for snorting copious quantities of cocaine than for achieving marijuana reform. Stroup was busted twice—once coming into Canada in 1977, for a joint in his pocket (he was fined $100), and once leaving Canada after his trial, for another joint in his pocket and a vial containing traces of cocaine (he was fined $300, spent the night in jail and was deported). Not that Stroup hid those sins—the conference media kit included a lengthy profile of him detailing all his peccadilloes.

Those days are long behind him. He hoped the ascendancy of thirty-nine-year-old Allen St. Pierre, a soft-spoken, intense archivist with the group since 1991, would reinvigorate the organization. As we shared a spliff on the deck of the Waterfront Restaurant, Stroup looked at the lights of the Golden Gate Bridge and lamented his principal failure: he never found a sustaining revenue stream for NORML. The organization continued to limp along on about $750,000 in annual dues from twelve thousand members.

NORML had spent much of its history in internecine squabbles and scrambling for cash. There had been Hefner's donations. And Tom Forcade, the legendary pot smuggler who founded *High Times* in 1974 and committed suicide in 1978, gave it $10,000 in 1976. But there had been no sustaining sugar daddy.

St. Pierre's challenge would be to carve out a new role for NORML, now that the Drug Policy Alliance and the Marijuana Policy Project (MPP) were leading the fight for reform. Both had solid funding.

Two billionaires—insurance mogul Peter Lewis and investment guru George Soros—are pumping millions into the campaign to legalize marijuana and liberalize drug laws globally. Lewis is backing Rob Kampia and the MPP.

Kampia, who was attending the NORML conference, had left NORML in 1995 to found the MPP. He thinks NORML's days are over; his own organization has usurped its place. He is definitely the most important pro-marijuana lobbyist in the world, and he may be right.

But the main man globally in the fight for saner drug policies and legalized marijuana is Ethan Nadelmann, the brilliant educator plucked from Princeton University by Soros. He created the Lindesmith Center for drug policy change in 1994, and the Drug Policy Alliance in 2000. You are as apt to find him in Buenos Aires, Belfast or Vancouver promoting needle-exchange programs, anti-AIDS measures and other progressive health policies to combat drug addiction. He arrived on the bridge of the marijuana movement in 1996.

Nadelmann had been summoned that summer by Ed Rosenthal, after the medical-marijuana Proposition 215 campaign in California stalled. Lacking money and in danger of falling apart because of personality conflicts, the coalition supporting the proposition needed money and help, Rosenthal said. Nadelmann organized emergency financing and raised another $2 million to allow them to finish and win. Today, he had come to the conference to tell the delegates— and Kampia—to quit the infighting and focus on the goal.

To effect change in the marijuana laws in particular and drug policy in general, Nadelmann believes the activists must adopt the very strategy their foes railed against. "Never use the Z-word, legalize," he said, brandishing a copy of the right-wing *National Review* that scoffed at drug czar John Walters and urged reform. "Never say legalize. Talk about patients' needs. Talk about medicine."

Marijuana is on the front line of sensible drug policy and that's why Nadelmann was on board. But he had come to give this audience the hard truth about changing policy—saying it was a long-term task and required a thoughtful, sophisticated, multi-year strategy.

"People should not be punished for what they put in their bodies if it causes no harm to others," Nadelmann insisted. "But the flip side of that is responsibility. Any psychoactive substance can be both enabling and disabling for some people."

For nearly a decade, he has been a key player behind Vancouver's adoption of the Four Pillars approach to drug policy. That's how I knew him. It was a template for successful political change.

He believed there was no substitute for a courageous politician, so he cultivated a relationship with Vancouver mayor Philip Owen and his successor Larry Campbell. Nadelmann carefully educated Owen and changed his mind on drug policy; Campbell arrived converted after years of seeing the drug war's carnage as a cop and a coroner.

"Basically, our message was do this to defeat AIDS and overdose deaths—that was the first message," Nadelmann said. "That's why we pushed safe-injection sites and needle-exchange programs. Then the next year we come in with the treatment message. Look at the changes this produces. Then, when we come in with the medical marijuana, we are credible. We have clout. We have bona fides. Once we have medical marijuana . . ."

The same approach is being tried in the United States.

"I always know when we are getting close to winning a medical initiative at a state level," Nadelmann said. "The big money arrives. It's the same old big business, status quo alliances—the drug-testing and rehab industry, pharmaceutical firms, police and corrections, big oil, tobacco . . ."

It was going to take time, but he was sure he was going to win. He did not believe people could continue to embrace so disastrous a policy as prohibition. It caused too much damage. More education was needed, more positive examples.

"San Francisco and Oakland have a leadership role now," he said. "But people must be responsible. Don't be a target. Be a place we want to bring people to show them what works—not a place for their side to bring people and say, 'Look at this disaster.'"

"Big Mike" Straumietis was on the phone. "I'm getting out of a Seattle halfway house Monday and I've got an apartment in Everett," he said. "Come on down."

After he left Canada in October 2004, he returned a few months later to see his new daughter, and his ill wife. He stayed for five months. When the RCMP discovered him, they handed him to Canada Customs and Immigration officers, who gave him the bum's rush to the U.S. border and kicked him out of Canada.

We met in Everett, and he sat with tears rolling down his cheeks as he recounted the tale. "What they did was absolutely illegal and there should be an inquiry or an investigation into what happened there," he complained. "I think they should lose their jobs."

Carmella stroked his hand. "This has been a nightmare. He was just visiting his family."

Straumietis saw it as another example of law enforcement animosity toward his firm, Advanced Nutrients. He figured the Mounties engineered his latest removal to harass him for embarrassing them in court in 2003. It began about 4:30 p.m. on St. Patrick's Day. Several marked and unmarked

RCMP cars surrounded the Chilliwack Mountain house in which he was staying.

"Someone turned me in," Straumietis said. "I was very low-key. I didn't go out or go to bars. I stayed there, saw my wife, watched my child grow."

The RCMP hailed him through a bullhorn, he said, so he dressed and went out. They handcuffed him and drove him about 130 metres down the rural road to waiting Customs and Immigration officers.

"I said hi to them since I knew who they were," said Straumietis. "They told me they were taking me straight to the border and handing me to the Americans. I said, 'What you are doing is wrong. Under due process, I should be taken to Surrey Pretrial.' I said, 'No, no, no, you can't do that. I have to have a hearing. I have a seven-month-old Canadian daughter. You just can't take me to the border. You have to give me due process, you have to do things the right way. You're basically kidnapping me.'"

They ignored his protestations.

At the Abbotsford–Sumas border crossing, Straumietis was handed to U.S. Homeland Security officials. Several hours later, he learned he was being charged with passport fraud.

"I thought all this was finally behind me—and then they do this," he said.

"Here's a businessman providing employment and they're kicking him out," Carmella added. "We need a system that works for the people."

"This is nuts," Straumietis continued. "This wasn't legal—if it was, where is the paperwork? Why wasn't I charged with returning to Canada illegally?" He wiped the tears from his cheeks.

He accused the customs agency of violating his legal rights in Canada. But he received little sympathy. "I should have been taken before a judge and given a chance to tell my story—about my sick wife, my child, about coming through the border legally," Straumietis said. "It would have been better for me to have been an Eastern European prostitute or a Honduran crack dealer."

He finally calmed down. The good news, he said, was that he faced a stretch of probation for the passport violation and then he would be legitimate for the first time in more than a decade.

"And business is going great," he said, flashing a grin. "We're in the process of forming another company— Advanced Plant Sciences. It will be nutrient products aimed at the commercial greenhouse industry."

In the meantime, he planned to be more involved in running his firm's manufacturing plant in Longview, California, and to develop a closer relationship with his U.S. distributors. He also had applied to be readmitted to Canada to live with his family.

"I love that country. I want to come back and I want to raise my family there," he said. "I want to come back there. I want to be there. That's where I want to die and be buried."

In a tiny Irish bar in Vancouver's Gastown, Charles Scott washed down a plate of bangers and mash with a Harp lager. Then he giddily made his way through two large grocery bags filled with mail. Another of his strains had come first in another prestigious European growers' competition.

"I did $100,000 worth of business last month," he said. "I just cashed $15,000 U.S. worth of money orders. It's unbelievable. I've got another $34,000 U.S. in my jeans. But I'm being smart and declaring it all. I've got my accountant paying Revenue Canada already. It's just great, man."

His seed business skyrocketed as a result of his win in Amsterdam and the full-page advertisements in *High Times*. Advanced Nutrients was also touting his use of their products on its website. Nearly 90 per cent of his business was American. He got hundreds of thousands of hits a day on his own website. Scott figured he now was among the top five global seed retailers—maybe even number one.

"Four years ago, man, I was sleeping in a teepee with my kids," he said. "Now I've just ordered a huge one for the back-yard as a plaything. Times have changed."

He was paying down his mortgage, leasing a new car, buying stuff he had always wanted, such as a new green-house, and opening a store—Toys for Boys—to put some of his money to work. Still, there was a downside. He and Emery were battling each other—the Internet was ablaze with their flame-throwing.

Emery considered Reeferman's decision to go retail and compete head-to-head to be a declaration of war. He told the world Reeferman was a pariah and declared Scott persona non grata soon after the welcome-home-from-Saskatchewan party.

"I feel like I have been betrayed by Reeferman Seeds," Emery told the world on his website. "He hasn't restocked us in his seeds for over 4 months . . . Even though I was in jail for two months since then, and continued to pay him, he has-n't restocked us. Insultingly, even though I have paid him over $160,000 over the past five years ($40,000 this year) for his seeds, and my catalog in my magazine has promoted him for five years, Reeferman (formerly Prairie Fire Seeds) has never bought an ad in *Cannabis Culture* magazine, ever!

"I am thunderstruck . . . Wow! Complete betrayal in every possible way . . . It infuriates me every time I think about him . . . I have already dumped the three thousand seeds of Reeferman's I have in stock into the Indoor or Outdoor Mixes."

Emery pulled the curtain back on Scott's unsavoury white-supremacist past—a revelation to many in the marijuana community. Scott called his friends and me after it happened, shaken and worried the information would cripple his business.

He said that initially he worried his conflict with Emery and the release of the details of his past would cause him loss of face with his connections in Holland and New York, many of whom were Jewish. But all stood by him, he said, and most said they had known all along; they preferred to judge him for who he was, not who he had been.

"And look—" He held up a shopping bag bulging with orders. "Hey, Emery at least trained the clerks at Money Mart so I can go in and cash $15,000 U.S. in money orders without a problem." He chuckled. "The chartered banks give me a real hassle. I don't care what he says any more . . . I'm off to China in a few weeks to fill a container full of goods for my store."

Before I left, I asked him what he thought of the most recent events and where things were going. I wondered if he was still as optimistic. He shook his head. He didn't think the signs indicated a quick end to prohibition.

Obvious evidence included the rabid anti-pot rhetoric that followed the killing of the four Mounties in Alberta. Although the murders were the work of a psychopathic chopshop owner who also happened to grow a little dope, RCMP Commissioner Giuliano Zaccardelli, Public Safety Minister Anne McLellan, B.C. Solicitor General Rich Coleman and U.S. drug czar John Walters blamed marijuana growing. It did not augur well for change.

Easton's predictions—a return to the Roaring Twenties and all the violence and corruption that entailed—were coming to life more and more every day.

A thirty-five-year-old motorcycle gang leader under indictment in connection with a Hells Angels–run smuggling ring was executed in Prince George. His hands were bound to the steering wheel of his pickup deliberately parked so he could watch his mansion-like home burn to the ground; he was then shot several times.

The Angels are much more than a motorcycle gang because of the money provided by marijuana and other illegal activities. They are a massive, multi-tentacled international crime conglomerate with expensive lawyers and accountants on the payroll. The membership controls an impressive array of legal companies and has interest in scores more—cafés and tanning salons, tattoo parlours and clothing boutiques, grocery stores and trucking companies, motorcycle shops and restaurants, travel agencies and real estate firms.

But they are not alone. Large ethnic-Chinese, ethnic-Italian, ethnic-Vietnamese and ethnic-Indian gangs are involved in the marijuana trade. There's room for all of them and they all have their customers—most in the United States. And cities across the continent could see the fallout of the trade in schoolyards, on street corners, in the morgue.

Marijuana is the anchor tenant in organized crime's shopping mall of vice. With legalization, the criminals won't disappear, but their wealth, their scope and their reach will be significantly diminished. I believe legalization is needed, even though it will bring its own set of problems.

Right now, society gets all of the headaches, none of the benefits and scant share of the prodigious profits. In spite of the mounting evidence that the pot prohibition is not working, Ottawa continues to push a ticketing regime for users and tougher sentences for growers and traffickers. It remains to be seen whether the courts will change tack and get onside.

Worse, the U.S. Supreme Court again upheld Washington's tough stand on pot, saying it was okay for federal law enforcement agencies to charge medical patients for smoking cannabis in spite of state laws providing protection for them. The result was a wave of high-profile raids on medical marijuana growers and providers across the U.S. and a more aggressive stance internationally. In May of 2005, a secret grand jury in Seattle indicted Marc Emery, Michelle Rainey and Greg Williams.

In late July, Emery was arrested in Nova Scotia, where he was on a speaking tour. Rainey and Williams were picked up in Vancouver. All three were detained on warrants, issued at the request of the U.S. government, charging them with selling cannabis seeds, conspiracy to manufacture marijuana and money-laundering. An 18-month DEA investigation had concluded Emery was shipping an estimated $3 million in annual seed sales to nearly every state in the union. Uncle Sam had brought the campaign against cannabis to Canadian soil.

Emery and his associates face life imprisonment if they are handed over to the Americans, given the broad anti-pot statutes that allowed Washington to jail Tommy Chong. The extradition fight could be a high-profile brawl that might last years, a long and lengthy battle that will be a lightning rod for the debate about cannabis policy and American hegemony on Canadian social and cultural mores.

I don't think Canadian courts will begin aggressively jailing growers and traffickers or agreeing to requests to send citizens to face trial and lengthy jail terms in the U.S. I think this is the last gasp of the prohibition and that the damage the criminal law is causing is becoming more and more evident to everyone, especially since the government continues to send mixed messages. Vancouver mayor Larry Campbell was appointed to the Senate in August 2005. The long-time activist for saner drug policies immediately said he would use his position there to press for marijuana legalization. His predecessor Philip Owen was on his way to Afghanistan, the latest stop on his agenda as an international advocate for drug policy reform and an end to the prohibition. He told audiences around the globe that they could witness proof that such an approach works by visiting Vancouver.

Charles Scott agrees the prohibition should end. "Everything from the sex trade to just about every evil we have in society is profiting off this prohibition," he says. "It's wrong. It's horrible that it has gone on this long."

One way or another, Scott figured, medical marijuana would win the day. It will take time—years probably. But Canada and every other country must find a workable system that allows patients and researchers ready access to a standardized supply of quality marijuana, he insisted, and he was ready to fill that massive need.

"I look at this as an investment in my kids' future," Scott said. "That's how I feel about my seed company. I'm not going to stop because I know eventually the prohibition is going to end and my business will be fantastic. It's already fantastic. I am going to be the Seagram's of the pot industry."

I left him counting his money.

ACKNOWLEDGEMENTS

A LOT OF PEOPLE MADE THIS BOOK POSSIBLE. Most especially I would like to thank those who shared their time and experience with me—Marc, Michelle, David, Rielle, Renee, Chris, Don, Carol, Lorne, Tim, Charles, Mike, Dick, Nol, Ben, Henk, Tony, Robert, Paul, Andrew, Ethan, Stephen, Barb, et al. Of course, thanks to all those whose names could not be included in the text.

As well, this book would not have been possible without the backing of *Vancouver Sun* Editor-in-Chief Patricia Graham, who has long encouraged my journalism. My Sun colleagues, too, especially David Bains, Kim Bolan, Chad Skelton, Neal Hall and Lori Culbert, all have contributed hugely to my understanding of the black market with their reporting on the underground world of drug dealing, money laundering and the rising power of gangs such as the Hells Angels.

Of course, I am greatly indebted to my agent Robert Mackwood for believing in the idea, Random House publisher

Anne Collins for having incredible confidence in me and editor Tanya Trafford for her insight and unstinting efforts. My friends—Kevin Mooney, Rod Kay, Janet Ingram-Johnson, Michael Medjuck, Doug Mills, Doug Hayman, Sasha McInnes, Roberta Staley, Andrew Stones, Jack Danylchuk, Donald MacNeil, Maureen Kelleher, Peter Ritchie, Dan Smith, David Beers, Shane and Janna Lunny, Andre and Bev Gerolymatos, Kirk Tousaw, Jim Macdonald, Elaine Graham, Sam Pybus, Aja and Georgia Mingay, David Hogben, Edward and Marion Mulgrew, and the late Tony Campbell—were unflinching in their understanding and support, too. I'm sorry my dear friend Don Graham died before I could plague him with this effort.

My sons Paul and Alexander deserve praise for putting up with me throughout the book's composition. And lastly, Rona Gilbertson has my undying gratitude. I would have dedicated the book to her, but she can't stand the smell of pot.

SELECTED BIBLIOGRAPHY

THIS BOOK IS NEITHER ENCYLOPEDIC nor the first to tackle the subject. An incredible amount of material on cannabis exists on the Internet, on library shelves and in the ephemeral media. Great websites cover the plant's myriad aspects and the issues that surround it. John Conroy's, for instance, contains all of the important Canadian legal decisions. I drew on much of this material in my research.

Here are a few books and references that I found notable, useful, informative or just plain fun, as well as selected links to people, companies or organizations mentioned in the book or that are worth a visit. Of course, regardless of the source, I am responsible for any mistakes, errors and misperceptions in the final text.

BOOKS
Booze: A Distilled History, by Craig Heron (Between the Lines, Toronto: 2003).
The Cannabible, by Jason King (Ten Speed Press, Berkeley: 2001).
Cannabis: A History, by Martin Booth (Bantam Books, New York: 2004).
High Society: Legal and Illegal Drugs in Canada, by Neil Boyd (Key Porter Books, Toronto: 1991).

Justice Defiled: Perverts, Potheads, Serial Killers and Lawyers, by
    Alan N. Young (Key Porter Books, Toronto: 2003).
Pot Planet: Adventures in Global Marijuana Culture, by Brian
    Preston (Grove Press, New York: 2002).
*Reefer Madness: Sex, Drugs, and Cheap Labor In the American
    Black Market*, by Eric Schlosser (Houghton Mifflin Company,
    New York: 2003).
Sex, Drugs, Violence and the Bible, by Chris Bennett and Neil
    McQueen (Forbidden Fruit Publishing Co.: Gibsons).
Spliffs: A Celebration of Cannabis Culture, by Nick Jones (Black
    Dog &Leventhal Publishers Inc, New York: 2004).
The Little Book of Pot, by Dr. V.S. Ganjabhang (aka Michael
    Anderiesz), (Pan Macmillan Ltd., London: 2001).
The Primo Plant: Growing Sinsemilla Marijuana, by Mountain
    Girl (Leaves of Grass/Wingbow Press, Berkeley, Calif.: 1977).

PAPERS

Crimes of Indiscretion: Marijuana Arrests in the United States, by
    Jon Gettman, Ph.D, National Organization for the Reform of
    Marijuana Laws Foundation, March 2005.
Drug Threat Assessment: United State-Canada Border, October
    2004, a jointly prepared paper by the governments of Canada
    and the U.S.
Marijuana Availability in the United States and Its Associated
    Territories, Dec. 1993, a report prepared by the U.S. federal
    research division, Library of Congress, under an interagency
    agreement with the National Guard Bureau Counterdrug
    Office.
Marijuana Growing Operations in B.C. Revisited (1997–2003), by
    Darryl Plecas, Aili Malm and Bryan Kinney, International
    Centre for Urban Research Studies, University College of the
    Fraser Valley, March 2005.
Marijuana Growth in B.C., by Stephen Easton, A Fraser Institute
    Occasional Paper, No. 74, May 2004.
"The Last Radical," by Kevin Gillies, *Vancouver Magazine*, Nov.
    1998.

WEB LINKS

www.advancednutrients.com
www.cannabisculture.com
www.cannabishealth.com
www.cannabisnews.com
www.cannasat.com
www.drugpolicy.org
www.eddysmedicinalgardens.com
www.ganjaland.com
www.hc-sc.gc.ca/hecs-sesc/marihuana/index_e.html
www.hempcity.net
www.hightimes.com
www.jackherer.com
www.johnconroy.com
www.medicalmarihuana.ca/phytocan
www.medicalmarijuana.org
www.mpp.org
www.norml.org
www.reefermanseeds.com/
www.safeaccess.ca
www.safeaccessnow.org
www.thevics.com

INDEX

Award-winning journalist Ian Mulgrew has worked for newspapers and magazines, authored three books and co-authored another. He has also produced and hosted numerous broadcast programs. He is currently the legal affairs columnist for the *Vancouver Sun*.